AA004360

MODERN SYSTEMS 2022

International Conference of Modern Systems Engineering Solutions

July 24th – 28th, 2022

Nice, France

MODERN SYSTEMS 2022 Editors

Alan Martin Redmond, CSTB, France

Printed from e-media with permission by:

Curran Associates, Inc.
57 Morehouse Lane
Red Hook, NY 12571

Some format issues inherent in the e-media version may also appear in this print version.

Printed with permission by Curran Associates, Inc. (2023)

International Academy, Research, and Industry Association (IARIA)
412 Derby Way
Wilmington, DE 19810

Phone: (408) 893-6407
Fax: (408) 527-6351

petre@iaria.org

Additional copies of this publication are available from:

Curran Associates, Inc.
57 Morehouse Lane
Red Hook, NY 12571 USA
Phone: 845-758-0400
Fax: 845-758-2633
Email: curran@proceedings.com
Web: www.proceedings.com

Table of Contents

Investigating the Conditions of Emerging Requirements of Advanced Technologies for BIM-SPEED Platform 1
Alan Martin Redmond, Sonia Alvarez-Diaz, and Nicolas Pastorelly

Developing European Defense Strategy for Electromagnetic Resilience Infrastructure Network 8
Alan Martin Redmond and Alexandru Georgescu

Ensure a Stable Power Grid when using Renewable Energy 15
Aleksander Kulseng and Mo Mansouri

Applying Systems Thinking for Early Validation of a Case Study Definition: An Automated Parking System 21
Haytham B. Ali, Mo Mansouri, and Gerrit Muller

Applying Conceptual Modeling and Failure Data Analysis for "Actual Need" Exploration: Case Study for an Automated Parking System 27
Haytham B. Ali, Gerrit Muller, and Fahim A. Salim

Preventing E-Government Tragedy Of The Clouds Using System Thinking Methods 35
Geoffrey Lichtenheim and Mo Mansouri

User-centered Data Driven Approach to Enhance Information Exploration, Communication and Traceability in a Complex Systems Engineering Environment 39
Fahim Salim, Haytham Ali, Gerrit Muller, and Kristin Falk

State of Affair in terms of Big Data Utilization in Complex System Engineering Organizations 45
Fahim Salim, Haytham Ali, Tommy Langen, Andreas Wettre, Gerrit Muller, and Kristin Falk

AutoDrone - Use of Autonomously Operated Drone Technology in Forest Inventory 50
Robert Richter, Christopher Dunkel, and Oliver Michler

Implementation of the RAM Analyses into a Discrete Event Simulation of a Process in Early Stages of its Development 56
Martin Kubic and Maurice Pendola

VR-SysML: SysML Model Visualization and Immersion in Virtual Reality 61
Roy Oberhauser

A Systematic Mapping of Natural Gas Transportation Systems' Reliability and Risks Analysis 67
Yefeng Liang and Mo Mansouri

Multi-Protocol Interoperability Between Distributed Cyber-Physical Systems Towards Industry 4.0 Collaborative Optimization 73

Md Sabbir Bin Azad and Christophe Danjou

Achieving City Intelligence - A Systems Engineering Approach 80
Yaw Adom-Mensah and Mo Mansouri

MODERN SYSTEMS 2022

Forward

The International Conference of Modern Systems Engineering Solutions (MODERN SYSTEMS 2022) inaugurates a series of events focusing on systems development considering the variety of combination between requirements, technologies, and the application domains. The conference was held in Nice, France, July 24 - 28, 2022.

We are witnessing a paradigm shift in systems engineering approaches caused by several facets of society and technology evolution. On one side, the mobility, the increase in processing power and the large storage capacity created the capacity needed to deliver services to everybody, everywhere, anytime. On the other side, new computation approaches, data gathering, and storage combined with advances in intelligence-based learning and decision-making, allowed a new perspective for systems engineering.

The advanced pace of technological achievements is supported by Cloud/Edge/Fog-based computing, High Performance Computing (HPC), Internet of Things (IoT), Big Data, Deep Learning, Machine Learning, along with 5G/6G communications (integration of terrestrial/special systems) and mobility. As such, deployment, operation and technologies, integration, maintenance became a cornerstone for developing systems complying with functional and non-functional requirements.

We take this opportunity to thank all the members of the MODERN SYSTEMS 2022 Technical Program Committee as well as the numerous reviewers. The creation of such a broad and high-quality conference program would not have been possible without their involvement. We also kindly thank all the authors who dedicated much of their time and efforts to contribute to the MODERN SYSTEMS 2022. We truly believe that, thanks to all these efforts, the final conference program consists of top quality contributions.

This event could also not have been a reality without the support of many individuals, organizations, and sponsors. We are grateful to the members of the MODERN SYSTEMS 2022 organizing committee for their help in handling the logistics and for their work to make this professional meeting a success.

We hope the MODERN SYSTEMS 2022 was a successful international forum for the exchange of ideas and results between academia and industry and to promote further progress with respect to modern systems. We also hope that Nice provided a pleasant environment during the conference and everyone saved some time for exploring this beautiful city

MODERN SYSTEMS 2022 Chairs

Romania
Chunguo Li, Southeast University, China
Oliver Michler, Technische Universität Dresden, Germany

MODERN SYSTEMS 2022 Liaison for Certification on Systems
Paul Martin, SE – Scholar, USA

MODERN SYSTEMS 2022

COMMITTEE

Zhonghao Wu, Shanghai Jiao Tong University, China
Rui Xu, East China Normal University, China
Enrico Zero, University of Genova, Italy
Qing Zheng, Los Alamos National Laboratory, USA
Han Zhou, Synopsys Inc., USA
Francesco Zirilli, Sapienza Universita Roma, Italy

Copyright Information

Investigating the Conditions of Emerging Requirements of Advanced Technologies for BIM-SPEED Platform

Alan Martin Redmond
Information Technologies Directorate (DTI),
Centre Scientifique et Technique du Bâtiment
Sophia Antipolis, France
email: alan.redmond@cstb.fr

Nicolas Pastorelly
Information Technologies Directorate (DTI),
Centre Scientifique et Technique du Bâtiment
Sophia Antipolis, France
email: nicolas.pastorelly@cstb.fr

Sonia Álvarez-Díaz
Energy Division,
CARTIF Technology Centre
Boecillo, Valladolid, Spain
email: sonalv@cartif.es

***Abstract*—As society is becoming more and more aware of the negative environmental impact of our living environments there is a need for interoperability of a full range of Building Information Modelling (BIM) tools for renovation that will be accommodated on an innovative BIM cloud platform. The use of BIM will be the catalyst for a more intelligent and efficient method of deep renovation for the residential building sector. This paper is based on the deliverable report 'Strategies for user acceptance, collaboration support, and BIM data maintenance' of the BIM-SPEED project, an H2020 research project. This report aimed to investigate and define the conditions for improving the use of the BIM-SPEED platform and fostering its adoption by the largest community of stakeholders. The methodology is based on two complementary aspects: i) feedback provided by the first end-users of the BIM-SPEED cloud platform, the necessary functionalities required to be implemented in the future versions of the platform to support renovation projects that have been collected and synthesized; and ii) by using end-user expectations regarding BIM content and update during Operation and Maintenance (O&M) of buildings. The result of this paper provides general recommendations for improving such an Integrated BIM Platform to guarantee its usability over time by advancing future versions, such as the services offered, user needs (user friendliness, user interface and ease of use), performances, flexibility, and availability.**

Keywords-BIM; Renovation; Agile Development; Collaboration; Platforms; Usability Testing, O&M.

I. Introduction

The current trend in the use of digitalization of built assets to support in the deep renovation of buildings has led to the development of many tools based on Building Information Modelling (BIM), both desktop and cloud-based. This paper aims to investigate and define the conditions for improving the use of the BIM-SPEED platform and fostering its adoption by the largest community of stakeholders. This platform is part of the Horizon 2020 project BIM-SPEED (harmonized Building Information Speedway for Energy-Efficient Renovation) [1], which aims to improve the performance of building stock by developing a combination of techniques and tools with one central information source at its core: the use of BIM.

The BIM-SPEED platform is part of an ambitious work package 'Implementing BIM cloud platform and data management' whose objective is to develop and deploy an operational cloud platform for collaboration and exchange of BIM data and other project documentation between all stakeholders in the whole cycle of European Environmental Bureau renovation projects [2]. For this purpose, there are several points that were analyzed:

- The functionalities or services offered by the platform and how they meet the needs of different end-users' profiles to support renovation projects.
- The user-friendliness of the platform, in particular the user interface and ease of use.
- The robustness, reliability, performance (e.g., response time for certain actions), security of data (e.g., in case of system failure).
- The flexibility and evolution of the platform (its capacity to adapt to the real needs of the end-users).
- The availability of a user support service.
- And finally, the data maintenance and update in the long term during the building operation.

In order to investigate the conditions of emerging requirements of advanced technologies needed to improve the BIM-SPEED platform, a study was conducted to select the most viable components and what and how to update in practice, explained in Section II of this paper. In Section III is explained the first part of the methodology followed, and the second part focused on the development of an agile platform is explained in Section IV. Some BIM recommendations are included in Section V, and the conclusions and future exploitation of the BIM-SPEED platform are explained in Section VI.

II. Ease of Use

The following section addresses the selecting of the components for advancement and the use of a desktop study.

A. *Selecting the Components for Advancement*

The first aspect was developed through an online survey by the end-users of the 13 demonstration sites of the BIM-SPEED project, complemented with some face-to-face interviews. The main result of the survey was that the BIM-SPEED platform, in its current version (i.e., the launch version with mainly collaborative features had a limited set of BIM-based renovation-oriented services) was mainly used as a file repository and document sharing service. In this initial version in which it was at the time of the first survey, the platform did not show significant innovative features compared to many other products available on the market, according to user's answers. However, very valuable information on the expected developments had been collected during the survey, amongst which the most demanded ones were predefined folder structure specific to renovation projects, workflow management, online Industry Foundation Classes (IFC) viewer, and integration of BIM services for renovation (scan to BIM, energy simulation, checklist of BIM object properties at different stages of the renovation process, connection with BIM objects libraries, etc.). Specific feedback was provided on the level of information needed for some BIM objects (e.g., Heating, Ventilation, and Air Conditioning (HVAC) system components) during the building operation phase, which allowed to make the link with the second part of this study.

B. *The Integrity of the Desk Review*

This second part of the study was about the update of BIM during building operation and maintenance, and the central role that BIM is called upon to play during the operation of a building, in relation to traditional O&M tools and emerging initiatives like Digital Building Logbooks or BIM Passports. The study was informed by a desk review combined with the contributors' own experience. It resulted in a set of recommendations for updating BIM during renovation operations, even for smaller changes.

III. Methodological approach (Phase I)

The methodology followed relied on a two-step approach (Figure 1"). In a first step (1), conduct a survey among the users of the platform to better know how they use the platform in practice, and what are their expectations in terms of data organization, work progress monitoring, functionalities, and required BIM content for renovation projects. The results of this survey were used, on the one hand, to inform future developments of the platform, and on the other hand, as input to the second step.

The second step (2) consists in setting up recommendations for the BIM update and maintenance. This work relied on a desk review of relevant techniques, standards, and initiatives such as the building Logbook, the BIM Passport, IFC annotation mechanisms, on-site information acquisition, etc.

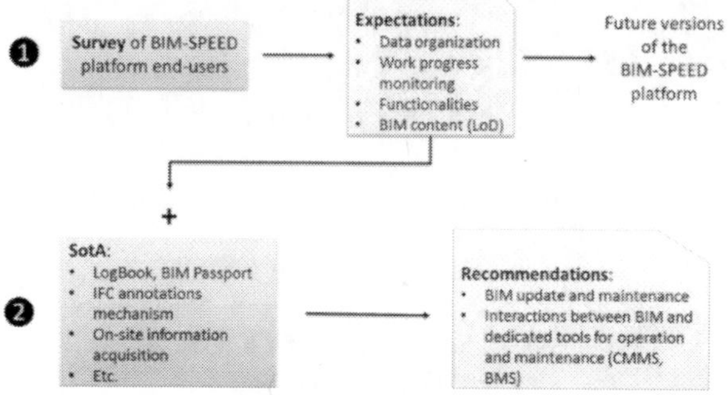

Figure 1. Methodology followed

A. *User Survey*

An online questionnaire was set up in April 2020 (as the project originally started in November of 2018 with a duration of 48 months). The questionnaire was re-launched in March 2021 for additional answers. The objectives were:

- To collect data on how end-users practically use the BIM-SPEED cloud platform.
- To get some qualitative information on their level of satisfaction.
- To identify current strengths and weaknesses.
- And to collect their expectations for future versions of the platform.

Two main target groups were identified for the survey: a) the BIM-SPEED partners who are the contacts for the 13 demo projects and b) the registered users of the platform outside the BIM-SPEED consortium. In all, this represented a sample of 41 people. This online questionnaire consisted of some 30 questions organized in several sections such as: identity (Table I), background in BIM, and expectations (Table II).

B. *Results*

Only a small part of the 41 identified end-users (between 7 and 12, pending the question) of the project had provided fully exploitable answers to the online survey. This is mainly because at the time of the survey, some of the pilots had only just started, so end-users did not have enough insight into the use of the platform to provide informed responses.

C. *Main characteristics of the BIM-SPEED pilot project and background in BIM*

Including the 2021 re-launch, the respondents represent 12 (9 from the first questionnaire, 3 from the second) from the 13 BIM-SPEED pilot projects in Italy, Romania (x2), Poland (x2), The Netherlands, Bulgaria, Spain, Germany (x2) and France (x2). All these projects included a residential part (sometimes beside other activities like hotel or commerce). These are mostly private projects, of very different sizes (from less than 1,000 m^2 up to 20,000 m^2). Half of them have a renovation budget lower than 100,000 € but one project has a budget higher than 10,000,000 €. Three-quarters of respondents had already good experience with BIM (through several projects), the others having participated once to a BIM project. Except in one case, all respondents' organizations have plans to develop the use of BIM internally.

TABLE I. YOUR IDENTITY

Structure	*Profile*
Type	• Company: 66,7% • Research and Technology Organization: 25% • Public Community: 8,3%
Size of Organization	• <10 (VSE): 8,3% • 11<250 (SME): 41,7% • 250><5,000: 25% • >5,000: 25%
Business Area	• Promoter: 8,3% • Building owner: 16,7% • Project manager: 33,3% • Architect: 25% • Engineering Office: 33,3% • Main contractor (builder): 8,3% • Subcontractor (crafts): 8,3% • Consultant (crafts): 8,3% • Surveyor: 0% • Real estate information manager: 8,3%
Using another platform	• Yes: 66;7% (Dalux Box, BauApp, C&C, Bim Server Center, BIM 360) • No: 33,3%

TABLE II. BACKGROUND IN BIM

Structure	*Results*
Participation in projects using BIM	• Never: 16;7% • Only once: 25% • Several times: 58,3%
Organization BIM expertise/experience	• No experience: 8,3% • <1 year: 0% • 1<2 years: 33,3% • 2<5 yeas: 25% • >5 years: 33,3%
Training sessions to BIM tools	• No yet: 25% • Yes, on need base: 41,7% • Yes periodically: 25%% • Yes, and every post has a BIM training roadmap: 8,3%
Have you used the BIM-SPEED platform yet?	• Yes: 75% • No: 25%

D. Appreciation of the BIM-SPEED Platform

The BIM-SPEED platform questionnaire implemented in this Phase I, used multiple methods or data sources to develop a comprehensive understanding of the stakeholders needs. The questionnaire, interviews and observation of the usability testing sites provided the inductive reasoning results, shown in TABLE III. Whereas Phase II outlined the deductive reasoning 'the act of backing up the BIM-SPEED platform applications with specific scenarios – observations learnt from existing case studies and analysis from inductive reasoning, leading the product progression to BETA stage.' The BIM-SPEED platform server was in an ALPHA development stage, and in this phase no functionalities of the software are tested, it is a previous stage of a BETA version, something of which respondents were unaware. For that reason, the stakeholder's requirements were still unclear. The survey and interviews were apart incremental and iterative methods to represent a practical and useful approach to promote initial capabilities that will be followed by successive deliveries to reach the product development phase.

TABLE III. BIM APPRECIATION

Structure	*Results*
BIM-SPEED Satisfaction	• Satisfied: 11,1% • Partially satisfied: 55,6% • Not satisfied: 11,1%
BIM-SPEED Platform meet your expectations?	• Yes: 22,2% • No: 77,8%
Main teamwork features used	• Document sharing: 100% • Task scheduling: 33,3% • Calendar: 33,3% • Meeting scheduling: 33,3% • Chat: 11,1% • Videoconferencing: 0%
Use the invitation function to invite a partner	• Yes: 55,6% • No: 44,4%
Using of Basic Services	• File naming convention: 80% • Model checking: 60%
Using EveBim Viewer	• Yes: 22,2% • No: 7,8%
Time using the BIM-SPEED Platform	• Every day: 0% • 1 to times a week: 22,2% • 3 to 5 times a week: 0% • Once a month: 66,7% • Once a certain period: 0%
BIM-SPEED Platform Advice	• It speeds up the renovation process: 60% • It reduces the renovation costs: 20% • It improves the quality of the renovation: 80%

In summary, the following results provided in TABLE IV. represent comments that contributed constructively to identifying future requirements and deductive comments that enabled the desired features and capabilities to be the target focus of future development

TABLE IV. SUMMARY OF RESULTS

Summary of future requirements	*Summary of key deductive comments*
No predefined folder structure specific to renovations projects. No tool to manage the BIM workflow. Limited size of files that can be uploaded (e.g., large cloud points). Lack of business functions and support tools integrated into the platform (the platform is mainly used as a file repository).	In response to what features does the platform lack the most: "energy calculations, management of the document, checklist, issue tracking, cost analysis, time analysis, in fact soon every employer's information requirement specification will demand Common Data Environment platform".
No online BIM viewer – eveBIM is integrated into the platform but it is a desktop application.	In response to what are the main types of tool/services to be integrated into the BIM-SPEED platform: BIM

Summary of future requirements	*Summary of key deductive comments*
	passport, model checker, energy analysis/ simulation/ calculation was all mentioned extensively in the survey. And "file naming, scan to BIM tools – that creates LOD 100-200 model (also referred to as a schematic design stage), and renovation scenarios results."

The overall endgame ('the final stage') is to present a platform that provides a streamlined process that overrides existing challenges, faster exchanges, easier sharing of files and managing of data. However, in order to reach this stage, the summary of the results shown in TABLE IV. must be taken into consideration to identify current obstacles.

IV. Agile Platform Development (Phase II)

The generalized comparison of commercial versus contract/task development domain is that the former requires the anticipation, innovation, developing and applying new or emerging technologies to create new products in a fast-paced time to market environment before the competition seizes on the opportunity spaces [3]. Whereas European H2020 projects recognize the importance of the commercial market while heavily leaning towards contract/task development domain ('the latter') which focuses on the dependency of the customer (project officer) satisfaction concerning results of performance-based outcomes (Key Performance Indicators - KPIs, Measurement of Effectiveness (MOE), and Measurement of Suitability (MOS)).

The Agile Platform Development Method had been adapted from the traditional contract/task schedule that is illustrated in a step sequence of events in Figure 2". During this stage of the development, the BIM-SPEED project had been involved in the ALPHA design stage of the platform which had partially incorporated the end-user anticipated needs. However, to further evolve the platform step 2 *User defined needs* required step 3 *User Cases*, to achieve step 4, identify features & capabilities. In reference to this paper, these stages are acknowledged by the questionnaire, and face-to-face meetings that were organized with professionals involved in some real-time usability testing (on specific user sites). These meetings were conducted by the BIM-SPEED partners defined as contact points for the user sites in Germany, Italy, and Spain.

In Figure 2", the importance of step 3 *User Cases* has been defined by a two-way directional arrow. This indicates that BIM-SPEED development process incorporated an agile platform development method at this stage (shown by the number 3 *User tested sites* on the right-hand side of the diagram). The reason for implementing this technique was to allow the platform developers to perform two incremental tests. The first evaluation at step 3 and the second evaluation at step 6. The results of the first evaluation helped to advance the development of the architecture (requirements & functional) referring to step 5 as outlined in Section IV. Step 6 *Rapid prototyping* will be conducted after the project partners accumulate the results provided from each of the site tests and incorporates them into an updated version of the BIM-SPEED Platform.

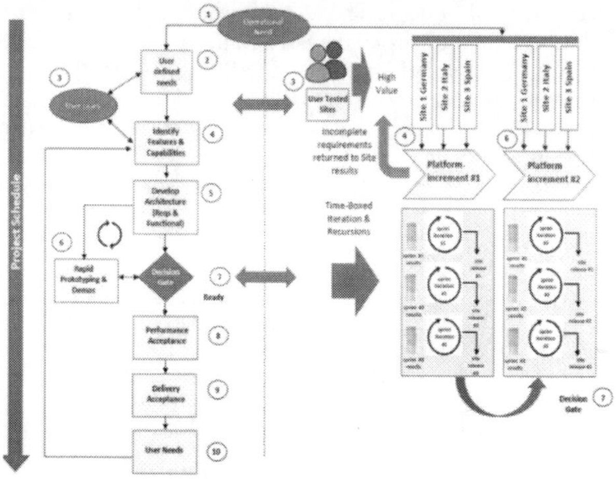

Figure 2. Agile Platform Development Method

The identified incomplete requirements and constructive comments will be revisited and tested on the existing sites via performing rapid prototyping & Demos. The outcome of these incremental (step by step process that loops back to refine the platform - iteration) and incursion (where the outputs at one level become the inputs for the next successive level), will lead to step 7 'decision gate'. At this stage the consortium will decide whether the platform has advanced to BETA testing. The agile technique enables short testing cycles rather than trying to implement one final test. It allows the platform to grow/evolve in a heuristic manner after two cycles. The process also assists in achieving the technical measures; MOE – the acquirer's key indicators and the process of MOS – the most suitable applications to be provided for the BIM-SPEED platform

A. *Real-Time Usability Testing*

In most cases usability testing requires four key areas to be examined: i) what features need to be improved; ii) what are the biggest obstacles to using the prototype; iii) what goals do you require when you come to the platform; iv) what did you learn from the usability test. However, as previously identified, the platform was a part of an agile development process, meaning that at this stage of the first incremental test, learning material was created to demonstrate the features available at that time, such as naming conventions. The survey results had highlighted this feature as necessary component of the platform and CSTB had responded (Figure 2"). According to [4], specifying the electronic data file format for information deliverables is critical.

If the data models of the export/import applications don't match, some modification of exported BIM data may be needed before it can be imported into the Computerized Maintenance Management System (CMMS)/ Integrated Workplace Management System (IWMS) software. Analyzing and addressing these data format compatibility issues before creating any data in the BIM model can greatly minimize these issues. If both applications support Construction Operations Building Information Exchange (COBie) format, as a non-proprietary data format, you can specify that data from the BIM can be delivered in a COBie-compliant format."

B. *Summary of Sprint Iteration*

A compilation of the three individual sprints (usability testing) are listed below. These results are based on the analysis of the problems and opportunities arising from the usability test. The following step 5 of Figure 2, *Develop Architecture,"* incorporates the patterns (systems thinking) identified to advance the architecture of the BIM-SPEED platform. The three user sites results are composed into two sections: usability study experience summary and summary of views on future changes/improvements. The results are displayed in a manner to find the patterns and traceability between the different tests user requirements and future design requirements. Usability Study Experience Summary:

a) *Germany*: the layout of the platform offers useful extensions through the versioning and chat function; very beneficial to publish data (models, reports, versions) which therefore can represent official, trustworthy documents; and the platform is only effectively usable for data storage so far.

b) *Italy*: the platform was mainly used as a platform for file sharing; tools used and from different data formats were also placed on the platform: AutoCAD (Autodesk), Revit (Autodesk), Thermus (ACCA Software), Primus (ACCA Software).

c) *Spain*: the main use of the platform has mostly been like a repository to exchange information; BIM model viewer has been implemented which turned out to be helpful.

Evidently the user experience in all three sites recognized at this stage the platform is an efficient repository for exchanging files. The use of additional extensions such as versioning and chat function for communication is beneficial. The BIM model viewer option and the semantic checker for elements etc., were also recognized as positive applications. Integrating different tools with different data formats streamlined the usability experience. Again, the naming convention was highly recommended.

C. *Summary of Views on Future Changes/Improvements*

The process of validating files, changing names, and modifying several files simultaneously, structuring files into folders and file checking for clearer workflows was highlighted in both Germany and Italy usability tests as areas for improvement. The SemChecker had been previously acknowledged as a positive contribution, however for future changes it was suggested that more information be provided. Likewise, the model viewers were viewed as positive contributor, however in the future an online viewer is deemed essential. The site usability test in Spain produced some constructive comments such as: missing a functionality to follow the site, like a logbook which allows to register all the issues during the site through the 3D model; linked annotations inside the model to different parts of it; and missing the possibility to link different documents like pdf or jpeg with different elements of the model. Both Spain and Italy recommended higher level of detail for objects. *Next Steps:* The information obtained from the survey and usability testing formed the basis of the key focus areas to advance the BIM-SPEED platform. The following suggestions address the main future services.

V. BIM Recommendations

The Level of Development (LOD) had been defined as a crucial process to initialize and update all information during renovation operations. Indeed, a process that would be too complicated can make this data structure unusable. On another hand, when smaller changes have been made to the building, they are often not integrated into the model. This issue can be linked to the development and management of the building Logbook which must list all operations made on the building. In this context, the use of BIM is often seen as a data sink for initializing CMMS software. However, one also must think of the opposite way, it means, how to update BIM following operations directly managed in the CMMS software. Indeed, if we can use BIM as an operational support of the Digital Building Logbook (DBL) (two ways communication between BIM and dedicated tools for maintenance), this will ensure the transmission of information about building operation including when the operator changes (using possibly different asset management tools).

Alternatively, we also looked at how BIM can be used to provide information to DBL or maintenance management systems, or conversely, how BIM can be updated from them. The challenges are to keep the BIM up to date during maintenance/renovation operations, even for small changes, and to ensure the transmission of information on building operations, even when the building operator changes and uses a different asset management tool.

A. *Digital Building Logbook*

The 'Digital Building Logbook' is defined as a digital traceable container for all the data of a building, including all the documents and information regarding design, structure calculation, system implementation, materiality, costs, maintenance, energy efficiency (including possible certifications), Life Cycle Assessment (LCA), urban conditions, property, etc. The DBL belongs to the building owner and can be shared with public entities (e.g., municipalities), AECOM professionals, energy certifiers, etc., to facilitate processes of review and management of the building, as well as to carry out future renovations on it. In more advanced scenarios it is also possible to use the DBL as a container for energy measurement data from the building, so that results that differ from the numbers in the digital twin's energy analysis can be a symptom of a breakdown in the air conditioning systems or a problem in the thermal envelope. Due to the relevance of this topic, some European initiatives related with the Building Logbook are already being developed in Germany (Gëbaudepass), Portugal (CASA+), France (Carnet numérique du logement) or Belgium (Woningpas), with the aim of bringing building owners and stakeholders together. The DBL is already starting to be implemented in countries such as France, Germany, or Belgium, as detailed in the European study BUILDING RENOVATION: Customized roadmaps toward deep renovation and better homes [5].

B. *BIM Passport*

The automated evaluation of information contained in the DBL holds great potential in supporting (future) building owners and operators to assess the quality and completeness of the given information to implement certain use cases related to deep building renovation. There are several (research) projects developing BIM-based Material Passports (MP) to increase the efficiency and sustainability in the construction sector, promoting circular solutions for building design and operation, as proposed by the HOUSEFUL project [6], which is supported by the MADASTER platform, a cloud platform that allows the generation of Material Passports for buildings [7].

The concept of the BIM Passport would be applicable to any type of construction project, however, in BIM-SPEED the focus lies on enabling (future) building owners and service providers to make informed decisions based on the information contained in the DBL regarding the implementation of certain use cases presented (Baseline and Use Cases for BIM-Based renovation projects and KPIs for EEB renovation) [8].

C. *BIM Collaboration Format (BCF – IFC Annotations)*

BIM Collaboration Format (BCF) is a buildingSMART International openBIM standard to communicate about the 'issues' of a BIM model during its live cycle. The development of BCF started in 2009 and was originally conceived by two members of the buildingSMART International Implementation Support Group (ISG), Solibri and Tekla, along with the Institute for Applied Building Informatics at the Munich (Germany) University of Applied Sciences. Their desire to leverage open communication technology for IFC-based workflows led to prototyping and eventually fully developing BCF with other ISG members [9].

BCF allows software to activate interoperable information workflows. The exchange of information in construction projects already benefits from the ISO 29481 IDM (Information Delivery Manual) standard. BCF's assessment of compliance with this ISO standard will help to further expand its use when quality management involves full adoption of ISO standards. Discussions within the buildingSMART association are underway to define BCF as a standard compliant with ISO 29481.

BCF was introduced to allow an intelligent communication workflow between BIM tools and a workflow communication capability connected to IFC formats, where the purpose was to separate the virtual communication from the model into a BCF format based on XML schemas. BCF process focuses on the support to comments and status of issues across platforms instead of focusing on a single discipline and its own product.

VI. CONCLUSION

The survey conducted as part of the BIM-SPEED project, whose methodology has been explained in this paper, showed that construction stakeholders have a strong expectation for user-friendly BIM platforms, where project information can be collected and structured in a logical way that corresponds to professional practices and project progress. In these platforms, the ability to trace the history of different changes with their various contributors can be included. In addition, a set of basic services (e.g., to track and control workflow, or check the completeness of the BIM model at each stage of the process) can also be offered, as well as business services dedicated to renovation projects. At the time this survey was conducted, within the BIM-SPEED project, the BIM platform made available to the pilot sites was the launch version, mainly offering a generic Common Data Environment (CDE) with still few renovation-oriented BIM services (except for a model checker). It is therefore not surprising that the survey showed that early users of the platform used it mainly as a file repository and document sharing tool. However, the expectations gathered through this survey had been very useful and helped guide future developments such as a weather data service, a service to link IoT data with BIM, a GIS data collector, a 'Material' service (to enrich IFC4 files with material properties), and a LoDlifter service (to enrich IFC files with object properties and values).

As a final recommendation, the integration into the BIM of all the necessary information to be able to undertake a renovation operation in a well-informed way (the so-called BIM PASSPORT, which differs depending on the intended use, for example an energy or structural renovation operation), is essential.

ACKNOWLEDGMENT

This research work has been funded under the research project BIM-SPEED. This project has received funding from the European Union's Horizon 2020 research and innovation programme under grant agreement No. 820553. This research work reflects only the author's view, and the Commission is not responsible for any use that may be made of the information it contains.

The authors would like to say thank you to the BIM-SPEED Project Partners (CSTB, TUB, CARTIF, CYPE, PB40, STRESS, VISESA) involve in deliverable 6.3: Strategies for user acceptance, collaboration support, and BIM data maintenance [10].

REFERENCES

[1] BIM-SPEED Project Partners, "Harmonised Building Information Speedway for Energy-Efficient Renovation (BIM-SPEED Project)," 2018. https://cordis.europa.eu/project/id/820553 (accessed June. 20, 2022).

[2] European Environmental Bureau, "EEB website", 2022. https://eeb.org/ (accessed June. 20, 2022).

[3] C. S. Wasson, 'System Engineering; Analysis, Design, and Development, 2nd', Published by John Wiley & Sons, Inc., Hoboken, New Jersey, 2016.

[4] M. Tardif, "Establish Uniform Naming Conventions to Best Use BIM for FM" Second part of a three-part Green Building Report., 2021. *https://www.facilitiesnet.com/facilitiesmanagement/article/Establish-Uniform-Naming-Conventions-to-Best-Use-BIM-for-FM--17072* (accessed June. 20, 2022)

[5] M. Fabbri, M. De Groote, and O. Rapf, "Building Renovation Passports", Customised Roadmaps Towards Deep Renovation and Better Homes, Published in October 2016 by the Buildings Performance Institute Europe (BPIE), Second Edition (November 2016), ISBN: 9789491143175, pp. 10-20

[6] HOUSEFUL project, "Material Passports based on advanced 3D Model", https://houseful.eu/solutions/material-passports-based-on-advanced-3d-model/ (accessed June. 20, 2022)

[7] Madaster Training, "Material Passports Training the Arc", Published by Sander Beeks, 11/12/2020 https://madaster.com/wp-content/uploads/2020/12/Material-Passport-The-Arc-EN.pdf (accessed June. 20, 2022)

[8] BIM-SPEED Project Partners, "BIMSPEED results, D4.1: Baseline and Use Cases for BIM-based renovation projects and KPIs for EEB renovation", 2019, https://www.bim-speed.eu/en/Project%20Results%20%20Documents/Deliverables/D4.1.pdf (accessed June. 20, 2022)

[9] buildingSMART International, "BIM Collaboration Format (BCF) - An Introduction", https://technical.buildingsmart.org/standards/bcf (accessed June. 20, 2022)

[10] BIM-SPEED Project Partners, "BIM-SPEED results: D6.3: Strategies for user acceptance, collaboration support, and BIM data maintenance," 2022. https://www.bim-speed.eu/en/Project%20Results%20%20Documents/Deliverables/D6.3.pdf (accessed June. 20, 2022).

Developing European Defense Strategy for Electromagnetic Resilience Infrastructure Network

Alan Martin Redmond,
Centre Scientifique et Technique du Bâtiment, Sophia Antipolis, France
email: alan.redmond@cstb.fr

Alexandru Georgescu,
The National Institute for Research and Development in Informatics ICI Bucharest, Romania
email: alexandru.georgescu@ici.ro

***Abstract*—As part of the Design Process Model that includes systematic methods for the 'Developing European Defence Strategy for Electromagnetic Resilience Infrastructure Network' this paper focuses on the analytical phase. In essence, the paper presents inductive reasoning (develop a theory), while also examining deductive reasoning (proposed solution) to promote the need and resources of the creative phase (development of such a strategy). The paper focuses on Spectrum capabilities in defense and acknowledges that the development of European Defense strategy for Electromagnetic Resilience Infrastructure is necessary. Issues such as interoperability, and ability to keep pace with technological advances by potential adversaries will require Europe to emulate recent developments by DoD to advance the USA superiority in EM warfare. The result of this paper will identify opportunities, risk and challenges within the scope of the European Defence Strategy for Electromagnetic Resilience Infrastructure Network.**

Keywords—Electromagnetic Spectrum; Resilience; Strategy; Infrastructure; Networks; Energy; Standards.

I. Introduction

In physics, Electromagnetic Radiation (EM radiation or EMR) refers to the waves (or their quanta, photons) of the electromagnetic field, propagating (radiating) through space, carrying electromagnetic radiant energy. It includes radio waves, microwaves, infrared, (visible) light, ultraviolet, X-rays, and gamma rays. In applications across civil, commercial, and government sectors, the characteristics of the waves used often drive the use [1] . Table 1 is an extraction from [2] and cross-referenced by the author to identify the specific use of the spectrum in Space and Defence. It highlights the theme of the paper's magnitude for reflection on Spectrum capabilities in defence.

In February 2021, the Congressional Research Service Report outlined DoD use of the EMS (Electromagnetic Spectrum) based on: (i) Interoperability, (ii) Ability to keep pace with technological advances by potential adversaries, (iii) The private sector's increasing interest in using frequencies traditionally reserved for the military (for example the 5G spectrum), (iv) Spectrum Sharing, (v) The interagency process for spectrum allocation – such as the Federal Communications Commission (FCC) authorisation of the Ligado 5G network, which could affect the global positioning system's radio signals, and (vi) Anticipating future spectrum needs for both commercial and military users. These principles have called the DoD to action and develop a strategy to control and enable these 6 principles in order to advance the USA superiority in EM warfare.

TABLE I. ELECTROMAGNETIC USES AND APPLICATIONS (EXTRACTED FROM [2])

Directed-Energy (DE) Weapons	**Concentrated EM energy** rather than kinetic energy to incapacitate, damage, disable, or destroy enemy equipment, facilities, and/or personnel examples include ground forces in Counter Rocket, Artillery, and Mortar (C-RAM), Counter-Unmanned Aircraft (C-UAS), or Short-Range Air Defense (SHORAD) missions.
Radio frequency waves	Can be used to transmit messages between electronic devices. Low frequency radio waves can travel long distances, and can penetrate seawater, but cannot support high data rates. These waves are useful for communications with submarines. long distance waves can pass through solid objects, like buildings and trees, making them useful for mobile communications.
Microwaves	Microwaves are used in radars—systems that send out pulses of high frequency waves that reflect off an object and back to the source. Microwaves are also used in satellite communications, which experience few obstacles in their transmission path.
Infrared radiation (IR)	Receives and converts light signals to electrical signals that instruct microprocessors to carry out commands, similarly infrared lasers can be used for point-to-point communications over short distances to provide high-speed, reliable connections.

The paper comprises of 7 main sections: i) introduction - observation and addressing the problem; ii) scope & objectives - what is required and measured; iii) project analysis - evaluation 'why it is needed'; iv) methodology - development of EMC standards and specification; v) proposed solution - how it will be achieved; vi) impact, opportunities & risks - the added value gained from such a strategy and risks associated with trying to achieve it; and vii) way ahead - funding. Overall results of the paper present a summary, synthesize, critique, and use of information as "background" for a research proposal.

II. Scope and Objectives

This section will address the overall scope of the projects contribution and outline the objectives.

A. Scope

This project is a contribution to the development of the European Defence Strategy for Electromagnetic Resilience Infrastructure and raises the profile of its activities in particular by working on the following: i) support the operation of the European Defence Agency (EDA) governance structure; ii) conduct national and regional based process for preparing a Research and Innovation investment Roadmap and priorities by involving research and industry stakeholders, and engaging in wide dissemination of the Electromagnetic Resilience Infrastructure results; iii) organise outreach events and engage in structured discussions with the general public, including on the social implications and ethics of Electromagnetic technology development and innovation, particularly with regard to privacy and security, public trust and acceptance; iv) provide research dissemination services to projects; v) identify relevant training, education and infrastructure needs. The results should be compared with best practices of international cooperation partners of similar governance (e.g., USA and Canada), and shared based on mutual exchange.

B. Objectives

1. Investigate and map best practice activities in European and international spheres - where Electromagnetic technologies will play a major role in the near future and where resilience in such fields can enhance existing capabilities, protection and offer a competitive advantage to Europe.
2. Increase the adoption of standards and regulations in Electromagnetic Warfare - either in existing standardisation activities and bodies and where relevant, by contributing to creating and testing new standardisation activities in existing groups and/or creation of new groups.
3. Open Innovation Days – mobilise the whole value chain (research, standardisation and the industry sectors, and defence sectors) at innovation days and advance the discussions at European level to achieve impactful results promoting the European interests in Electromagnetic standardisation.
4. Perform an extensive mapping of current and future resilient requirements for Electronic Warfare education and training; define standards for implementing appropriate educational strategies; host existing and newly developed teaching materials and resources within a European Defence repository.
5. Develop strategies for scaling up training programmes across Europe in the use cases of advanced Electromagnetic Spectrum Management; and establish a network between science, civil society, and industry to exchange ideas, needs, and human resources.
6. Develop the European Defence Strategy for Electromagnetic Resilience Infrastructure Network - involve and be driven by representatives of the relevant actors of the field (e.g., academia, RTOs, and industry, including SMEs, and intermediaries).

III. Project Analysis

The project focuses on the capabilities of electromagnetic waves and how the infrastructure for supporting such emissions is protected such as **Data Centers and 5G Networks**. EM waves in basic principle carry energy, momentum, and angular momentum away from the source particle and radiates without the need for continuing charges. EMR is sometimes referred to as far field because it achieves sufficient distance from such charges whereas near field are close to charges and the current that produces them. In reference to the incredible evolution of communicating systems; "the deployment of Internet and mobile networks, connected objects and sensors, has brought about the emergence of silicon photonics to meet these new major challenges" [3].

In essence, fiber optical communications have revolutionized the telecommunications industry as well as the data networking community. Fiber optic cables have enabled telecommunications links to be made over greater distances, with lower levels of transmission losses and enabled higher data rates. "As a result, fiber optic communication systems are widely employed for applications ranging from major telecommunications backbone infrastructure to Ethernet systems, broadband distribution, and general data networking [4].

Why is this important? The need for high speed, more capacity and longer distances has made Dense Wavelength Division Multiplexing (DWDM - is an optical multiplexing technology used to increase bandwidth over existing fiber networks) the technology of choice for greenfield installations, for upgrading existing networks, and is compulsory for transmission of 100G and above. In fact, the DWDM C-band 1525nm – 1610nm spectrum supports up to 96 wavelengths spaced at the standard ITU grid of 50GHz [5]. At higher data rates, including 400G and 1T, the signals will be transmitted over multiple subcarrier channels [6]. From a 5G commercial aspect, Intel acknowledged the benefits of their 100G silicon photonics transceivers that are optimised to meet the bandwidth requirements of next-generation communications infrastructure while withstanding harsh environmental conditions. Furthermore, their market opportunity projection for its connectivity business, which includes silicon photonics, is to grow from $4 billion today to an estimated $11 billion total addressable market by 2022 [7].

However, Spectrum Sharing is an issue with emerging technologies and policies are demonstrating commercial systems can use the same frequencies without degrading defense capabilities. Such policies, best practices, standards, and regulations must be referenced within the European Defence Agency context. **Integrated quantum, Photonic Devices, 5G security Networks (such as QKD and system lockout chip)** are not only a part of defence resilience strategies, but also of the cities of the future. Data centers bandwidth for communication and the use of silicon such as Insulated-Gate Bipolar Transistor (IGBT) and Metal–Oxide–Semiconductor Field-Effect Transistor (MOSFET) by STMicroelectronics to discharge batteries in electric and hybrid vehicles **indicate the dependency on the Electromagnetic spectrum and thus the need for protection from advanced Electronic Warfare Systems and Electromagnetic Interference in urban areas such as**:

- Electronic Support, Networking & Cyber Enabling – i) networks with Tactical Radios, ii) electronic support (detect, direction finding and geo-location, iii) cyber-enabling platform.
- Counter Unmanned Aerial Systems (CUAS) – i) integrates with radars, sensors, and fire control solutions, ii) stationary and on-the-move capable, iii) configurable for dismounted, mounted, fixed site and airborne platforms.

IV. METHODOLOGY

In practice Electromagnetic Compatibility (EMC) is the engineering discipline concerned with the behavior of a system in an Electromagnetic Environment (EM). According to INCOSE [8]: "A system is considered to be electromagnetically compatible when it can operate without malfunction in an EM environment together with other systems or system elements and when it does not add to that environment as to cause malfunction to other systems." The term electromagnetic interference (EMI) is recognised when a system causes interference, and in EMC the EM environment includes all effects classically attributed to electromagnetics (such as radiation) and electrical effects (conduction).

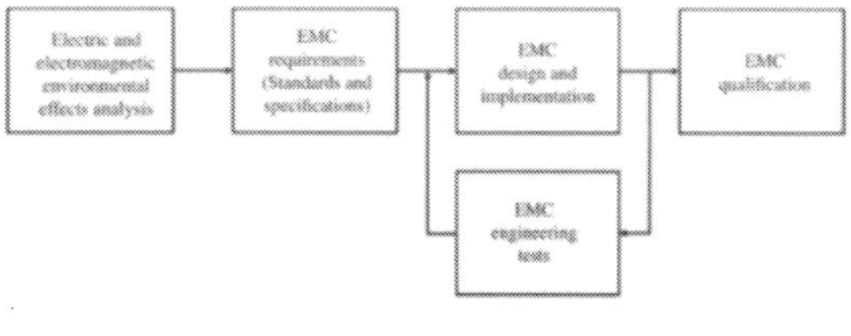

Fig 1. Process for achieving EMC (Arnold de Beer, cited by [8]: INCOSE page 219)

Arnold de Beer developed the Business Process Map (BPM) in Fig 2 which outlines how EMC will be successfully achieved during system development. It has 5 main areas: i) electrical and electromagnetic environmental effects (E4) - this analysis describes all the threats (natural and man-made) that a system may encounter during its life cycle, furthermore MIL-STD-46C [9] is still been used to determine requirements of a system such as installation; ii) EMC requirements (Standards and Specifications) – are used to regulate the EM environment in which a system is operating, however the process acknowledges that existing standards and specifications (whether commercial, military, avionic, automotive, or medical) can be used as EMC requirement based on its class or category according to the outcome of the E4 analysis; iii) EMC Design and Implementation – overall EMC requirements are inputs for the concept and development stages of design that includes both mechanical and electrical/electronic hardware implementations, the use of zoning for system elements with similar emissions or sensitive circuits require a control of interface and the EMI control plan includes EMC requirements, zoning strategy, filtering and shielding, mechanical and electrical design to EMC; iv) EMC Engineering Test – prequalification testing is done on a system element level and even as low as the single circuit board assembly level during the development stage; v) EMC qualification – EMC qualification tests verify the EMC design of a system against its requirements, the first part of such tests is to compile an EMC test plan and map each requirement to a test and a test set up.

Given the severity of EMI and the urban dependency on the Electromagnetic spectrum, the overall methodology is based on re-engineering the process for achieving EMC for urban interoperable design. For instance, challenges exist when testing for EMC qualification as the process must be in operational mode during emission testing to predict malfunctions during susceptibility. Just like EMC standards and specifications when it is impractical to test a large system such as ship, aircraft, or complete industrial plant, the qualification tests are based on the systems elements. In the opinion of this author, there needs to be an updated review EMS based on a similar international structured principle; (i) Interoperability, (ii) Ability to keep pace with technological advances, (iii) The private sector's increasing interest in using frequencies, (iv) Spectrum Sharing, (v) The Interagency process for spectrum allocation and (vi) Anticipating future spectrum needs for both commercial and military users.

V. PROPOSE SOLUTION

As part of a trains protection system, Delft University have been testing ERTMS/ETCS Hybrid Level 3 and ATO: A simulation-based capacity impact study for the Dutch railway network [10]. A EEIG ERTMS Users Group has been focusing on the implementation of ERTMS/ETCS Level 3, the Hybrid Level 3 concept. "The main characteristic of the concept is that it uses fixed virtual blocks for the separation of trains which are fitted with a Train Integrity Monitoring System (TIMS), while a limited installation of trackside train detection is used for the separation of trains without TIMS, as well as for the handling of degraded situations" [11] (EEIG ERTMS Users Group, page 5).

The common theme here for testing EM designs in reference to requirements is the creation of user's groups, the analysis of best practices (case studies) and the use of personas. In order to 'Develop European Defense Strategy for Electromagnetic Resilience Infrastructure Network', the project must build upon existing networks and create similar Special Interest Groups (SIGs).

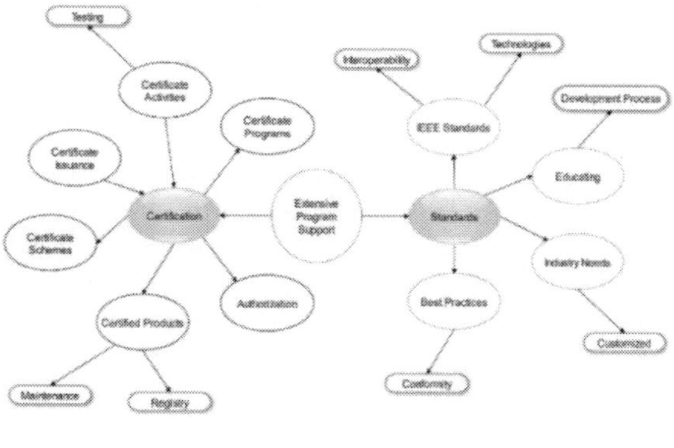

Fig 2. IEEE Standard Association ICAP (Adaption of this Authors, Interpretation)

Figure 2 is a graphical mind map representation of IEEE Conformity Assessment Programs based on the following 10 main points of their ICAP working group Extensive Program Support [12]:

- ICAP is a facilitator and administrator of certification programs.
- Full oversight for testing and certification activities.
- Certificate issuance.
- Development and management of test plans, test suites and certification schemes.
- Maintenance of certified products registry.
- Test laboratory assessment and authorisation.

- Technical and logistical support services to industry groups executing interoperability demonstrations of specific technologies related to IEEE standards.
- Educating IEEE Working Groups on conformity assessment to ensure conformity assessment is injected early in the standards development process.
- The development of customised conformity assessment programs that meet industry needs.
- Defining and designing conformity assessment best practices.

The concept for the Developing European Defence Strategy for Electromagnetic Resilience Infrastructure Network is to build similar SIG groups to the IEEE Standard Association ICAP (IEEE Conformity Assessment Programs) but concentrate on attributes of the DoD 6 pillars.

VI. Impact, Opportunities & Risks

The following section will outline the impact of advancements associated to the Electromagnetic Spectrum, the opportunities relating to technologies and infrastructure, and the current known risks and challenges.

A. *Impact*

Advancements in Electromagnetic Spectrum have revolutionised how we manage, control, use and distribute data that affects our digitally operated devices in order to advance our health and well-being on a daily basis. Optronics (the combination of optical and electronics) such as fiber optic communication and in particular fiber optical receivers have presented opportunities through wide band width devices. With the inclusion of WDM multiplexing technology the capacity to enable bidirectional communication over one strand fiber exists. This is just one example; other added advantages include:

- **Security** – quantum communications such as WDM have been operating through the protection of Quantum Key Distribution (QKD) can offer communication with unconditional security).
- **Speed** – multiplexing enables high speed capacity and high-speed telecommunications.
- **Energy** – i) charge pumps circuits are capable of high efficiencies, sometimes as high as 90–95%, while being electrically simple circuits; ii) MOSFETs and IGBTs are powered by Charge pumps in H bridges in high-side drivers for gate-driving high-side n-channel power [13] ; The Silicon Micro-Ring Resonator (MRR) has gained significant attention for use in an energy-efficient and high-bandwidth photonic system and is ideally suited for both inter- and intra- data center communication [14].
- **Cost** – the use of DWDM (referring to optical signals multiplexed within 1550Nm) leverages cost and capabilities of Erbium Doped Fiber Amplifiers (EDFAs) for wavelengths between C-Band and L-Band, 1525nm – 1565nm and 1570nm – 1610nm.

B. *Opportunities*

According to RADIO WAVES [15], "Massive Multi-Input Multi-Output (MIMO) antennas provide access to wide frequency bands for very high-speed connections. Their 'agile' technology gives them the ability to direct their beams to countless moving devices thanks to their multifocal technology. As a result, they enhance a better direct signal to the user, by following them as they move. Furthermore, they provide:

- reduced energy consumption.
- the handling of a larger number of users, and increased speeds.
- a significant improvement in signal quality to the user while also reducing superfluous surrounding emissions.

There have been many studies on the role that photonics, particularly microwave photonics, can have in implementing 5G networks. Currently, there are several general disruptive technologies needed for 5G cellular networks, such as small-cell architectures, the utilisation of the millimeter-wave (mmWave) spectrum, and the implementation of MIMO systems at mobile base stations [16]. Other benefits of fiber include the fact that "the mmWave frequency band is a "sweet spot" for Radio Frequency over fiber and mmWave signal with broadband data can be easily transported over large distances with minimal loss [17].

However, interoperability will always be the main issue when exchanging information and standards are the key mechanism to achieving interoperable solutions when developing systems and providing ICD (Interface Control Document). The U.S. Defense Advanced Research Projects Agency (DARPA) has been working on "developing 100 Gb/s RF Backbone (100G) program whose goal is to design, build, and test an airborne Millimeter based RF communications link with fiber-optic equivalent capacity and long reach capable of propagating through clouds and providing high availability." DARPA's focus is to provide a system comprising 100 Gb/s capacity at ranges of 200 km for air-to-air links and 100 km for air-to-ground links when installed in a high-altitude (e.g., 60,000 ft) aerial platform [18]. And these types of systems will adhere to DoD military specifications, therefore if commercial interests are also using frequencies traditionally reserved for the military there needs to be the inducement of technologies such as AI-enabled dynamic spectrum sharing. Such technologies will require best practices regulation and standards to achieve the end game.

C. *Risks & Challenges*

- The main risks are related to not being able to build upon existing networks and create similar Special Interest Groups (SIGs).
- Another risk is the fact that typical military specifications and commercial specifications would need to be reviewed in order to proceed with a joint strategy for developing European Defense Strategy for Electromagnetic Resilience Infrastructure Network.
- This ambitious project will require collaboration between the Energy Consultation Forum's Working Groups (CF SEDSS), the largest defence energy community in Europe, and support from Institutes such as the European Telecommunication Standard Institute (ETSI) and the *International Telecommunication Union* (ITU). While the CF SEDSS working groups do not implement projects, they can address conceptual design and, through the Forum, EU and Member States funding could be mobilized to produce tangible results.

- Many of the disruptive technologies already exist for implementing the key systems but there is a significant lack of training and open collaboration that can involve all major players that will utilise the EMS with particular reference to resilience system engineering. For instance, the defence and private sectors may not wish to share information.
- To appreciate the challenges, all of the supply chain actors (Large enterprises, Mid-Caps, SMEs) must be included in the discussions at the innovation days.
- There will be challenges and risks associated with tests, particularly the new development of European Defense Electromagnetic Compatibility documents.

VII. Way Ahead

This section will focus on the core theme 'a possible project', case study, and funding mechanisms.

A. *Theme*

A possible project would be to develop a framework for assessing EMS resilience in power plants in the context of hybrid threats that can be offered to Member States, along with a toolkit of best practices, guidelines and technical solutions to ameliorate the risks. The project could have a practical implementation at the level of 1 or 2 power plants volunteered by one of the participating Member States. It can also propose to deliver a network of stakeholders, including developers, beneficiaries, expert groups and research labs, to serve as a resource for supporting future efforts.

B. *Case Study*

According to [19] a case study is a strategy used to research an experimental theory or topic using set procedures. The authors are of the opinion that testing a case study starting at TRL2 (technology concept formulated) and finishing at TRL 4 (technology validated in lab) will add significant value to any potential funding key performance. Figure 3 below shows how pre-existing components (databases, platforms) and concepts of EMC for BIM model structure topology can be configured to developed 'Resilience System for Electromagnetic Resilience Infrastructure'.

The following points identify the requirements:

- According to [20] the starting point is to identify what we are looking for! Example: unauthorised, unlicensed wireless devices, new wireless services turning on in an area of interest, keeping up with changes in the spectral landscapes. Furthermore, a signal development environment is required to; a) enable rapid development, test, and optimisation of signal (or device) detection and isolation capabilities; b) utilise commercial tools and software; c) can be setup in a secure or open environment; d) can be configured as portable, rugged, or transportable system. In essence for EMC the basic question to answer is there a frequency plan and should frequency plan be statutory for cities with buildings of interest (civilian infrastructures etc.).
- [21] Created a European project based on two phases: phase 1 consisted of assessment scenarios concerning IEMI - intentional malicious generation of electromagnetic energy introducing noise or signal into electric and electronic systems, NEMP – an electronic pulse produced mainly from gamma rays from a nuclear explosion, HEMP – a series of electromagnetic waveforms generated from a nuclear detonation at altitudes above 30km and the propagate to the earth surface, **and HPEM which produces intense electromagnetic radiated fields or**

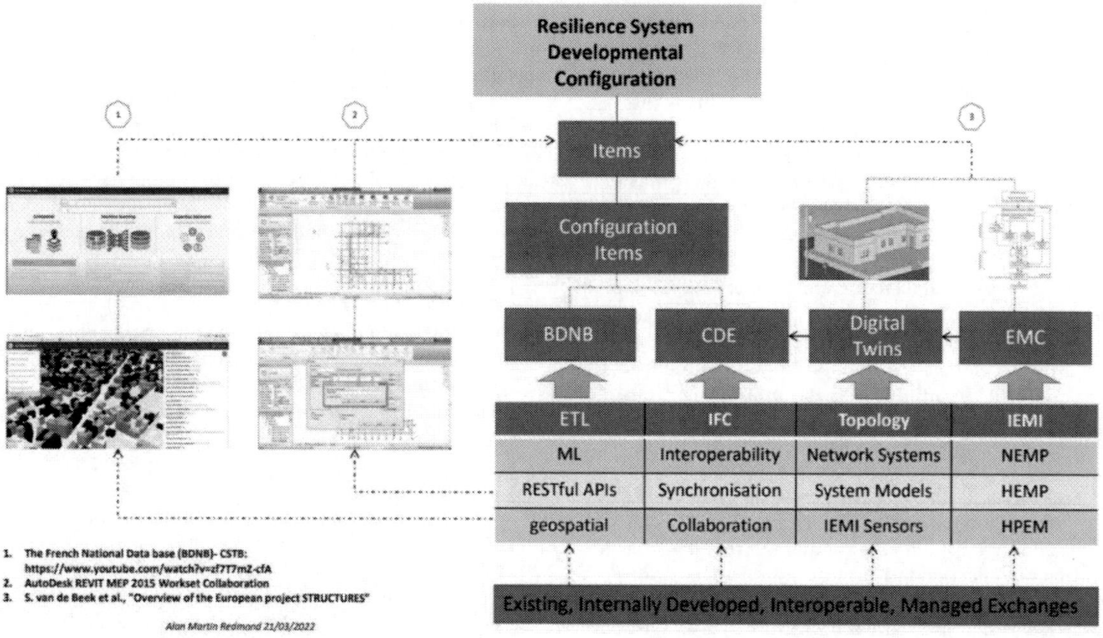

Fig 3. Resilience System Developmental Configuration Architecture, Legend: Common Data Exchange (CDE); Extract, Transform, Load (ETL); Machine Learning (ML); Application Performance Interface (APIs); Industry Foundation Classes (IFC); Intentional ElectroMagnetic Interference (IEMI); Nuclear ElectroMagentic Pluse (NEMP); High Altitude Electromagnetic Pluse (HEMP); High Power ElectroMagnetic Pulse (HPEM)

conducted voltages and currents with the capabilities to damage or upset a city infrastructures. Phase 2 investigated IEMI risks and introduced protection strategies based on sensor design, characteristics of susceptible devices and simulation tests.

- Figure 3 illustrates such requirements under the EMC column. Investigating such requirements can be enacted and enhanced via Digital twins, while interoperability as previous identified will be provided through Common Data Exchange (CDE) using IFC (BIM open data exchange files), under point 2 Autodesk in the diagram it shows how collaborative workstations are implemented in modeling design and this type of collaboration allows various actors/stakeholders to review the model sections referring to their needs and any changes can be synchronised to a central sever, or unsynchronised and shared as an independent file.
- The French National Database (BDNB) is a database built by joining multiple building-stock databases, including energy performances diagnostics, and energy consumption. BDNB concentrates on the Extraction, Transformation, and Loading (ETL) that refers to collecting raw data from disparate sources, transmitting it to a staging database for conversion, and loading prepared data into a unified destination system. This allows all the previous disjointed databases to be consolidated into a centralised system where analytics and calculations can be performed [22].
- The concept is to build upon [21] and create at national (French) and European level a centralised database that monitors HEPMs for civilian infrastructures.

C. Funding

To take the project forward will require a partnership built on trust and mutual respect. Securing funding for such research will be an onerous task. However, there are existing funding mechanisms such as HORIZON EUROPE – Work Programme 2021-2022 Digital, Industry and Space. Other funding mechanisms include the European Defence Fund – EDF (information superiority and disruptive technologies) and the European Defence Industrial Development Programme (EDIDP) which has five priorities:

- Facilitating operations, protection, and mobility of military forces.
- Information, secure communications, and cyberspace.
- Ability to conduct peak operations.
- Innovative defence technologies and SMEs.
- Innovation in defence research in materials

Actions of finance:

- Development of CBRN threat detection capabilities or anti-drone systems.
- Development of the next generation of precision ground strike capabilities, ground combat capabilities, aerial warfare capabilities and future naval systems.
- Solutions in the field of artificial intelligence, virtual reality and cybertechnologies.

VIII. Conclusion and Future Work

The papers' main objective was to illustrate a process model based on Developing European Defense Strategy for Electromagnetic Resilience Infrastructure Network. The paper highlighted the need/background for such a strategy by examining existing international strategies of reasoning such as the DoD Congressional Research Service Report that outlined the use of EMS. The capabilities of electromagnetic waves and how the infrastructure for supporting such emissions is protected such as **Data Centres and 5G Networks** is the background of the paper. The paper has also addressed KETs such as photonics in particular reference to Si photonics with CMOS electronics and bandwidth challenges. However, advancements in how we use standards to design a process that will achieve EMC taking into consideration EMI, needs to be addressed and function as part of an overall EMS strategy. The paper has outlined potential solutions such as the project must build upon existing networks and create similar Special Interest Groups (SIGs). The paper identified opportunities, risk and challenges and presented opportunities and the added value associated with utilising EMS, security, speed, energy and cost. In essence, the paper is a medium for identifying research opportunities within the scope European Defense Strategy for Electromagnetic Resilience Infrastructure Network.

ACKNOWLEDGEMENT

The ideas of this article originated in the works of the Consultation Forum for Sustainable Energy in Security and Defence Sector (CF SEDSS) of the European Defence Agency (EDA), in its Working Group 3 on the Protection of Critical Energy Infrastructures (PCEI). The authors would like to address special thanks to Dr. Constantinos Hadjisavvas, Project Officer Energy at EDA and CF SEDSS Project Manager, Ioannis Chatzialexandris, CF SEDSS PCEI WG3Team Leader, and Dr. Nicolas Mazzucchi, CF SEDSS PCEI WG3 moderator.

References

[1] Purcell and Morin, Harvard University. (2013). Electricity and Magnetism, 820p (3rd ed.). Cambridge University Press, New York. ISBN 978-1-107-01402-2. p 430:

[2] J.R. Hoehn, J.C. Gallagher, and K. M. Sayler, "Overview of Department of Defense Use of the Electromagnetic Spectum," Congresssional Research Service CRS Report; Prepared for Members and Committees of Congress, http://crsreport.congress.gov R46564

[3] L. Vivien, D. Marris-Morini, E. Cassan, C. Alonso-Ramos, C. Baudot, F. Bœuf, and B. Szelay, "Circuits Intégrés Photoniques Silicium, Photoniques, EDP Sciences, 2018. Pp. 18-22. 10.1051/photon/201893/18. Hal-02413568

[4] Electronicnotes, "Optical Fibre Cable – an overview or tutoroial covering fibre optic cabling, the construction of the fibre optic cables, how they work, their applications and specifications, electronics-notes.com/articles/connectivity/fibre-optics/optical-fibre-cable.php (access 13/04/2021)

[5] F. Maze, M. Traetta, M. Bentivegna, F. Kaiser, D. Aktas, W. Zhang, C. Alonso-Ramos, L. Bin-Ngah, T. Lunghi, E. Pichelle, N. Belabas-Plougonven, X. Le Roux, E. Cassan, D. Marris-Morini, L. Vivien, G. Sauder, L. Labonté, and S.Tanzilli, "High-quality photonic entanglement for wavelength-multiplexe of quantum communication based on a silicon chip," Opt. Express 5128731 (2016) DOI: 10.1364/OE.24.028731, arXiv:1609.00521 [quant-ph].

[6] LIGHTWAVE, "Evolution to flexible grid WDM, WDM networks operate by transmitting multiple wavelengths, or channels, over a fiber simultaneously, Each channel is assigned a slightly different

wavelength, Nov 26th, 2013, (access 14/04/2021) https://www.lightwaveonline.com/network-design/dwdm-roadm/article/16649471/evolution-to-flexible-grid-wdm

[7] M. Alleven, "Intel takes aim at 5G infrastructure with latest silicon photonics technology", FIERCE Wireless, Sep 24, 2018, https://www.fiercewireless.com/wireless/intel-takes-aim-at-5g-infrastructure-latest-silicon-photonics-technology (access 14/04/2021)

[8] INCOSE 2015, Systems Engineering Handbook, A Guide for Systems Life Cycle Processes and Activities, 4th Edition

[9] DoD Military Standard, MIL-STD-46C (4 August 186), Electromagnetic Emission and Susceptibility Requirements for the Control of Electromagnetic Interference. M. Young, The Technical Writer's Handbook. Mill Valley, CA: University Science, 1989.

[10] R. Vergroesen, "ERTMS/ETCS Hybrid Level 3 and ATO A simulation based capacity impact study for the Dutch railway network", Master Thesis: TU Delft Civil Engineering and Geosciences; TU Delft Transport and Planning, 2020-06-10, http://resolver.tudelft.nl/uuid:971cdcde-1a9a-490a-b72c-8490f2f668ed

[11] EEIG ERTMS Users Group, "Hybrid ERTMS/ETCS Level 3", Ref: 16E042, Version: 1A, Date: 14/07/2017, 123-133 Rue Froissart, 1040 Brussels, Belgium, http://www.ertms.be/sites/default/files/2018-03/16E0421A_HL3.pdf

[12] IEEE Standards Association, "The ICAP Advantage", IEEE Conformity Assessment Program (ICAP), https://standards.ieee.org/products-services/icap/index.html, (access 14/04/2021)

[13] Toshiba, "MOSFET Gate Drive Circuit, Application Note", Toshiba Electronic Devices & Storage Corporation, 2018-07-26

[14] Z. Wang, D. Paez, A. I. Abd El-Rahman, P. Wang, L. Dow, J. C. Cartledge, and A. P. Knights, "Resonance control of a silicon micro-ring resonator modulator under high-speed operation using the intrinsic defect-mediated photocurrent," Opt. Express 25, 24827-24836 (2017)

[15] Radio Waves, "The Key role of antennas", Orange, https://radio-waves.orange.com/en/the-key-role-of-antennas/ (access 14/04/2021)

[16] R. Waterhouse and D. Novack, "Realizing 5G: Microwave Photonics for 5G Mobile Wireless Systems," in IEEE Microwave Magazine, vol. 16, no. 8, pp. 84-92, Sept. 2015, doi: 10.1109/MMM.2015.2441593.

[17] A. L. Swidlehurst, E. Ayanogolu, P. Heydari, and F. Capolino, "Millimeter-wave massive MIMO: The next wireless revolution?" IEEE Commun. Mag., vol. 52, pp. 56–62, Sept. 2014.

[18] R. Uppal, "DARPA Developing Millimmter Wave Wireless Communications to Connect Dismounted War fighters using UAVs and Provide 100 GB/S RF Backbone (100G) using high-altitude, Long-endurance Platforms", Oct 13, 2018, https://idstch.com/technology/communications/darpa-developing-milimmter-wave-wireless-communications-connect-dismounted-warfighters-using-uavs-provide-100-gbs-rf-backbone-100gusing-high-altitude-long-endurance-platforms/, (access 14/04/2021)

[19] R. Fellows and A. Liu, Research Methods for Construction (2nd edition), Blackwell Publishing, Oxford, 2003.

[20] I.C. Tillman, "Accelerating Signals Development for the Modern Specturm Warrior " BDM, RF/uW Senors, Geo Keysight Technologies, September 2019

[21] S. van de Beek et al., "Overview of the European project STRUCTURES," in IEEE Electromagnetic Compatibility Magazine, vol. 3, no. 4, pp. 70-79, 4th Quarter 2014, doi: 10.1109/MEMC.2014.7023202.

[22] M. Thorel and P. Schetelat, Construction de la base de Données Nationale des Bâtiments, June, 2021, https://datafoncier.cerema.fr/sites/datafoncier/files/inline-files/03_base_donnees_nationale_batimentaire_0.pdf

Ensure A Stable Power Grid When Using Renewable Energy

Aleksander Kulseng
Department of Science and Industry Systems
University of South-Eastern Norway (USN)
Kongsberg, Norway
e-mail: aleksanderkulseng@gmail.com

Professor Mo Mansouri
Department of Science and Industry Systems
University of South-Eastern Norway (USN)
Kongsberg, Norway
e-mail: Mo.Mansouri@usn.no

Abstract— **How can we ensure that we do not overload the power grid as we use more renewable energy sources, charging more electric vehicles and using more home electronics? In this paper we will investigate the limitations in the power grid, the consequence of using more renewable energy and charging more electric vehicles. We will also look into ways that smart home technology can make the grid more efficient, and reduce the need for infrastructure upgrades.**

Keywords- Systems Thinking; Systemigram; Power Grid; Smart Electricity; Sustainability; Renewable Energy; Electric Vehicle; Smart Charging; Smart Home Technology

I. INTRODUCTION

The Nordic Transmission System Operators (TSOs) Svenska kraftnät, Statnett, Fingrid and Energinet.dk has identified the following challenges for the Nordic power system: climate change, development of more Renewable Energy Sources (RES), technological development, and a common European framework for markets, operation and planning [1].

Before we continue, renewable energy is according to U.S. Energy Information Administration [2]: energy from sources that are naturally replenishing but flow-limited: renewable resources are virtually inexhaustible in duration, but limited in the amount of energy that is available per unit of time. The major types of renewable energy sources are:

- Biomass
  - Wood and wood waste
  - Municipal solid waste
  - Landfill gas and biomass
  - Ethanol
  - Biodiesel
- Hydropower
- Geothermal
- Wind
- Solar

The Nordic power system have experienced trouble during cold winter days with high consumption and limited generation and transmission capacity. It is easy to predict when these conditions will occur, and to implement corrective actions. In addition to days with high consumption, the power grid may also have hours with low load and high wind production. The power system (illustrated in Figure 1) needs to keep production at the same level as consumption at all times. To be able to do this, flexibility is required. This can be used to change the input or output for balancing purposes. Irregular renewable production is a main driver to increase the flexibility compared to today. Flexibility can be achieved through utilizing transmission capacity more efficient, utilize information from Automatic Metering System (AMS) to further develop demand response and new technology. As the world shifts for more renewable energy production, a new problem emerges. With some green energy, comes more unreliable production and with the increasingly bi-directional flow of power, there is a need to update the infrastructure. With the emerging number of prosumers (households and Electric Vehicles (EV) that consume power from the grid, but also produce electricity from their rooftop solar panels or wind turbine) installation of smart technology will be required to ensure flexibility [3].

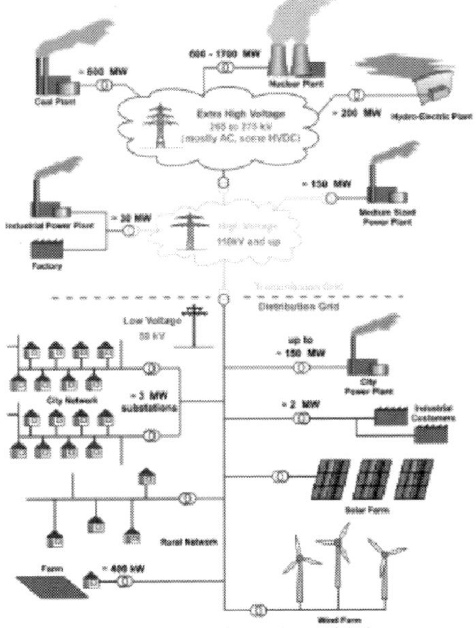

Figure 1. Example of electrical grid [15]

In this paper we will investigate the limitations in the power grid, the consequence of using more renewable energy and charging more electric vehicles.

The reminder of this paper is organized as follows, Section II investigates the current limitations in the power grid. Section III investigates the consequences of using more renewable energy. Section IV investigates how agents can be applied. Section V investigates in to how we can achieve a holistic view of challenges. Section VI looks into how smart technology can be used for grid efficiency.

II. CURRENT LIMITATIONS IN THE POWER GRID

Most of the Norwegian transmission grid is built from 1950 – 1980 and the last part of the transmission grid connecting northern Norway with southern Norway was finished in 1994 (see Figure 2). Large parts of the power production happens in western Norway and in norther Norway, but eastern Norway has the highest consumption with limited local production. This is reflected in the transmission grid, where the flow of power basically flows from west to east and north to south (Figure 3). The government sees a need to modernize, restructure and expand the capacity in the transmission grid. This is to increase the security of supply in some areas, more RES, higher consumption in industry and rural areas with population growth [4].

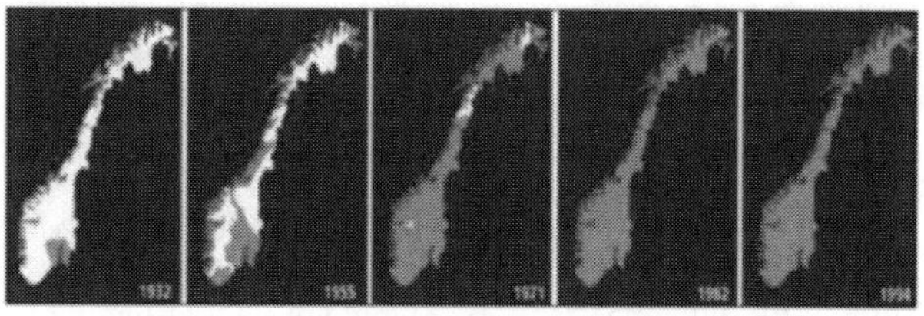

Figure 2. Development of the Norwegian transmission grid.

Figure 3. Overview of the Norwegian transmission grid [4].

III. CONSEQUENCE OF USING MORE RENEWABLE ENERGY

To be able to reduce initial infrastructure cost its recommended to exploit the current transmission grid in relation to available transmission capacity, so that renewable energy production is localized in areas with low capacity or areas in need of more capacity. This may mean a more geographical distributed development.

Renewable energy draw power from natural sources; solar, wind, ocean, hydroelectric and geothermal. This means that it is affected by environmental, seasonal and daily cycles that can limit their efficiency. This means that production will vary during all hours of the day and be less predictable. Because of this there is a need to store the energy, *grid energy storage*. There are multiple ways to store energy depending on the source; dammed hydroelectricity, batteries, thermal energy storage and mechanical energy storage. Dammed hydroelectricity is the largest way to store energy, using both conventional hydroelectricity generation and pumped storage hydroelectricity. Recent years the research and development of battery storage technology has enabled commercially viable projects to store energy during periods with low consumption and high production. Thermal energy storage is another way to store renewable energy using liquids or solid materials to store and release thermal energy. Water tanks in buildings are a simple example of thermal energy storage systems. Storage of energy may give the TSOs and grid operators the flexibility and ability to maintain security of supply.

As a consequence of high electricity bills, lower cost for solar panels and the security of supply more and more consumers become prosumers. Not only do they consume power, they also generate their own (Figure 4).

Figure 4. Consumer vs. Prosumer [3].

The increase in electrical appliances and charging of EVs is making some cities experiencing higher peak loads. Increasing peak loads will lead to grid enhancements and increased cost. Some of this cost may be reduced if local generation, batteries or other *demand flexibility resources* reduce the required capacity during peak load hour.

IV. Application of Agents

The problem domain can be viewed as a system containing various agents. The agents and their characteristics can change based on the area that's being researched or analyzed. The Energy Hub [20] has made some good examples of this, they present all consumers and producers of electricity are represented by an agent, connected to a power matching auctioneer agent (Figure 5).

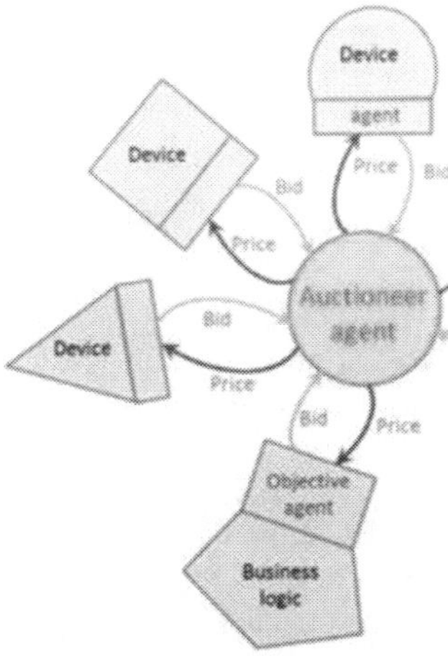

Figure 5. Agents representing devices operating in a market with an auctioneer agent [20].

The report "NIST Framework and Roadmap for Smart Grid Interoperability Standards" written by The National Institute of Standards and Technology (NIST) [16] has useful illustrations showing the agents and domains that could exist in the problem domain. This is a good basis to understand the different stakeholders (Figure 6).

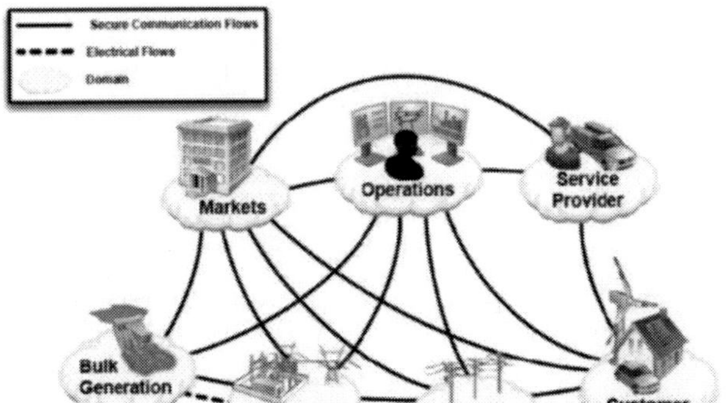

Figure 6. NIST domains and agents for a Smart Grid [17].

V. Achieving a Holistic View of the Challenges

A central approach in Systems Thinking is the holistic approach, which looks at the interrelationship between the parts in its environment [5]. We want to use this approach, and to get a holistic view, we model the problem domain and its relationship in a Systemigram. The Systemigram can be seen in Figure 7 below, and the full-scale Systemigram can be seen in Figure 8 at the end of this paper. From the Systemigram, we can see that there are many complex and complicated relationships and not individual problems. The Systemigram contains many stories, and every story has an unique color, and the reading direction is appointed by the arrow. By the help of the Systemigram, we get a holistic view of the problem domain. This is helpful because, as stated earlier, new solutions bring new challenges to the table, but with the Systemigram one can get an idea of how the other relationships are affected, so one can take precautions and make a more robust solution. From the Systemigram we can see that there is more than one system in action.

Figure 7. Systemigram of the problem domain.

VI. Using Smart Technology for Grid Efficiency

In recent years, there has been multiple research projects focusing on utilizing smart technology for grid efficiency. The focus has been to give TSOs and grid operators the flexibility needed to maintain security of supply and minimizing the impact on the customers. These research projects have been cooperation between different technology companies, grid owners and TSO.

A. *NorFLex*

Cooperation between Agder Energi, Statnett, Glitre Energi, Mørenett and NODES to develop new technological solutions to get a more flexible power consumption [6]. The solutions shall contribute to avoid overload in the power grid. The goal of the project is to find the smart technological solutions for the power grid that smooths out the peak loads over the hole day. One of the technologies used in this project is smart adapters for panel heaters and smart EV chargers connected to Tibber. Tibber then pooled together the flexibility from these two device types in multiple homes and offered this aggregated flexibility to the local grid owner Agder Energi in an automated process.

B. Electric vehicles and buildings keep the power grid in balance

This is a cooperation project between Tibber, Entelios and Statnett to use electric vehicles and large buildings to maintain balance between the production and consumption of electric power [7]. Entelios and Tibber are working to deliver flexibility from a wide range of technologies. Tibber has now contributed flexible power consumption from EVs in Greater Oslo, while Enelios has tested automated flexibility from electric central heating boilers in industrial, commercial and public buildings in the eastern part on Norway, according to Statnett. Both research projects conclude that to be able to safeguard the supply of power in the future, there is a need for smart technological solutions.

Tibber is currently using smart chargers for electric vehicles as load balancer in the real power grid in large scale in Sweden as they have moved into the Swedish balancing market for frequency containment reserve (FCR), using the capacity offered by electric vehicles [8] [18].

The U.S. Department of Energy´s Office of Electricity states that [9]: "The Smart Grid is not just about utilities and technologies; it is about giving you the information and tools you need to make choices about your energy use. If you already manage activities such as personal banking from your home computer, imagine managing your electricity in a similar way. A smarter grid will enable an unprecedented level of consumer participation. For example, you will no longer have to wait for your monthly statement to know how much electricity you use. With a smarter grid, you can have a clear and timely picture of it. "Smart meters," and other mechanisms, will allow you to see how much electricity you use, when you use it, and its cost. Combined with real-time pricing, this will allow you to save money by using less power when electricity is most expensive. While the potential benefits of the Smart Grid are usually discussed in terms of economics, national security, and renewable energy goals, the Smart Grid has the potential to help you save money by helping you to manage your electricity use and choose the best times to purchase electricity. And you can save even more by generating your own power."

VII. Conclusion

Norway is committed to achieving its emission reduction target under the Paris Agreement, which sets a target of reducing emissions by at least 50% and towards 55% below 1990 levels by 2030 [10]. Smart Grids are the digitalized and smart power grids of the future. They are also essential to Norway's electrification efforts and success with the necessary reduction of greenhouse gas emissions [11].

Norway, the Nordic countries and the EU are all shifting from large, centralized coal- and gas power plants to de-centralized wind- and sun power plants. It is estimated that from 2010 to 2025 the total capacity of wind power is quadrupled to 24.000 megawatt, or 22% in the Nordic. The most important challenges for the TSO and grid operators is to secure a stable power grid. One of the means to ensure this is flexibility; the possibility to get industry or households to reduce their consumption during peak load hours [12].

The Nordic TSOs has published a report "The Way forward – Solutions for a changing Nordic power system" where they summarize the key solutions that are needed to meet the challenges affecting the Nordic power system in the period leading up to 2025. One of the key areas is balancing the power system, with a new Nordic balancing concept called the Modernized Area Control Error (MACE) [13]. Compared to ACE control, MACE control utilizes modern IT solutions and optimization algorithm, automatic reserves and available transmission capacities in order to exchange reserves between zones [14].

There are multiple research projects underway or finished related to the topic we have investigated in this paper. All projects conclude that smart technology, used right, gives the flexibility needed to help balance the power grid as more RES are integrated. Tibber is doing this in Sweden using only smart charges for electric vehicles, this can be expanded to utilize other smart technology to balance the power and to postpone the need for infrastructure updates. The implementation Tibber is doing in the Swedish power grid can easily be expanded to Norway and Germany where Tibber also has established their business [19].

References

[1] Svenska kraftnät, Statnett, Fingrid, and Energinet.dk, ``Challenges and Opportunities for the Nordic Power System," https://www.fingrid.fi/globalassets/dokumentit/fi/yhtio/tki-toiminta/report-challenges-and-opportunities-for-the-nordic-power-system.pdf, August 2015. [retrieved: June, 2022].

[2] U.S. Energy Information Administration, Renewable energy explained, https://www.eia.gov/energyexplained/renewable-sources/, May 2021. [retrieved: June, 2022]

[3] U.S. Department of Energy Office of Energy Efficiency \& Renewable Energy, Consumer vs Prosumer: What's the Difference?, https://www.energy.gov/eere/articles/consumer-vs-prosumer-whats-difference, May 2017. [retrieved: June, 2022].

[4] The Royal Norwegian Ministry of Petroleum and Energy, ``Meld. St. 14 (2011–2012) Vi bygger Norge – om utbygging av strømnettet", https://www.regjeringen.no/contentassets/19472ee2fcc54a0eaae169972fd61c98/no/pdfs/stm201120120014000dddpdfs.pdf March 2021. [retrieved: June, 2022].

[5] J. Gharajedaghi, ``Systems Thinking: Managing Chaos and Complexity" Burlington, MA 01803, USA: Elsevier, Inc., 2011. [retrieved: June, 2022].

[6] Agder Energi, Hva er NorFlex? https://www.ae.no/var-virksomhet/fornyelse/norflex-prosjektet/hva-er-norflex/, August 2019. [retrieved: June, 2022]

[7] Statnett, Electric vehicles and buildings help keep the power grid in balance, https://www.statnett.no/en/about-statnett/news-and-press-releases/news-archive-2020/electric-

vehicles-and-buildings-help-keep-the-power-grid-in-balance/, June 2020. [retrieved: June, 2022]

[8] E. Barbiroglio, A Swedish Energy Startup Wants To Make Electricity Consumption Smarter. Forbes, https://www.forbes.com/sites/emanuelabarbiroglio/2020/08/28/a-swedish-energy-startup-wants-to-make-electricity-consumption-smarter/?sh=f2dd38528175, 2020. [retrieved: June, 2022].

[9] U.S. Department of Energy´s Office of Electricity, The Smart Grid, https://www.smartgrid.gov/the_smart_grid/smart_grid.html, [retrieved: June, 2022].

[10] The Royal Norwegian Ministry of Climate and Environment, Norway's comprehensive climate action plan, https://www.regjeringen.no/en/aktuelt/heilskapeleg-plan-for-a-na-klimamalet/id2827600/, January 2021. [retrieved: June, 2022]

[11] SINTEF, Smart Grids, https://www.sintef.no/en/shared-research-areas/smart-grids/. [retrieved: June, 2022].

[12] K. M. Hovland, Ruster opp kraftnettet for milliarder: – Et historisk høyt nivå, https://e24.no/olje-og-energi/i/gPm10B/ruster-opp-kraftnettet-for-milliarder-et-historisk-hoeyt-nivaa, E24, August 2018. [retrieved: June, 2022].

[13] Svenska kraftnät, Statnett, Fingrid, and Energinet.dk, The Way forward – Solutions for a changing Nordic power system, https://www.statnett.no/globalassets/om-statnett/nyheter-og-pressemeldinger/the-way-forward---solutions-for-a-changing-nordic-power-system_lowres.pdf, March 2018. [retrieved: June, 2022].

[14] Statnett, A new balancing model for the Nordic power system, https://www.statnett.no/en/about-statnett/news-and-press-releases/News-archive-2017/a-new-balancing-model-for-the-nordic-power-system2/, October 2020. [retrieved: June, 2022].

[15] Wikimedia Commons, Electricity Grid Schematic English, https://commons.wikimedia.org/wiki/File:Electricity_Grid_Schematic_English.svg, March 2010. [retrieved: June, 2022].

[16] "NIST Framework and Roadmap for Smart Grid Interoperability Standards , Release 1.0. United States National Institute of Standards and Technology," 2010. [retrieved: June, 2022].

[17] D. Saraansh, M. Sooriyabandara, and M. Yearworth, A Systems Approach to the Smart Grid, http://www.bristol.ac.uk/media-library/sites/eng-systems-centre/migrated/documents/s-dave-paper.pdf , 2011. [retrieved: June, 2022].

[18] Tibber, IMPACT REPORT 2020, https://tibber.com/en/impact-report, 2021. [retrieved: June, 2022].

[19] Tibber, About Tibber, https://tibber.com/en/about-us, 2021. [retrieved: June, 2022].

[20] Energy Hub, Agent based technology, http://www.e-hub.org/agent-based-technology.html, 2022. [retrieved: June, 2022].

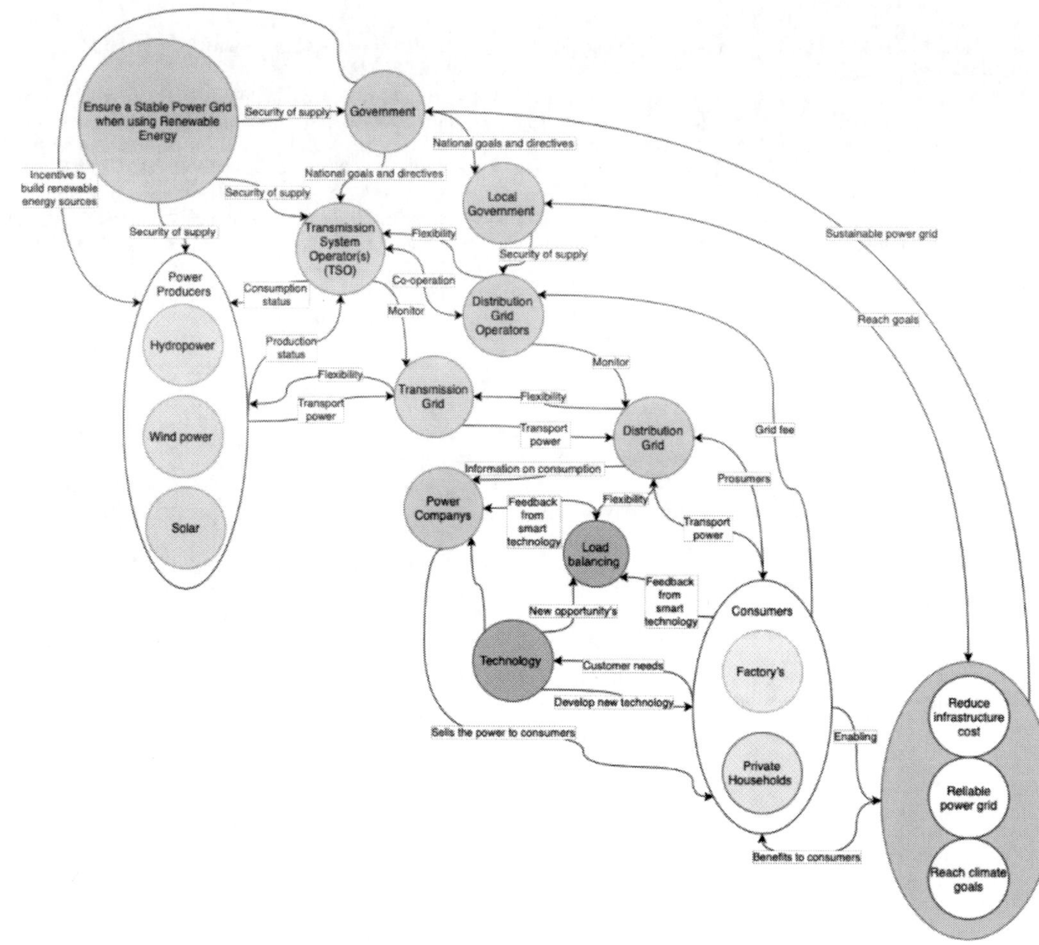

Figure 8. Systemigram of the problem domain.

Applying Systems Thinking for Early Validation of a Case Study Definition: An Automated Parking System

Haytham B. Ali
University of South-Eastern Norway
Kongsberg, Norway
haytham.ali@usn.no

Mo Mansouri
Stevens Institute of Technology
Hoboken, USA
mo.mansouri@stevens.edu

Gerrit Muller
University of South-Eastern Norway
Kongsberg, Norway
gerrit.muller@usn.no

***Abstract*—Case study research and industry-as-laboratory research are well-known research methods in industry–academia collaboration research projects. Defining a case study well in the early phase of an industry–academia complex sociotechnical and data-oriented research project is crucial for success. This success can be measured by the Company's active participation and sharing of all data needed for the research project. In this paper, we apply systems thinking and its tools to validate the Company's need in an early phase to define the case study in the research project. We use systemigrams for early validation. The foundation for the systemigram is system thinking tools. These tools include stakeholder analysis, context diagram, and Customers, Actors, Transformation, Worldview, Owner, and Environment (CATWOE) analysis. Systems thinking and its tools aid in communicating and sharing a common understanding of the Company's case study and support further exploration of the value proposition for the Company's actual needs.**

***Keywords*—early validation; systems thinking; CATWOE analysis; systemigram; company's need; visualization.**

I. INTRODUCTION

A lack of available land and a need for more parking places, especially in urban cities, triggers the need for an Automated Parking System (APS) [1]. However, the APS fails mostly for two main reasons: when the system is used at a high rate and when the end-user is unfamiliar with it. In addition, the APS fails due to some mechanical failures[2][3]. The failure rate of an APS is higher than that of the traditional system. Thus, there is a need to increase the reliability of APSs [4].

In this paper, we investigate the application of systems thinking to validate the Company's need in an early phase as part of defining the case study within the harvesting value from big data and digitalization through the Human Systems-Engineering Innovation Framework (H-SEIF 2) research project. Defining a case study well during the early phase of a complex sociotechnical research project is crucial for the success of a research project. This success can be measured by the Company's participation and data sharing. Data sharing is an essential factor in this research project. We systematically analyze the needs and investigate how external forces affect the project's development [5].

1) The case. The H-SEIF 2 project is a research project aiming to enable data-supported early decisions in the early design phase of the New Product Development (NPD) process. Today, an enormous amount of data is available. With the right approach, suitable algorithms, and structure, Norwegian companies can use big data to provide a decisive competitive advantage in the international market. This research project is an ongoing project that investigates how companies that deliver complex systems can streamline their innovation and NPD processes by using big data and digitalization more effectively [5].

2) The Company. The Company is small and medium-sized enterprise that delivers APSs, including maintenance, primarily for land developers and building owners. The APSs include fully and semi-automated car parking systems. The Company is transitioning from selling to developing, producing, and marketing. Their systems are not designed with enough sensors to achieve proper condition monitoring, and they require proper data management. Company management believes that other parking systems are far behind this solution.

The Company has stored data, also called big data. Big data refer to datasets whose size or complexity exceeds the capability of current or conventional methods within the Company. However, the challenge for companies is to explore value from their stored big data [6]. The application of big data will increase the reliability of APSs by making more data-driven decisions for the early design phase within the NPD and maintenance processes [7]. The paper reminder is as follows: Section II illustrate the study's research method. Section III shows systems thinking application in a case study. Section IV provides a thorough discussion, and ultimately Section V wraps up the study with a conclusion.

II. RESEARCH METHOD

A. Case Study Research

We use case study research, as we use industry-as-laboratory research during the research project [8][9]. Case study research includes the following three steps: defining the case study well, selecting the design, and using theory in design work [9]. In this paper, we focus on the first step through applying systems thinking. A case study usually includes multiple units of analysis. We collected mainly qualitative data. The qualitative data include direct observations, participant observations, open-ended (nonstructured) interviews, and physical artifacts.

The direct and participant observations resulted from the authors as researchers involved in a real-life context by participating in events and meetings within the Company-of-Interest. We also conducted open-ended interviews as part of the observation and part of the workshops we performed with the Company. Moreover, we identified and collected stored data within the Company as physical artifacts. These data were downloaded by the Company's employees and provided to the main author of this paper.

Having different sources of evidence permits us, as researchers, to investigate and reinvestigate the consistency of the findings from various sources of evidence. Furthermore, we can converge these pieces of evidence, also called data triangulation, to increase the robustness of the results [10].

B. *Checkland's Soft Systems Methodology*

Applying systems thinking in a case study within the industry-as-laboratory enables soft systems methodology (SSM) and supports systems engineering. Boardman et al. (2009) [11] argue that systems thinking is the foundation of systems engineering, SSM, and applied complexity science.

Figure 1 depicts Checkland's SSM. We modified the methodology to be iterative, excluding the phases between the steps and emphasizing that there was no one right path. Further, we use the systemigram as a conceptual model, structured text as the root definition of relevant systems, and dramatization and dialogue as a comparison of steps 2 and 4. This modification was inspired by Sauser et al. (2011) [12], who called the SSM that includes those modifications Boardman's SSM (BSSM).

SSM allows for individuals' different perspectives and different desirable outcomes of the case study. In addition, SSM bridges the real world and systems thinking [12]–[14]. The SSM consists of the seven steps visualized in Figure 1. Steps 1 to 7 are repeated until consensus is reached among the individuals involved in the in the case study. In other words, the process including the steps is repeated until the Company's need as part of the case study definition is verified and validated.

III. Applying Systems Thinking Methodology in a Case Study

There are several definitions of systems thinking. However, Barry Richmond, one of the leaders of systems thinking, emphasizes that systems thinkers look at the tree and the forest simultaneously [15]. In this context, the tree is the Company, and the forest is the H-SEIF2 research project as the project includes other companies. We investigate the similarities and synergies between those companies further during a co-creation process. In this paper, we adopt Arnold and Wade's definition of systems thinking: "Systems thinking is a set of synergistic analytic skills used to improve the capability of identifying and understanding systems, predicting their behaviors, and devising modifications to them in order to produce desired effects. These skills work together as a system" [16].

To get a better understanding of the context, we describe the system. Furthermore, we define system boundaries with a context diagram. We then identify the stakeholders and their interests in a stakeholder interests map. We use systems thinking tools: CATWOE analysis and systemigram.

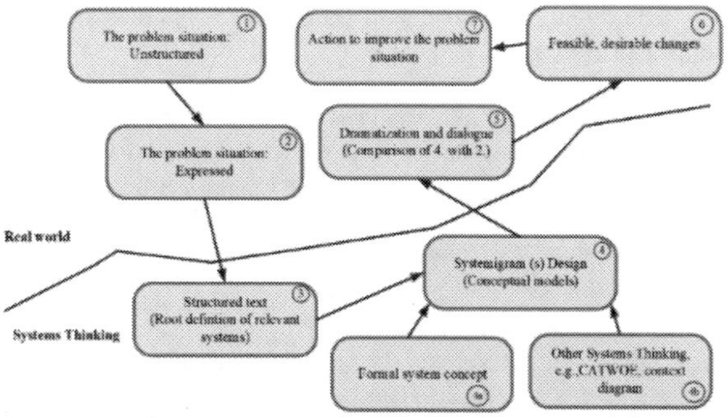

Figure 1. Checkland's soft systems methodology (SSM) based on [12]–[14].

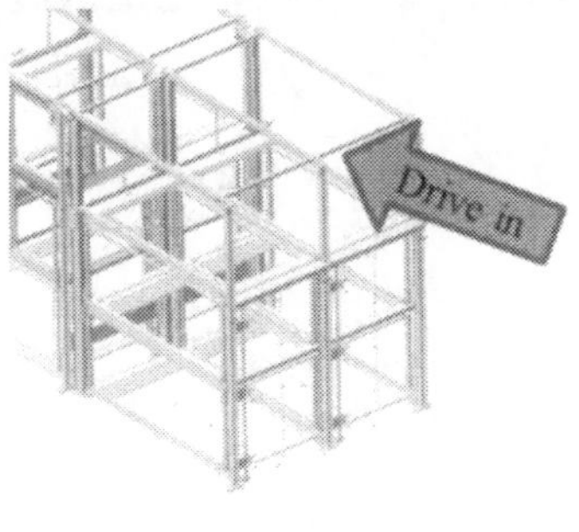

Figure 2. The SOI: the semi-automated parking system.

A. *Description of the APS*

The APS is a complex system due to its multiplex hardware and people's interactions with the system [4]. Problems that occur include not retrieving the right car or no a car at all. Figure 2 shows the System-of-Interest (SOI): a semi-automated car parking system (garage). Figure 2 also depicts a drive-in indication. The car entrance can be a straightforward or inclined plane. The SOI has different configurations. These configurations include different heights, breadths, and depths. The car entrance and the SOI's configurations depend on the building and its architecture. In addition, the SOI includes many parts, such as the gate, control unit, platform, wedges, and so forth.

B. *System Boundaries*

We can understand systems in the context within their environment [17]. The system context helps us to understand the openness of the system. Figure 3 depicts a context diagram for the SOI.

The context diagram illustrates three variables:

1) *Controllable variables* are variables in which we identified the SOI. Having the SOI within the innermost circle means that it is necessary to act sufficiently to achieve the needed outcome.

2) *Influencing variables* are uncontrollable variables that we can influence. We identified the critical stakeholders within the influencing variables. The critical stakeholders are Company management, land developers, building owners, suppliers, local authorities (communes), maintenance personnel, development team, and car owners. We discuss the stakeholders more in the following subsection.

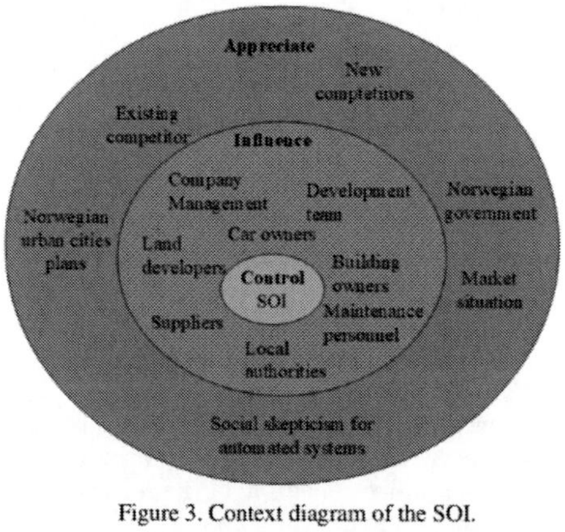

Figure 3. Context diagram of the SOI.

3) Appreciating variables are uncontrollable variables that we cannot influence; thus, we need to appreciate them. The *appreciating variables* include the following:

a) *Existing competitors*. To date, there has been only one competitor in the Norwegian market.

b) *New competitors*. Any new competitor can emerge and enter the market. We included new competitors, although the barrier to entry makes that problematic.

c) *Norwegian urban cities plan*. Norwegian cities have their own development plans, including construction of new buildings and the architecture of old and new buildings [18].

d) *Market situation*. The market situation is crucial, as many Norwegian cities (including Oslo) aim to have car-free downtowns [19]. In addition, the Norwegian market is part of the global market and is highly affected by it.

e) *Norwegian government*. The Norwegian government is responsible for existing and future regulations and standards. The regulations include which level of authorities have the local authorities, also called communes.

f) *Social skepticism* toward automated systems. These automated systems include fully and semi-automated parking systems. Social skepticism is one of the challenges facing the SOI. Car owners may get the wrong car or no vehicle. Thus, increasing the system's reliability is necessary to improve social acceptance. Using big data analytics, including two different data sources to monitor and maintain the SOI, is crucial.

C. Stakeholders and Their Interests

Figure 4 shows the critical stakeholders for the SOI. The SOI in the middle of the figure. Furthermore, we connected the essential stakeholders with the SOI with two types of arrows.

The first type is a solid line and arrow, indicating an intense connection and a strong influence or interest in the SOI. The dashed arrows and lines indicate a weak association between the SOI and the stakeholders(s) and a weak influence on or interest in the SOI. For instance, we identified a weak connection between the government and the SOI, which has regulations, safety, and rules as their interest in the SOI. The government makes the regulations and standards for the systems, including the SOI. However, the government is not involved and does not strongly influence the development process. Thus, we chose to identify this relationship as a weak connection. Furthermore, we identified an intense relationship between the SOI and the following stakeholders: Company management, the development team, maintenance personnel, land developers, building owners, and car owners. This strong connection results from high involvement or influence in the SOI and its development process.

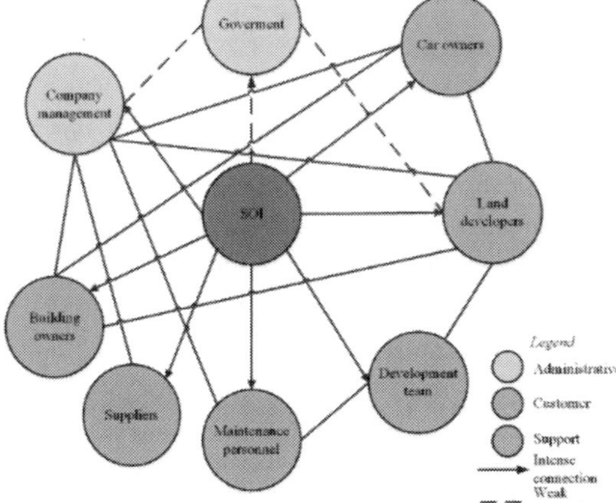

Figure 4. Stakeholder interests map.

We also identified relationships or connections among the stakeholders. For instance, there is a strong connection between car owners and Company management, as car owners are the end-users of the SOI. We present an intense relationship with a solid line between building owners, land developers, and Company management. The Company sells its SOI primarily to land developers. However, the Company also sells its SOI directly to building owners or land developers. Table I lists the stakeholders and their interests.

TABLE I. STAKEHOLDERS AND THEIR INTERESTS

Stakeholder	Interests (why)
Government	Urban city development, including building new buildings and car-free downtowns. The government has the authority for regulation and standards for the SOI and includes the Norwegian Competition Authority
Company management	A reliable SOI as the traditional parking system, customer satisfaction, profit maximation
Land developers	Operating Expense (OPEX) and Capital Expenditure (CAPEX)
Building owners	Operating Expense (OPEX) and Capital Expenditure (CAPEX)
Car owners	Availability of parking spots and reliability of the SOI (getting the right car without any damage at the right time)
Suppliers	Maximize profit by winning contracts and satisfying the Company, which is the supplier's customer
Maintenance personnel	Accessibility and usability of the SOI to conduct maintenance
Development team	Accessibility and usability of the SOI for car owners and maintenance personnel or anyone who uses the SOI

D. CATWOE Analysis

Customers, Actors, Transformation, Worldview, Owner, and Environment are called CATWOE. CATWOE analysis is an essential tool for understanding the different stakeholder perspectives. This understanding is the foundation of the systemigram that we present in the following section.

The CATWEO analysis tool aids in constructing the root definition of the proposed system [20]. This tool also provides an understanding of what the Company wants to achieve with the stored data, alongside their need as a case study. In addition, the CATWEO analysis identifies the problem areas and suggests how the proposed solution could impact the Company and its critical stakeholders.

We apply CATWEO analysis to the two main critical stakeholders in the case study: Company management and maintenance personnel. The results are shown in Table II and

Table III, respectively. The CATWOE illustrates the different aspects of the two main critical stakeholders. These different aspects show the different abstraction levels of the Company's need as part of the case study in the H-SEIF2 research project. Thus, we use the CATWOE analysis as a foundation of the following systems thinking tool: a systemigram.

TABLE II. CATWOE: COMPANY MANAGEMENT

Aspect	Description
Customers	Company management
Actors	Partners, suppliers, maintenance personnel
Transformation	Increase the reliability of the SOI
Worldview	H-SEIF2 research project: value from big data (provide data to the project) Maximize profit
Owner	Company management
Environment	Urban cities

TABLE III. CATWOE: MAINTENANCE PERSONNEL

Aspect	Description
Customers	Maintenance personnel
Actors	Suppliers, Company management, car owners
Transformation	Maintenance process and method
Worldview	Increase reliability and availability of the SOI
Owner	Department heads of service and maintenance
Environment	The Automated Parking System (APS), building, cars, traffic density, weather, city infrastructure

E. Systemigram

A systemigram, also called a systemic diagram, is a graphical visualization of the Company's need in terms of storytelling [13]. Using a systemigram aids in communicating understanding of the Company's need. The Company's need represents the surface of the problem definition, as well as the Company's case study in the H-SEIF2 research project. We developed a systemigram based on the analysis and discussion in the previous subsections. The systemigram represents the Company management's and maintenance personnel's perspectives, focusing on the SOI and Condition-Based Maintenance (CBM) system, CBM also seen as the System-Of-System (SOS).

The systemigram, showing the case study based on the Company's need, is visualized in Figure 5. The flow for the systemigram is from the top left to the bottom right. In the upper left is the Company management who presents the SOI for the systemigram, where the primary goal is at the bottom right, which is to maximize business viability. The systemigram is sorted into two main categories with two colors. The first category is the mainstay in dark gray blue. The other main category is big data, in light blue. We aim to have an overview of available stored data and possible needed data for the Company's proposed system (request) within the Company's case study: the CBM system (SOS).

The mainstay is diagonal and presents the central message of the systemigram. The mainstay can be read as follows: "Company management owns the SOI that comprises the NPD process that constitute sensor(s) that allow CBM system implementation, which permits observation of anomalies that aids mechanical failure detection and prediction in real-time which allows continuous monitoring of the SOI through a dashboard that maximizes business viability." Business viability includes many other nodes: increase in the reliability of the SOI, increase in availability in the SOI, and increase in customer satisfaction.

The SOI consists of parts and data. Data include service-log data (maintenance records data) that constitute internal data, which are part of big data that can be provided to data analysts. Service-log data can be analyzed to identify measurable critical parameters and the most critical parts that can be used to decide which sensors to install. Data analysts include mainly researchers, in addition to the Company and partners. Sensor(s) (already installed sensors and planned to install) generate sensor data that constitute internal data. Maintenance personnel who maintain the SOI have tacit knowledge, and researchers can transform part of it into explicit knowledge in terms of visualization (information) and data that also constitute internal data.

Researchers conduct data analysis. Researchers including the main author are in process of the data analysis as part of the Company's case study. Data analysis enhances decision-making regarding the maintenance process of the SOI. Data analysis includes the following steps (nodes): data storage and retrieval, data pre-processing, data analysis, and data visualization. Decision-making regarding the maintenance process includes implementing the CBM system for the SOI (Company's request as part of the case study).

CBM implementation permits observation of anomalies that aids in detecting mechanical failure events. However, CBM passes over electronic failure events. Failure event detection and prediction allow continuous monitoring of the SOI through a dashboard using a traffic light color code. Researchers also identify the external data needed to verify the analysis results from internal data. External data is a third part data that the Company is not storing internally at their databases. Internal data is the data that the Company owns and is available to be downloaded. Implementing the CBM system requires external data. CBM generates sensor and stream data.

External data and internal data constitute big data. Big data can be provided, as mentioned, to data analysts who conduct data analysis. Data analysis investigates patterns and trends. It also supports the decision-making of the SOI maintenance process, including CBM implementation.

A CBM system can have system failures. These failures include data anomalies and downtime (CBM downtime). CBM can also give a false positive and a false negative. System failures and false alarms decrease business viability.

F. Possible Leverage Points

Applying systems thinking and its analysis tools aids in communicating and sharing understanding of the case study definition. This communication occurs through visualization of the systemigram. We developed the systemigram through several iterations after applying other systems thinking tools. These tools are the foundation of the systemigram development and include stakeholder analysis, a context diagram, and CATWEO analysis.

The systemigram visualizes the case study, including its multiple-unit analysis. This visualization aids in defining the case study well and sharing mutual understanding of the Company's need as part of the case study definition. The systemigram also helps communicate the case study definition to the Company, scholars, and other partners in the complex sociotechnical research project. The Company and the researchers used the systemigram to prioritize the most significant unit analysis in the case study. For instance, we agreed that CBM system is a long-term vision to increase the SOI's reliability. The second short-term vision is data analysis to investigate the use case for developing the CBM system. This communication aided in early validation of the Company's need as part of the case study during the early phase of the research project.

Early validation contributed to the project's success. This observation results from the Company's active participation in the research project. In addition, the Company shared all the stored and needed data with the main author of this paper. Moreover, the systemigram helped explore the problem domain that define the case study and not only touching the surface of the problem. In other words, systemigram helped at dig deeper into Company's actual (real) needs, which continues this an ongoing case study.

IV. Discussion

We developed the systemigram through several iterations. These iterations resulted in several versions of the systemigram. Some of the iterations were conducted with other researchers in the H-SEIF2 research project. The researchers were also involved in some of the workshops and interviews conducted with the Company. However, we struggled to visualize the systemigram so that is readable, as it included many nodes and explanatory links. We had to perform several iterations and use various tools. The iterations include feedback as part of the validation process with the Company. This visualization represents how researchers' knowledge is chaotic and disordered, while the systemigram aims to visualize this knowledge in a nice storytelling way. Moreover, the systemigram aids in explaining all the aspects and key stakeholders' perspectives and communicating and sharing understanding of the case study definition, including its multiple-unit analysis.

One of the essential perspectives to evaluate is the profitability aspect of the Company's request (the proposed system): the CBM system from an economic perspective. This profitability includes a business plan, including the capital expenditure (CAPEX), operating expense (OPEX), and return on investment (ROI) of the proposed system. However, we made a quick iteration to develop a rough business plan. This plan is not included in this paper, as we focus on using conceptual modeling, mainly systems thinking and its tools, to validate the Company's need in an early phase as part of the case study definition. We could also evaluate it by using other conceptual models and could include the economic perspective, such as cost optimization and performance in the systemigram(s). However, including this perspective could make the systemigram unreadable.

The Company's key personnel, including Company management and department heads of service and maintenance, validated the systemigrams. The Company's feedback indicated that the systemigram aids in communicating a common understanding and includes all the aspects and perspectives of the Company's case study.

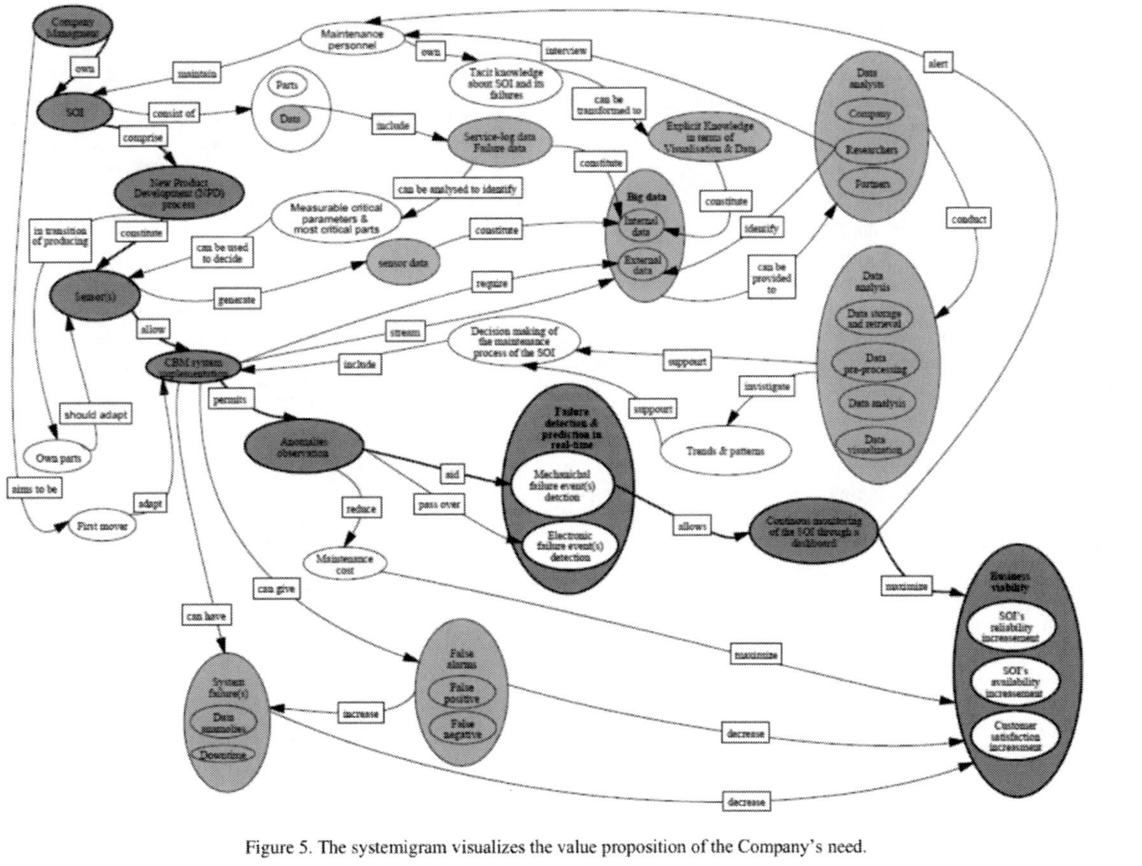

Figure 5. The systemigram visualizes the value proposition of the Company's need.

The main author tested the systemigram as a communication tool for the Company's case study with other companies in the H-SEIF2 research project. Company management also tested systemigrams as a communication tool for external stakeholders. The feedback indicated that the systemigram works as a communication tool. However, we may need to investigate further the need of other conceptual models that can be used as a supportive tool for systemigram(s). This support can be towards more concrete and specific solutions and technologies.

We could also apply other systems thinking tools to explore and increase understanding of the problem and solution domains from all perspectives and at different abstraction levels. These tools could include casual loop diagrams and conceptagon(s). We could use these tools to increase understanding of system behavior and dynamics and to organize system information and definitions. However, we believe that the systems thinking methodology and tools we applied in this paper achieved the goal of its application: early validation of the Company's case study definition.

V. Future Work

We aim to develop a financial model for the SOI. The model will investigate the profitability of implementing CBM in the short and long term. This model also aims to include the cost of the optimization and performance of adapting the Company's proposed system or request (the CBM system) as an option to increase the SOI's reliability.

Another option we plan to investigate is data analysis. We aim to analyze service-log data (maintenance record data) to increase the SOI's reliability. We believe that these data can support reliability engineering activities during the early design phase of the NPD process. In addition, we believe in using data analysis aids as input to discover the Company's actual needs. In other words, exploring the problem definition for the case study and not only touching the problem definition's surface by going forward for the Company's actual needs.

VI. Conclusion

Defining a case study well within the early phase of a complex sociotechnical research project is crucial for its success. This success can be measured by the Company's active participation and trust by sharing all needed data. We applied systems thinking and its tools to a real-industry case study. The tools include stakeholders' analysis, context diagram, CATWEO analysis, and systemigram. This application aims to validate the Company's need early as part of defining the case study well, including its several unit analyses. Feedback on the application of systems thinking methodology and its tools indicates that systems thinking aids in communicating and sharing understanding of all aspects and critical stakeholders' perspectives within the case study. This early validation helps researchers (academia) and Company (industry) investigate the Company's need and what triggers such a need to further explore the actual needs of the Company's case study.

Acknowledgment

This research is part of a larger research project, the second iteration of the Human Systems Engineering Innovation Framework (HSEIF-2), funded by The Research Council of Norway (Project number 317862).

References

[1] M. Nourinejad, S. Bahrami, and M. J. Roorda, "Designing parking facilities for autonomous vehicles," Trans. Research Part B: Methodological, vol. 109, pp. 110–127, 2018.

[2] G. Cudney, "Parking Today | Articles - Automated Parking: Is It Right for You?" Available: https://www.parkingtoday.com/articledetails.php?id=181&t=automated-parking-is-it-right-for-you (accessed June. 17, 2022).

[3] F. Robles, "Road to Robotic Parking Is Littered With Faulty Projects," The New York Times, Nov. 28, 2015. Accessed: Junev 17, 2022. [Online]. Available: https://www.nytimes.com/2015/11/28/us/road-to-robotic-parking-islittered-with-faulty-projects.html

[4] A. Mathijssen and A. J. Pretorius, "Verified design of an automated parking garage," in International Workshop on Parallel and Distributed Methods in Verification, 2006, pp. 165–180.

[5] "H-SEIF 2," Universitetet i Sørøst-Norge, Nov. 25, 2020. https://www.usn.no/english/research/our-research/technology/norwegian-industrial-systems-engineering-research-group/h-seif-2/ (accessed June. 17, 2022).

[6] H. B. Ali, "Unlocking the power of big data within the early design phase of the new product development process: A case study in a Company," 2021. [Online]. Available: https://www.gaudisite.nl/INCOSE2021_AliEtAL.pdf

[7] "Defining and Clarifying Reliability." https://www.reliableplant.com/Read/98/defining-reliability (accessed Aug. 15, 2021).

[8] C. Potts, "Software-engineering research revisited," IEEE software, vol. 10, no. 5, pp. 19–28, 1993.

[9] R. K. Yin, Applications of case study research. sage, 2011.

[10] M. Duneier and O. Carter, Sidewalk. Macmillan, 1999.

[11] J. Boardman, B. Sauser, L. John, and R. Edson, "The conceptagon: A framework for systems thinking and systems practice," in 2009 IEEE International Conference on Systems, Man and Cybernetics, 2009, pp. 3299–3304.

[12] B. Sauser, M. Mansouri, and M. Omer, "Using systemigrams in problem definition: A case study in maritime resilience for homeland security," J. Homeland Security & Emergency Mang.,

[13] J. Boardman and B. Sauser, Systems Thinking: Coping with 21st Century Problems. CRC Press, 2008.

[14] P. Checkland, "Systems thinking," Rethinking management information systems, pp. 45–56, 1999.

[15] B. Richmond, "System dynamics/systems thinking: Let's just get on with it," System Dynamics Review, vol. 10, no. 2–3, pp. 135–157, 1994.

[16] R. D. Arnold and J. P. Wade, "A definition of systems thinking: A systems approach," Procedia computer science, vol. 44, pp. 669–678, 2015.

[17] J. Gharajedaghi, Systems thinking: Managing chaos and complexity: A platform for designing business architecture. Elsevier, 2011.

[18] J. F. Nystad, C. B. Eckmann, and Gibbs, Walter, Building and urban development in Norway: a selection of current issues. 2004.

[19] Fast Company, "What happened when Oslo decided to make its downtown basically car-free?," Jan. 24, 2019. https://www.fastcompany.com/90294948/what-happened-when-oslo-decided-to-make-its-downtown-basically-car-free (accessed Sep. 28, 2021).

[20] A. Basden and A. T. Wood-Harper, "A philosophical discussion of the root definition in soft systems thinking: an enrichment of CATWOE," Systems Research and Behavioral Science, vol. 23, no. 1, pp. 61–87, 2006, doi: 10.1002/sres.689.

Applying Conceptual Modeling and Failure Data Analysis for "Actual Need" Exploration

Case Study for an Automated Parking System

Haytham B. Ali
University of South-Eastern Norway
Kongsberg, Norway
haytham.ali@usn.no

Gerrit Muller
University of South-Eastern Norway
Kongsberg, Norway
gerrit.muller@usn.no

Fahim A. Salim
University of South-Eastern Norway
Kongsberg, Norway
fahim.a.salim@usn.no

Abstract— **In complex sociotechnical research, organizations tend to plan to implement new technologies or solutions which may not fully address the actual need. This study demonstrates the use of conceptual modeling to explore an industry's "actual need" through a case study for a medium-sized company that delivers Automated Parking System (APS). Company plans the introduction of Condition-Based Maintenance (CBM). Conceptual modeling facilitated the exploration of the Company's actual need behind the plan, which is increasing APS reliability. We collected failure data to understand APS reliability in this context. We find that the combination of conceptual modeling and data analysis facilitates exploring and understanding the Company's actual need. The conceptual modeling supports communication and understanding, while the data analysis guides the modeling. This study concludes with suggestions regarding using a combination of data analysis and conceptual modeling as a short-term vision to increase the system's reliability. On the other hand, this short-term vision may support the CBM as a long-term vision.**

Keywords— Conceptual modeling; failure data analysis; case study; actual need; value proposition.

I. Introduction

This paper investigates an Automated Parking System (APS) as our System-Of-Interest (SOI). APSs operate mainly in urban centers. There is a need for APSs, especially in metropolitan areas, due to land scarcity, increasing numbers of vehicles, and urban mobility [1]. Shoup [2] states that between 1927 and 2001, studies show that finding a parking lot in a metropolitan city consumed between 3.5 and 14 minutes. The paper further mentions that research indicates that 8%–74% of traffic in urban areas was due to finding a parking for the car. Thus, APSs are needed to ease urban mobility. Internationally, there is a significantly increasing demand for semi-automated parking systems (garages). The value of APSs globally was 1.23 billion USD in 2019 and is expected to increase at a compound annual growth rate of almost 11% from 2020 to 2027 [3].

However, the SOI suffers from a variety of problems. These problems include end-user (car owner) mistakes, such as pushing or forgetting to push a button, which causes freezing of the SOI. In other words, end-users who are unfamiliar with the SOI can cause SOI failures. Furthermore, the SOI sometimes retrieves the wrong car, takes a long time to retrieve the vehicle, or does not retrieve the vehicle, especially during high-volume usage. In addition, there are mechanical failures related to the design of the SOI. These failures decrease the SOI's availability and increase downtime. Downtime increases costs. These costs include, but are not limited to, repair parts, and the fee for alternative conventional parking [4][5].

A. *Introduction to the Case Study*

The Company we use as a case study in this paper is a medium-sized enterprise that delivers APSs, including maintenance. The Company delivers fully and semi-automated parking systems. The Company starts its involvement before building. Nowadays, the Company is transitioning from only selling to developing, producing, and marketing APSs. The main customers for the Company are building owners and land developers. The main stakeholders to the case study are Company management, maintenance personnel, and car owners (end-users). The Company participates in a sociotechnical research project called H-SEIF 2. H-SEIF stands for "Harvesting value from Big data and Digitalization through a Human Systems-Engineering Innovation Framework." This project aims at enabling data-driven decision-making within the early design phase of the new product development (NPD) process. There are nine companies and two university partners within the research project. The company of interest in this case study came with a Condition-Based Maintenance (CBM) proposal as a case within the research project.

B. *Conceptual Modeling*

We use conceptual modeling to assist with the complexity of analyzing the Company's proposed CBM as a case study. Conceptual models are simple enough to share and communicate the understanding of needs, concepts, technologies, etc. These models are sufficiently detailed and realistic to guide system development. Conceptual modeling plays a vital role within various disciplines, such as simulations in the computer science domain, soft systems methodology (SSM), and systems engineering. Various types of conceptual modeling are in use, such as visualization and graphing of mathematical models (formulas), simulation models, and systems architecting models [6].

This study illustrates the use of conceptual modeling to explore CBM. Conceptual modeling is a way to find not obvious or "hidden" need of the Company; that is the actual problem that triggered the CBM. In other words, the employed conceptual modeling aids in communicating and sharing a common understanding of the Company's "actual need" and provides an overview of the case study. In addition, we support the conceptual model's discoveries with failure data analysis. Conceptual modeling, failure data analysis, and research data collected from interviews, observations, and workshops permit data triangulation in case study and thus increase the robustness of the results [7]. The research process aided in exploring how increasing the SOI's reliability is the actual need, while the CBM is an envisioned solution to address this need. The company sees CBM as the first step toward a digital twin for the SOI. The data analysis results can be used as feedback into the early design phase of the NPD process.

The research questions that the paper addresses are the following:

RQ1: How can conceptual models help the different stakeholders within a sociotechnical research project to formulate a shared understating of the Company's request and its consequences?

RQ2: How can shared understanding support reasoning and decision-making about options for solving the actual problem?

RQ3: How can data support common understanding, reasoning, communicating, and decision-making for the actual problem?

The reminder of the paper is as follows: Section II provides an informal literature review regarding conceptual modeling and reliability engineering. It continues with Section III that illustrates the case study. The case study section includes a description of the SOI and conceptual models from the case study. After the discussion in Section IV, the paper ends with a conclusion and suggestions for future work in Section V.

II. LITERATURE

This section discusses literature regarding conceptual models and reliability engineering.

A. *Conceptual Models*

Conceptual models have several definitions and origins. These origins include physics, simulations, tools for co-creation or collaborative sessions, and tools that aid conceptual design in systems engineering. The common aspect among these origins is that conceptual models aid in sharing and communicating common understanding and ways of thinking.

Co-creation sessions use conceptual models in several areas, such as design thinking, by focusing on human interactions [8]. Gigamapping, from system-oriented design, enhances communication and relates strongly to design thinking in its style [9]. Neely *et al.* [10] suggest a workshop for co-creation sessions for interdisciplinary teams; the workshop is similar to gigamapping.

The scientific simulation field includes several definitions of conceptual models. Sargent [11] defines conceptual models as follows: "the mathematical/logical/graphical representation (mimic) of the problem entity developed for a particular study." Many other authors link the use of conceptual models to simulation, such as [12]–[14]. Robinson states that conceptual models are an essential aspect of simulation projects and mentions that conceptual models are more art than science [12][15].

Systems engineering uses various types of conceptual models. This variety results from interdisciplinary engineering wherein each engineering field uses its domain-specific conceptual models [6]. For instance, Blanchard [16] uses several variations of conceptual models. Tomita *et al.* [17] consider conceptual system design and suggest using a systems thinking application to raise the consideration from the data and information level to the knowledge and wisdom level. Montevechi and Friend [14] put forward the use of an SSM to develop conceptual models. Using the SSM in this case study, part of a complex sociotechnical research project, makes sense; this research project aims to bridge soft aspects (including knowledge and wisdom) with hard aspects (data and information). Systems thinking plays a vital role in the development of conceptual models. For instance, Jackson [18] connects systems thinking to label complex problems. In another example, Sauser *et al.* [19] apply systems thinking to define a complex problem within a case study.

Muller's work illustrates bridging conceptual models with first principal and empirical models [20]. Empirical models aid in expressing what we measure and observe without the necessity of understanding what we observe. First principal models use theoretical science principles. These models are often mathematical formulas and equations. Conceptual models use a selection of first principles that explain measurements and observations. Conceptual models are a combination of empirical and first-principle models. This paper emphasizes that conceptual models need to be simple enough to reason and understand the case study. Simultaneously, conceptual models need to be realistic enough to make sense. This latter description of conceptual models emphasizes the need to balance between the simple, making sense, and the practical aspect when developing conceptual models.

B. *Reliability Engineering*

Reliability engineering is essential in systems engineering and quality management [21]. The main objective of reliability engineering is to prevent system failure. O'Connor and Kleyner [22] define reliability as "The probability that an item will perform a required function without failure under stated conditions for a stated period of time." This conventional definition of reliability emphasizes two aspects (scientific topics): statistics and engineering. The word "probability" emphasizes the mathematics and statistics aspects, whereas the phrase "required function, stated conditions, and period of time" emphasizes the engineering aspect.

One of the statistical methods within reliability engineering is determining the Mean Time Between Failures (MTBF). MTBF is the inverse of the failure rate: MTBF = (total system(s) operation time) / (total number of failures). MTBF can be used to measure a system's reliability by showing how long the system operates before it needs maintenance [23][24].

Developing a reliability program plan is a crucial within engineering aspect. This plan includes activities for reliability engineering and aids in determining which activities to perform. These activities depend on factors such as system complexity, life cycle stage, failure impact, etc. The *Systems Engineering Handbook* includes guidelines for developing a reliability program plan [25]. There are also reliability program standards, such as ANSI/GEIA-STD-0009. This latter standard supports the system lifecycle for reliability engineering. It includes three crucial elements: (1) understanding system-level operation and environmental and resulting loads, and understanding the stresses throughout the structure of the system; (2) identification of the failure modes and mechanisms; and (3) mitigation of surfaced failure modes [26].

There are also two types of reliability engineering: proactive and reactive. Proactive reliability engineering occurs during design and development, emphasizing failure prevention. In contrast, reactive reliability engineering happens during production, especially during maintenance and operations, emphasizing failure management [27][28]. Figure 1 visualizes these two types of reliability engineering: proactive and reactive reliability engineering. Figure 1 also depicts the development process. This process is an iterative one. It indicates that reliability engineering is also iterative in its nature. Systems engineering integrates reliability within the processes. Verification occurs before production proceeds and consists mainly of analysis, testing, inspection, and demonstration [27].

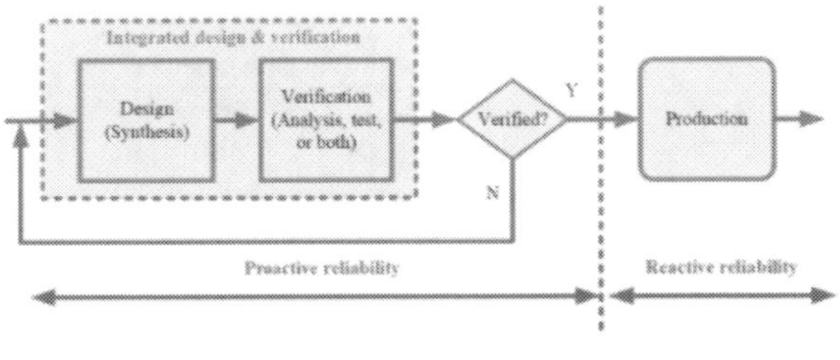

Figure 1. Proactive and reactive reliability engineering within the product lifecycle, including the new product development (NPD) process, redrawn from [27].

Shortly after reliability engineering was founded in 1957, Hollis stated a need for conventional statistical reliability. However, Hollis also emphasized that the statistical aspect is insufficient. There is also a need for other reliability activities or techniques to improve the feasibility and robustness of the designed system(s). In other words, statistical and engineering aspects complement each other [29][30]. Reliability influences other dependability attributes of the system, such as maintainability and availability. Thus, reliability affects return on investment, market share, and competitiveness. In other words, a reliable system provides a competitive advantage and increases market share by having a proven field design (good system reputation).

Reliability engineering includes different data sources [31]. These sources include the following:

1. data from the design synthesis,
2. testing and analysis from the verification process,
3. published information (literature),
4. expert opinion,
5. system operation data, and
6. failure data.

Failure data may come from maintenance record data or service-log data. Failure data analysis plays a vital role in increasing the system's reliability, due to the following reasons [31]:

1. increases knowledge regarding the system's design and manufacturing deficiencies;
2. estimates the reliability, availability, MTBF, and system failure rate;
3. improves reliability through design change recommendations;
4. aids data-driven decision-making through design reviews;
5. determining systems' maintenance needs and their parts; and
6. conducting reliability and life cycle cost trade-off studies.

In this study, we focus on closing the feedback loop from back-end data, represented by failure data, into the early design phase of the NPD process. Thus, it is also crucial to properly report and document the data, including failure data.

III. APPLYING CONCEPTUAL MODELING AND DATA ANALYSIS

This section starts by describing the SOI to give a contextual understanding for the case study. Further, the section illustrates the conceptual model application through the case study before it ends by analyzing failure data.

A. *Description of the System*

Figure 2 portrays the SOI: the semi-automated parking system and its configuration. Figure 2 visualizes a drive-in indication. The figure also visualizes a variety of SOI configurations. These configurations vary from $11 \times 2 \times 3$ to $4 \times 2 \times 2$ and $9 \times 1 \times 3$. The first number is the width, the second is the depth, and the third is the height. Depending on the building architecture, the car entrance can be a straightforward or inclined plane, as with the SOI's configurations.

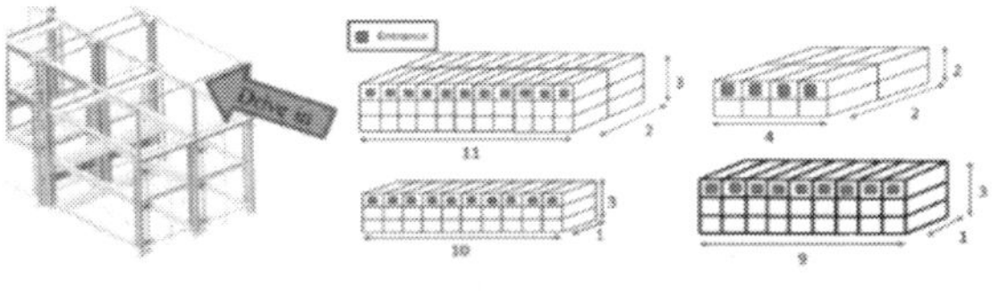

Figure 2. The System-Of-Interest (SOI): semi-automated parking system (left) and its configurations (right).

The SOI consists of numerous hardware parts. We mention here some of the main parts to give a better understanding of the SOI. We visualize these parts in Figure 3, which contains the following:

- The gate is the entrance and exit before and after parking.
- The control unit is a touch screen with operating instructions, including a key switch and emergency stop. The control is connected to the power unit through cables and fixed on a wall.
- The platform carries the car to the correct position.
- The wedge helps the driver position the car at the correct position.

Figure 4 and Figure 5 visualize the workflow from the user perspective for car entry and retrieval for the SOI, respectively.

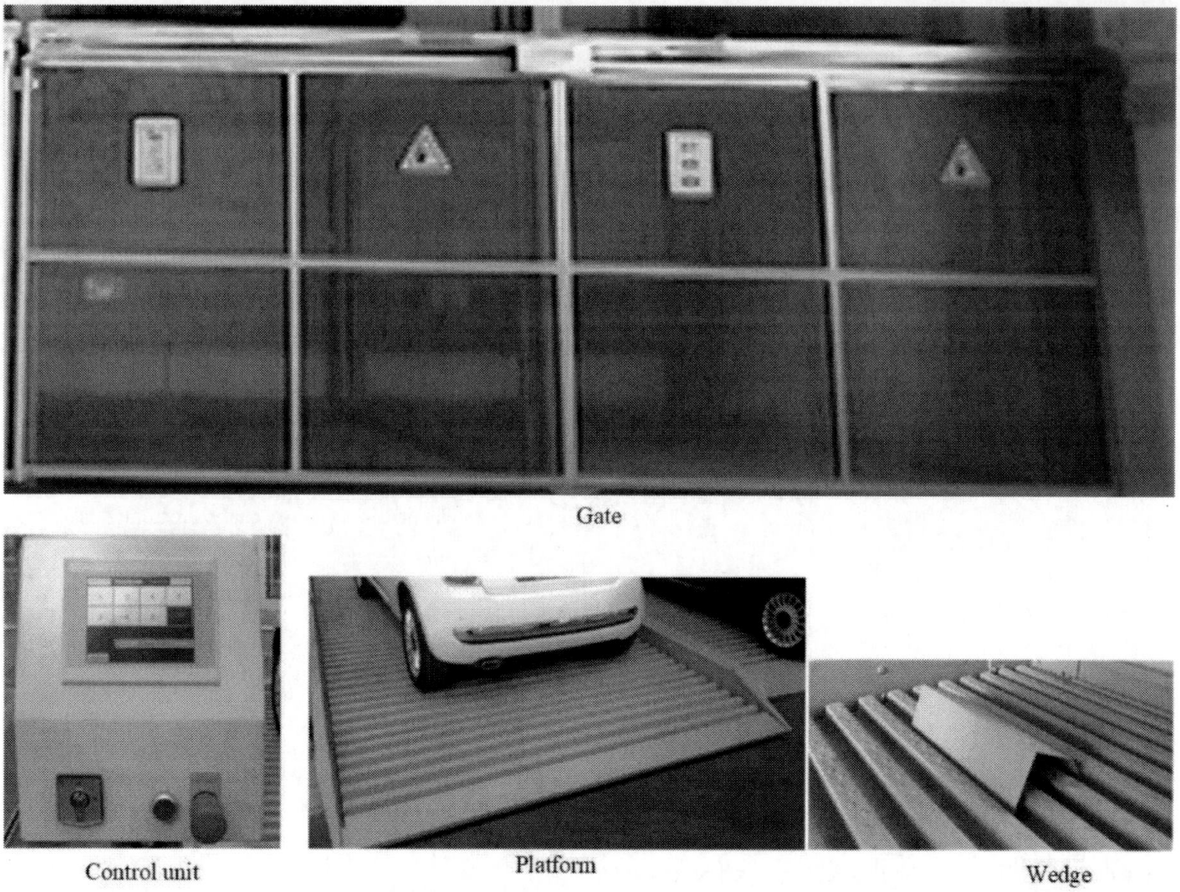

Figure 3. System-Of-Interest's main parts.

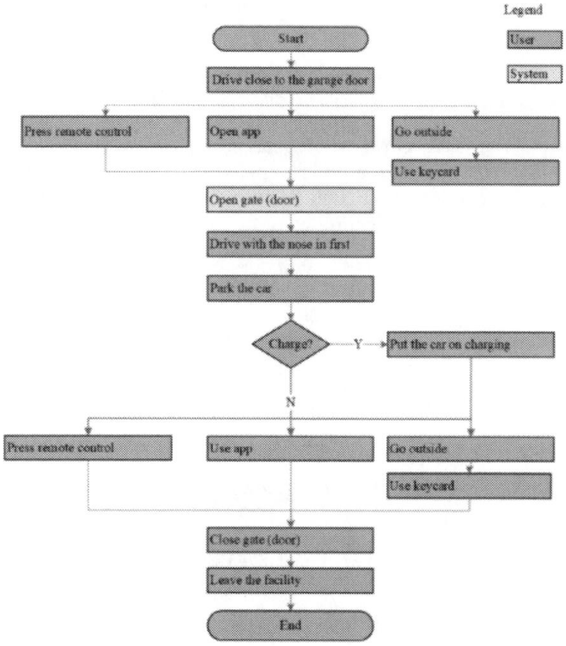

Figure 4. Workflow for car entry to the SOI.

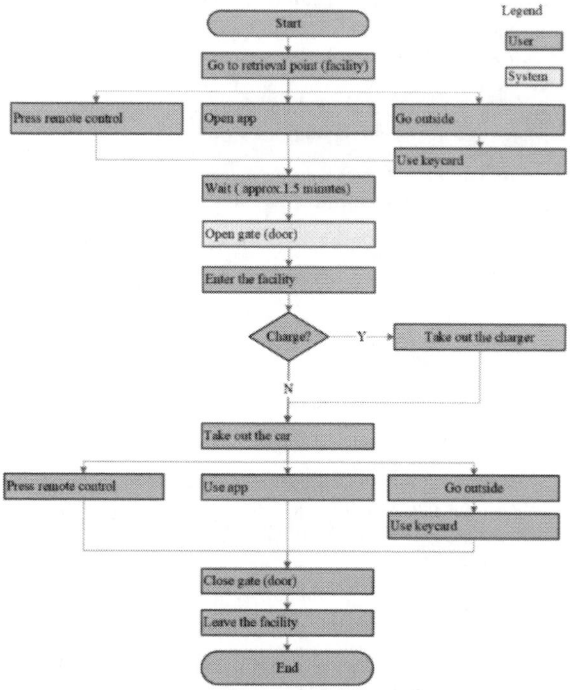

Figure 5. Workflow for car retrieval from the SOI.

B. Applying Conceptual Models Through Case Study

We applied conceptual modeling using multiple views on the SOI, the requested CBM, and its context to understand, reason, make decisions on, and communicate the system's specification and design [32]. This application ensures the Company's need fulfillment through eliciting customer value and business value propositions. These propositions drive the system's requirements, which further drive the system design. On the other hand, design and system requirements enable customer and business value propositions [33].

We used core principles, objectives, and recommendations in applying conceptual modeling. The main principles we applied are using feedback and being explicit. Using feedback indicated whether we moved in the right direction by moving back and forth from the problem domain and solution domain, as well as indicated whether our solution solved the problem. These principles facilitated reaching our objectives. In turn, the objectives were to establish understanding, insight, and overview, support communication and decision-making, as well as facilitate reasoning [34]. The main principles and objectives translate into ten main recommendations:

1. Timeboxing: We used timeboxing for developing several models. The timeboxing varies from 1 hour to days.
2. Iteration: We iterated using feedback from expert input. The experts included domain scholars and industry practitioners.
3. Early quantification: We translated the principle of being explicit into quantifying early. This quantification aids at being explicit and sharpening discussions through numbers. However, these numbers can evolve, as we conducted quantification at an early phase, and more confidence through validation may be needed.
4. Measurement and validation: We calculated and measured numbers for the proposed system: CBM and SOI, for the early quantification. We validated these numbers through evidence and arguments from the literature and the Company.
5. Applying multiple levels of abstraction: We considered the size and complexity within these levels of abstraction. We aimed at connecting a high level of abstraction to a lower level to achieve concrete guidance.
6. Using simple mathematical models: We used simple models to be explicit and understand the problem and solution domain. These models aimed at capturing the relation between the parts and components for the Company's proposed system, to be able to reason these relations.
7. Analysis of credibility and accuracy: We made ourselves and the Company aware of the numbers in such a way that these numbers were an early quantification that needed to be further verified and validated within more extended iterations.
8. Conducting multi-view: We applied six main (different) views. These views are customer objectives ("what" for the customer), application ("how" for the customer), functional view ("what" of the Company's proposed systems: black-box view the CBM), conceptual view, and realization view. The conceptual and realization views describe the "how" of the Company's proposed system (CBM).

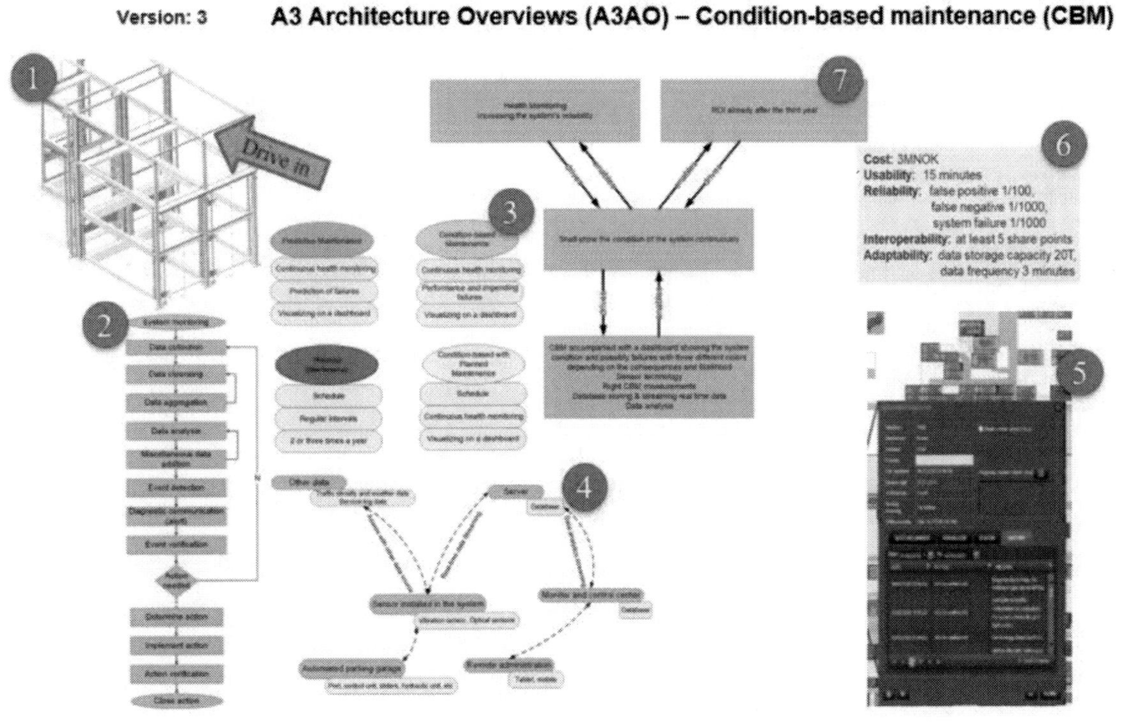

Figure 6. A3A0 shows the most significant results from applying conceptual modeling through the case study.

These six views include more relevant views. Muller [20] describes these views accompanied by a collection of sub-methods. We iterated over these views by using different abstraction levels.

9. Understanding the system in its context: We conducted several research data collection methods, including workshops, participant observation, and interviews, to understand the SOI context. We also conducted a literature review to understand the Company's proposed system (CBM) context. We needed to understand the SOI, CBM context for reasoning.

10. Visualizing: We used visualization to develop all the figures (models) conducting the multi-view. The visualization facilitated communicating common understanding, reasoning, decision-making, and stimulating discussions among the domain experts: scholars and the Company [35]–[38].

A3 Architecture Overview (A3AO) is an effective tool for communication [39]–[41]. Figure 6 visualizes the most significant results from applying conceptual modeling through the case study within an A3A0. The A3A0 (figure) content includes seven parts marked with a red numbered cycle in the figure. These parts are the following: 1) SOI; 2) functional model for the CBM system; 3) concepts for different maintenance systems, with a description. These systems include predictive maintenance, CBM, planned maintenance, and condition-based with planned maintenance; 4) CBM system context; 5) a prototype dashboard visualizing the CBM system functionality. This visualization includes traffic light color code indicating the condition for the different parts of the SOI; 6) key performance parameters for the CBM system; and ultimately 7) conclusion and recommendations. The conclusion and recommendations include the customer value proposition, business proposition, system requirements, and system design and technology for the Company's proposed system (CBM system). The lines between these parts illustrate the enables and drives among them.

C. *Failure Data Analysis*

This subsection illustrates the failure data analysis and its results. The failure data (also called maintenance record data) are unstructured. The maintenance personnel manually log failure events, using excel. In the excel file, there are several sheets. Each sheet belongs to a specific semi-automated car parking garage system. Each sheet's content includes the following columns, also called parameters: date (for a maintenance event), time, telephone number (for the maintenance personnel who investigated the failure event), place number (for which parking lot the failure event occurred), reason (possible reasons for the failure event), and reinvoiced yes/no (if the failure event is reinvoiced as it is not included within the maintenance agreement with the Company, or not). The main parameter within the failure data is the description of the failure event. The description includes data about what part of the SOI failed, possible reasons, and maintenance actions to fix the failure event.

The excel file contains several sheets. Most of the sheets belong to private semi-automated car parking systems, whereas others belong to a public car parking system. The main difference between the private and the public is that in the public parking system the users get different parking plot in the system each time they use the system, while in the private the users have their permeant parking lot each time. However, for both the private and public parking, the users are permanent users. The raw dataset for the public parking system is larger than that for the private ones. The period for the failure events varies from one parking garage to another. Most of the sheets contain data for the previous 6 years (2016-2021). Since the failure data are manually logged and include descriptions, especially the failure events, we employed an introductory natural language processing (NLP) method to analyze them.

NLP is a well-known method for analyzing text entry fields, such as the description field within the Company's failure data [42]. Manual pre-processing is necessary for data analysis and data quality. Here, pre-processing consumed approximately 80% of the data analysis. Figure 7 visualizes the data analysis results for the public parking system as a use case for the analysis results. (The most-repeated words are translated from Norwegian to English.) Figure 7 shows the frequency of the most-repeated words for failure events. "Gate" constituted approximately 50% of the failure events.

We dug deeper into the most frequently mentioned part: the gate. Figure 8 depicts the MTBF for the gate which is the inverse of the failure rate. We calculated MTBF per year for 6 years. The MTBF average is approximately 80 hours for the gate. Moreover, we analyzed and visualized the gate with other field data or parameters. The parameters included both date and time. However, we show here only the time bar chart as it makes most sense. It indicates that most failure events involving the gate occur at 07:00 and 15 to 18:00 h, which are the rush hours (see Figure 9). The other parameters need more investigation, and other data source integration.

We used Python for a customized code to analyze the failure data. We started by finding the most repetitive word in

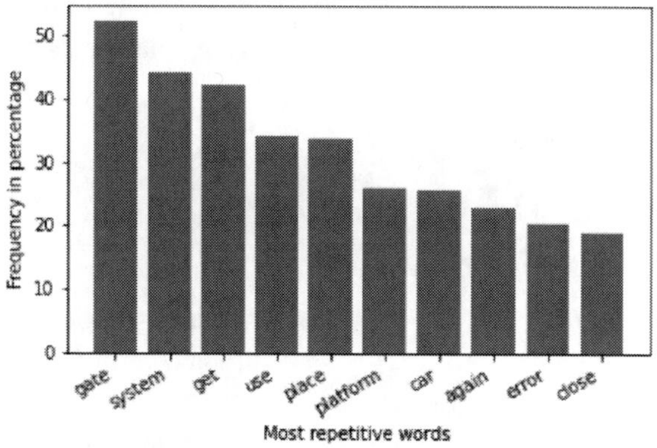

Figure 7. Percentages for most-repeated words for failure events.

the description text entry field. Further, we compared and linked the "most failed" part of the SOI with the other parameters (columns) and conducted some analysis and calculations such as failure rate and MTBF. Then, we discussed the results with the Company to determine whether the data analysis and results made sense.

IV. DISCUSSION

Applying conceptual modeling through a case study facilitates communication, understanding, and decision-making for a real industry problem within an early design phase of an industry–academia research project. A

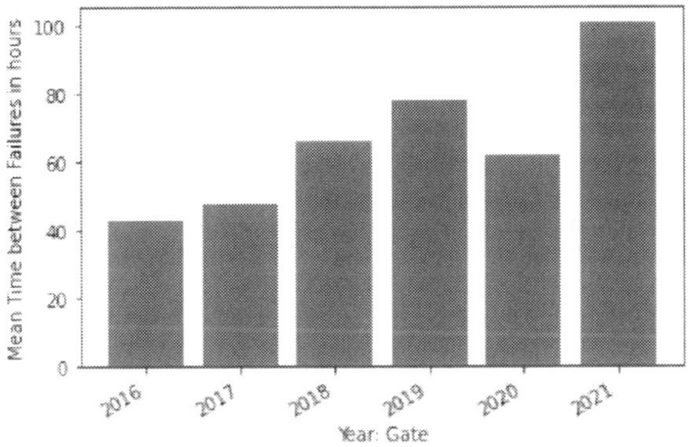

Figure 8. Mean Time Between Failures (MTBF) for 6 years period for the gate.

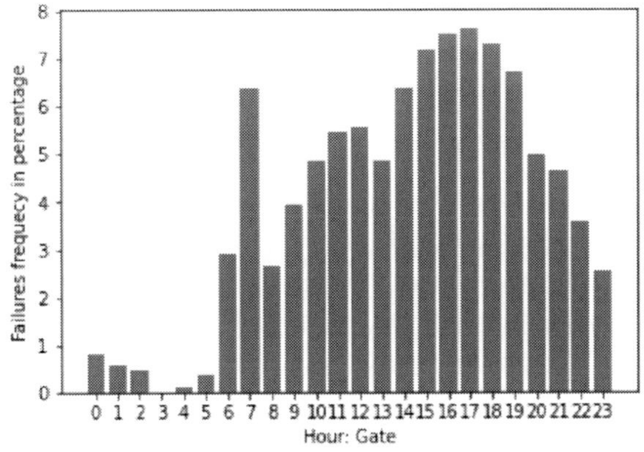

Figure 9. Gate failure events versus time of day (hour).

collaborative industry–academia project includes different stakeholders from industry and academia. Industry is more oriented toward "how" and developing their projects and systems. By contrast, academia is more oriented toward "what" and "why" with academic rigor, to understand, explore, and realize the problem.

Conceptual models aid in explaining the value proposition for the Company's proposed system (solution) that touch the surface of the problem for the case study and further explore the actual problem. However, there are several conceptual models that can be applied using multi-views and different levels of abstraction. The challenge is to develop the optimal number of conceptual models that gives a full and sufficiently realistic picture for the case study but does not overwhelm the researchers implementing the conceptual models. In this context, we found that following the principles, objectives, and recommendations mentioned in subsection B (under section III) aid early validation [34].

In addition, communicating the most critical results for the Company, including Company management, delivered effectively the full and detailed picture for the proposed system as part of a feasibility study. The company management gave feedback that they could see all the aspects for their proposed system as a case study (CBM) by using the A3A0 [39]–[41].

Collecting and analyzing failure data supported the conceptual model discoveries regarding the actual need that triggered the proposed system. The actual need was to increase the system's reliability, and the CBM was a solution to solve the Company's problem. The failure data analysis showed that the APS fails mostly during rush hours and due to the users' lack of familiarity with the system. This data analysis exploration concurs with state-of-the-art [4][5]. Failure data are one type of feedback data from the operation for the early design phase of the NPD process. We aim to investigate other data, such as the system's operation data, weather data, and so forth. This investigation aims to find a correlation to understand the data and their analysis in a way that makes sense.

Industry members tend to jump to the solution they believe can solve the problem, whereas academia tends to explore and understand the problem more in-depth. Conceptual modeling facilitates balancing between these two perspectives by jumping to the solution, back to the problem through several iterations, zooming in and out, and using different timeboxing and multiple levels of abstraction. However, the case study's (research) context plays a vital role in both the number of the conceptual models needed and time to develop and conduct them. Thus, domain (context) knowledge facilitates conceptual modeling implementation. In this context, being an employee in the Company aided conceptual model implementation. However, the main author used several data collection methods, including participant observation, interviewing, and workshops. This data collection helped implement conceptual models and collect the failure data. The collected research data supported the conceptual models and failure data analysis results. This support allows for data triangulation and increases the robustness of the results and evidence validity [7].

V. Conclusion

The combination of conceptual modeling and failure data analysis facilitated exploring and understanding the Company's actual need as a case study within an industry–academia, sociotechnical, systems engineering–focused, data-oriented research project. The conceptual modeling lifts customer value and business value on the one hand. On the other hand, conceptual modeling implementation encourages concrete, specific solutions and technologies. Here, conceptual modeling aided in communicating and sharing understanding of analysis of the value proposition of the Company's proposed system, CBM, which is formulated as a need. The Company's feedback indicated that they were able to see all aspects within feasibility study of implementing the CBM as a system for their SOI—also CBM as a system-of-system (SOS).

We also discovered that the Company's "actual need" (actual or real problem) relates to the inferior reliability of the SOI. This actual need is the key driver beyond the CBM, as is increasing market share and scaling up the operation 24/7. Applying conceptual modeling triggered this actual need discovery, alongside data collection including participant and direct observation, interviews, and workshops. In addition, we collected and analyzed failure data. The data analysis supported our discovery. We proceed with a feasibility study of the CBM as a long-term vision for the Company, using the most critical part (gate) as a use case. In addition, we supported the Company by enabling data-driven decisions through data analysis as a primary short-term vision. These decisions aid the early design phase in NPD and maintenance processes. For further work, we plan to include external data such as environmental data, mainly weather data to investigate any correlation between the failure events and environmental parameters such as humidity. We believe such further investigation would aid at facilitating decision making within the early phase in NPD and maintenance process, as well as, conducting new iterations with the conceptual modeling.

ACKNOWLEDGMENT

This research is part of a larger research project, the second iteration of the Human Systems Engineering Innovation Framework (HSEIF-2), funded by The Research Council of Norway (Project number 317862).

REFERENCES

[1] M. Nourinejad, S. Bahrami, and M. J. Roorda, "Designing parking facilities for autonomous vehicles," Trans. Research Part B: Methodological, vol. 109, pp. 110–127, 2018.

[2] D. C. Shoup, "Cruising for parking," Transport Policy, vol. 13, no. 6, pp. 479–486, 2006.

[3] Grand View Research, "Automated parking systems market size report, 2020-2027." Available: https://www.grandviewresearch.com/industry-analysis/automated-parking-systems-market (accessed June. 17, 2022).

[4] G. Cudney, "Parking Today | Articles - Automated Parking: Is It Right for You?" Available: https://www.parkingtoday.com/articledetails.php?id=181&t=automated-parking-is-it-right-for-you (accessed June. 17, 2022).

[5] F. Robles, "Road to Robotic Parking Is Littered With Faulty Projects," The New York Times, Nov. 28, 2015. Accessed: June. 17, 2022. [Online]. Available: https://www.nytimes.com/2015/11/28/us/road-to-robotic-parking-islittered-with-faulty-projects.html

[6] G. Muller, "Applying Roadmapping and Conceptual Modeling to the Energy Transition: A Local Case Study," Sustainability, vol. 13, no. 7, p. 3683, 2021.

[7] M. Duneier and O. Carter, Sidewalk. Macmillan, 1999.

[8] H. Plattner, C. Meinel, and L. Leifer, Design Thinking Research: Making Design Thinking Foundational. Springer, 2015.

[9] Wettre, A. Sevaldson, B. & Dudani P. "Bridging silos: A new workshop method for bridging silos,". In proceedings of Relating Systems Thinking and Design (RSD8) Symposium, 2019.

[10] K. Neely, M. Bortz, and S. Bice, "Using collaborative conceptual modelling as a tool for transdisciplinarity," Evidence & Policy, vol. 17, no. 1, pp. 161–172, 2021, doi: 10.1332/174426419X15468578119304.

[11] R. G. Sargent, "Verification and validation of simulation models," J. Simulation: JOS, vol. 7, no. 1, pp. 12–24, 2013, doi: 10.1057/jos.2012.20.

[12] S. Robinson, "Conceptual modelling for simulation Part I: definition and requirements," J. Operational Research Society, vol. 59, no. 3, pp. 278–290, 2008.

[13] O. Balci, J. D. Arthur, and R. E. Nance, "Accomplishing reuse with a simulation conceptual model," in 2008 Winter Simulation Conf., pp. 959–965.

[14] J. A. B. Montevechi and J. D. Friend, "Using a soft systems methodology framework to guide the conceptual modeling process in discrete event simulation," in Proc. of the 2012 Winter Simulation Conf. (WSC), pp. 1–12.

[15] S. Robinson, "Conceptual modelling for simulation Part II: A framework for conceptual modelling," J. Operational Research Society, vol. 59, no. 3, pp. 291–304, 2008.

[16] B. S. Blanchard, Systems Engineering and Analysis, 5th ed. Boston: Pearson, 2011.

[17] Y. Tomita, K. Watanabe, S. Shirasaka, and T. Maeno, "Applying design thinking in systems engineering process as an extended version of DIKW model," in INCOSE Int. Symp., 2017, vol. 27, no. 1, pp. 858–870.

[18] M. C. Jackson, Critical systems thinking and the management of complexity: Responsible Leadership for a Complex World, 1st ed. Hoboken, NJ: Wiley, 2019.

[19] B. Sauser, M. Mansouri, and M. Omer, "Using systemigrams in problem definition: A case study in maritime resilience for homeland security," Journal of Homeland Security and Emergency Management, Vol. 8 (Issue 1), pp. 000010220215477355 1773. https://doi.org/10.2202/1547-7355.1773, 2011.

[20] G. Muller, "CAFCR: A multi-view method for embedded systems architecting," Balancing Genericity and Specificity, 2004.

[21] H. N. Hosseini and T. Welo, "A framework for integrating reliability and systems engineering: proof-of-concept experiences," in INCOSE Int. Symp., 2016, vol. 26, no. 1, pp. 1059–1073.

[22] P. O'Connor and A. Kleyner, Practical Reliability Engineering. John Wiley & Sons, 2012.

[23] M. Krasich, "How to estimate and use MTTF/MTBF would the real MTBF please stand up?," in 2009 Annu. Reliability and Maintainability Symp., pp. 353–359.

[24] Ridgway, M., Baretich, M. F., Clark, M., Grimes, S., Iduri, B., Lane, M. W., ... & Lum, N. "A Rational Approach to Efficient Equipment Maintenance, Part 2: A Comprehensive AEM Program," Biomed. Instrum. & Technol., vol. 52, no. 5, pp. 350–356, 2018.

[25] D. D. Walden, G. J. Roedler, K. Forsberg, R. D. Hamelin, and T. M. Shortell, Systems engineering handbook: A guide For system life cycle processes And activities. John Wiley & Sons, 2015.

[26] E. A. Long and D. Tananko, "Best practices methods for robust design for reliability with parametric cost estimates," in 2011 Proc. Annu. Reliability and Maintainability Symp., pp. 1–6.

[27] R. W. A. Barnard, "3.2. 2 What is wrong with Reliability Engineering?," in INCOSE Int. Symp., 2008, vol. 18, no. 1, pp. 357–365.

[28] A. Barnard, "Reliability engineering: Value, waste, and costs," in INCOSE Int. Symp., 2016, vol. 26, no. 1, pp. 2041–2054.

[29] R. Hollis, "Put engineering Efforts Back in Reliability Techniques," IEEE Trans. on Parts, Mater. & Packag., vol. 1, no. 1, pp. 297–302, 1965.

[30] A. Coppola, "Reliability engineering of electronic equipment a historical perspective," IEEE Trans. Rel., vol. 33, no. 1, pp. 29–35, 1984.

[31] B. S. Dhillon, Robot System Reliability and Safety: A Modern Approach. CRC Press, 2015.

[32] G. Muller, "System and context modeling—The Role of Time-Boxing and Multi-View Iteration," in Systems Research Forum, 2009, vol. 3, no. 2, pp. 139–152.

[33] G. Muller, "Teaching conceptual modeling at multiple system levels using multiple views," Procedia CIRP, vol. 21, pp. 58–63, 2014.

[34] G. Muller, "Challenges in teaching conceptual modeling for systems architecting," in Int. Conf. on Conceptual Modeling, 2015, pp. 317–326.

[35] E. Engebakken, G. Muller, and M. Pennott, "Supporting the system architect: model-assisted communication," in Systems Research Forum, 2010, vol. 4, no. 2, pp. 173–188.

[36] Rypdal, Muller, G., & Pennotti, M. Developing the Modeling Recommendation Matrix: Model-Assisted Communication at Volvo Aero. INCOSE International Symposium, 22(1), 2012, 1870–1883. https://doi.org/10.1002/j.2334-5837.2012.tb01443.x.

[37] E. Polanscak, G. A. N. AS, and G. Muller, "Supporting product development: A3-assisted communication and documentation," unpublished master project paper at Buskerud Uni. Col., 2011.

[38] Stalsberg, & Muller, G. (2014). 8.3.1 Increasing the value of model-assisted communication: Modeling for understanding, exploration and verification in production line design projects. INCOSE International Symposium, 24(1), 827–842. https://doi.org/10.1002/j.2334-5837.2014.tb03184.x.

[39] W. Pesselse, T. Hofman, M. Simons, and G. Muller, "Applying and analyzing A3 Architecture Overviews in a complex and dynamic engineering environment," in INCOSE Int. Symp., 2019, vol. 29, no. 1, pp. 952–970.

[40] P. D. Borches Juzgado, "A3 Architecture overviews. A tool for effective communication in product evolution," 2010.

[41] G. Muller, D. Wee, and M. Moberg, "Creating an A3 architecture overview; A case study in subSea Systems," in INCOSE Int. Symp., 2015, vol. 25, no. 1, pp. 448–462.

[42] C. Stenström, M. Al-Jumaili, and A. Parida, "Natural language processing of maintenance records data," Int. J. COMADEM, vol. 18, no. 2, pp. 33–37, 2015.

Preventing E-Government Tragedy Of The Clouds Using System Thinking Methods

1st Geoffrey Lichtenheim
School of Systems & Enterprises
Stevens Institue of Technology
Hoboken, USA
email:glichten@stevens.edu

2nd Mo Mansouri
School of Systems & Enterprises
Stevens Institue of Technology
Hoboken, USA
email:mmansour@stevens.edu

***Abstract*—The purpose of this study is to propose the use of system thinking methods in E-Government systems and system of systems to drive greater efficiencies in the deployment of public cloud services. Qualitative methods such as a systemigram, causal loop analysis, as well as a novel cloud cost reduction model is used to map complexity, display the multidimensional nature of the system, as well as formulate an ontology. The "tragedy of the commons" economic concept is used to orient our research towards the sustainable consumption of digital resources for government agencies. Business and system dynamics concepts are used to both discover as well as propose solutions for the research problem, which is identified as E-Government cloud services efficiency and cost optimization. We conclude with additional ideas to further this research through the use of triangulation and additional quantitative research methods.**

Keywords*—*E-Government, E-Governance, Systems thinking, Systems Dynamics, Public cloud.

I. Introduction

State and local governments continue to embrace digital transformation initiatives that provide services and accessibility for both citizens as well as business in their respective jurisdictions. The emergence of E-Government, which is defined as the use of information and communications technology (ICT) to provide public services for government to government (G2G), government to citizen (G2C), and government to business (G2B) has become a shaping force for the use of cloud services [1] [2] [3]. Cloud computing, defined by NIST is "a model for enabling ubiquitous, convenient, on-demand network access to a shared pool of configurable computing resources (e.g., networks, servers, storage, applications, and services) that can be rapidly provisioned and released with minimal management effort or service provider interaction". This new technical consumption model operates similar to a public utility where resources are charged based on the amount of resources used by the agent. As E-governments continue to expand, so does their requirement for cloud computing services to host infrastructure platforms, applications, data repositories, as well as network interfaces [4] [5] [6]. This resource need, however creates a challenge as programs and projects for E-services grow so does the respective budget and spending. Government agencies now see value in digital services and choose to leverage them to deliver positive outcomes for constituents and businesses. This situation of competing priorities as well as consumption can create a modern-day "tragedy of the commons", which is the potential rapid deterioration or complete elimination of a resource due to overly aggressive demand without limitations or constraints [7] [8].

A. *Research Questions*

Research questions we aspire to answer are, firstly how do we represent the complexity and boundary of the system, its stakeholder interests, as well as multiple interconnections and dimensions? Secondly, how do we define causal relationships of the system to understand both virtuous, vicious, as well as balancing cycles and the effect of time delay. Finally, how can a cloud efficiency model applied to these public cloud resources limit the potential for budgetary overruns and ensure a resilient and sustainable E-Government service?

B. *Methods*

We leverage a qualitative system thinking method known as a systemigram to represent complexity and system boundaries as well as a causal loop analysis to display the effect system elements have on each other, both reinforcing as well as balancing [9] [10]. Finally, we address governance and the important role it will play in system dynamics to set thresholds and limits by using a novel cost reduction model.

C. *Structure*

A foundational conceptual understanding of cloud computing is provided in the primer section, followed by a view of the complex E-Government system of interest using a systemigram. Economics of cloud describes how this new computing utility is financially structured, and the unique ways that stakeholders and consumers can interact and consume the vast amount of technical resources. A new model developed for E-Government, provides high-level guidance in the form of capabilities, solutions, and respective outcomes, which we call the "cloud efficiency model" [11]. A Causal loop analysis is an instrument out of system dynamics and is used to display reinforcing behaviors, such as cloud spend and vendor revenue generation as well as balancing factors, such as budgetary constraints. The conclusion discusses ideas to enhance and extend this research effort.

II. Cloud Computing Primer

Today there are multiple large public cloud technology providers and services used extensively by both private as well as public sector customers [12] [13]. We list three major cloud providers, also known as "hyperscalers", as well as some of the most widely used services they host.

Public Cloud providers

- Amazon Web Services (AWS)
- Microsoft Azure Cloud (Azure)
- Google Cloud Platform (GCP)

Public Cloud Prominent Services

- AWS Services
  1) Elastic Compute Cloud (EC2)
  2) Relational Database Service (RDS)
  3) Elastic Container Service (ECS)
- Microsoft Azure Services
  1) Azure Active Directory (AD)
  2) Azure Content Delivery Network (CDN)
  3) Azure Data Factory
- Google Cloud Platform Services
  1) Database Services
  2) Big Data Services
  3) Machine Learning Services

III. E-Government System Complexity

Using a systemigram, we can see in Figure 1 how the mainstay represented in yellow displays primary system nodes, which include government services, operations, employees, and citizens, which are both important and relevant to our narrative. Branching off in red are public cloud services that connect to elements, such as third-party vendors, as well as the information system (IS) budget, which has multiple outflows and only a single inflow.

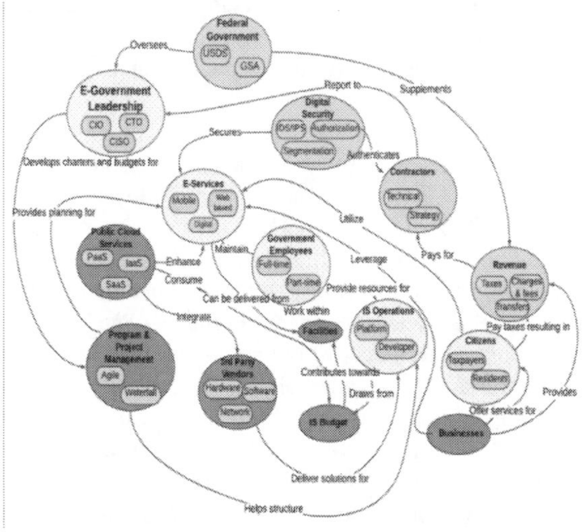

Fig. 1. Systemigram.

In the blue-colored section, we show the interconnections of the federal government, revenue, as well as digital security which in this environment is paramount to the success of the system. As we can see from Figure 1, E-government's use of cloud computing has an inherent complexity in its mission to provide secure, scalable, and resilient E-services to its citizens [14] [15].

IV. Economics of Cloud

The concept of cloud computing is to provide a simplified and consolidated platform hosted off-site that removes much of the operational overhead of traditional private cloud data center technologies. Many private and public sector IS teams are adopting this cloud-hosted model as it allows them to focus on the higher layer applications and remove the need to spend resource cycles with physical equipment maintenance and upgrade processes. This shifting of data center operations, in many cases, removes the need for dedicated operational staff; therefore operational expenditure budgets can be re-appropriated towards greater consumption of compute resources [16].

There are two ways to consume cloud-based services, the first is direct from the cloud provider, and the second is indirect via a third-party integrator. Entities that consume cloud services do so via a subscription that involves a legal contract or "terms of service" (TOS) that stipulates the rules and guidelines for the consumer. Vendors have multiple ways of selling cloud services, and one of the most popular is under a consumption plan agreement that define how much of a resource will be consumed over a certain period of time. An example is a government organization that signs a three-year multi-million dollar contract with a cloud vendor to use services such as email for their staff. The government agency benefits from the use of this highly scalable email system for its employees, and the cloud vendor receives revenue which is assumed to be allocated to fund ongoing research and development operations, finance, HR, as well as enhancing shareholder value due to its favorable earnings projections.

While this cloud-hosted IS strategy seems to be an advantageous relationship for all parties, there are some caveats to consider. One of the issues with the cloud is its seemingly endless supply of resources for end users of its services. The reality is that physical data centers with compute, network, and storage equipment are still required to host the infrastructure required to deliver cloud services. This means that there is a finite amount of resources from any cloud vendor, some customers have experienced hitting these limits when provisioning additional capacity. This was recently experienced due to pandemic-related supply chain shortages in microprocessors and hardware needed to expand hosted environments [4]. In addition to the constraints possible by cloud providers, government agencies have fixed budgets, and these can shift based on a multitude of factors such as government revenue or alternate priorities. A possible scenario could be the case where a government entity wants to expand its cloud services but cannot due to the hosting costs being greater than the allocated budget. The entity could request a budget enhancement or one-time over allocation however, this may take time to obtain requisite approvals or authorization, causing a potential delay [17].

As we have seen in the research, this issue of cloud economics, such as the panacea of cloud, requires careful planning and proper allocation of funds and resources to ensure the long-term effective use of the resources. Shaping forces are all around to turn a well-run environment into a security breach or system down emergency, negatively impacting mission-critical systems [18].

V. Cloud Efficiency Model

With the goal of ensuring the prolonged efficient use of cloud computing resources in E-Government, a novel model is created in Figure 2, which addresses the technical capabilities desired, solutions which can be employed, as well as positive outcomes which help in the conservation of budget. Based on the E-Government service being delivered, one or many of these solutions can be adopted, leading to outcomes that are oriented towards sustainability [19]. The technical capabilities are broad, high level domains spanning the most commonly requested infrastructure components and services. The solution for each respective capability provides more conceptual guidance as opposed to specific solutions. This is due to a rapidly changing landscape of technical solutions constantly entering and leaving the market.

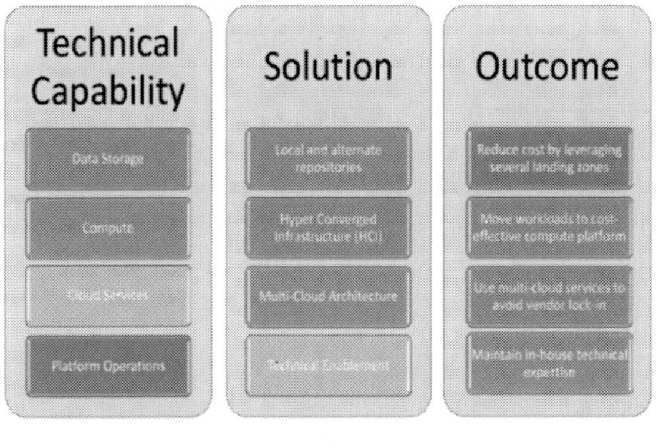

Fig. 2. Cloud Efficiency Model.

The outcome maps to business value and is intended to validate the goal of adopting the solution. Each outcome is directed towards cost efficiency, sustainability, and preservation of resources which can be technological, human, or monetary.

VI. Causal Loop Analysis

To obtain a graphical representation of how E-government spending on cloud computing affects other elements such as cloud vendor revenue, a causal loop diagram is developed [20] [21]. As we see in Figure 3, a reinforcing loop is established by E-government consumption of cloud resources which increases their digital service catalog and offerings. Similarly, as the cloud vendor providing services continues to grow, their offerings and revenue increases in another reinforcing loop. The balancing portion of this analysis comes via the finite E-Government budget that constrains both what is consumed as well as what is offered.

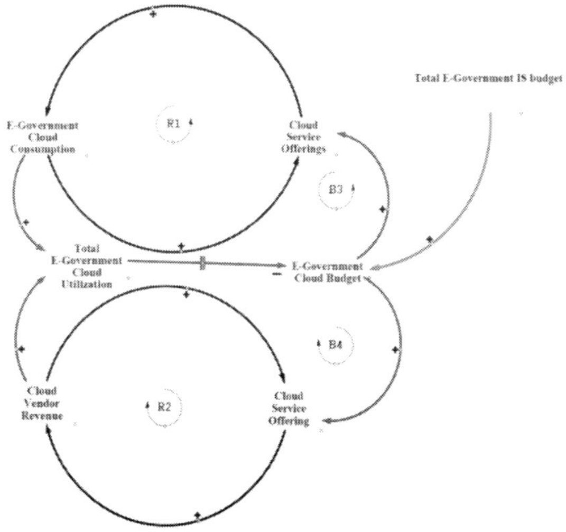

Fig. 3. Causal Loop Analysis.

There is a delay factor which in some cases could prove problematic if the consumption exceeds the budget or if the budget gets cut without timely notice to the operations team, which is provisioning new services. This situation could prove harmful if a sustainable resource management system was not planned for and executed. Also, having proper visibility to the cost of cloud services and discounted rates can help ensure continuity [22] [23].

VII. Conclusion

System thinking methods were employed in this study to analyze how cloud computing impacts E-Government services. First, we utilized the systemigram to map the complex relationship between E-Government agents, vendors, citizens, and the federal government [24]. This revealed different stakeholder interactions and provided insight into possible shaping forces that may impact how these digital services are fulfilled, operated, and delivered. Next, a novel model for E-Government cloud cost reduction was proposed to provide technical leadership with solutions and respective outcomes based on the capability being considered. Leveraged properly and given due consideration, these solutions may have a lasting impact on future costs associated with consumption of cloud services. Finally a causal loop analysis was developed to show the interconnections between E-Government use of cloud, reinforcing vendor revenue streams, as well as how budget constraints become balancing factors in this flow of resource and funds. This study lacks a complete quantitative analysis component with data that would have enhanced our models, specifically our causal loop. An idea for further study and enhancement of the contribution would be to gather data related to government spending on cloud computing platforms and use mathematical models as a triangulation technique to complement the qualitative components. Cloud technology will continue to grow in government, therefore, being able to find sustainable and responsible ways to ensure its prolonged use would provide value to those who are tasked with its operation [3].

REFERENCES

[1] F. M. Al-Balushi, M. Bahari, and A. A. Rahman, "Defining e-Government integration and its objective: A systematic literature review," *2016 3rd International Conference on Computer and Information Sciences, ICCOINS 2016 - Proceedings*, pp. 13–18, 2016.

[2] V. R. Prybutok, X. Zhang, and S. D. Ryan, "Evaluating leadership, IT quality, and net benefits in an e-government environment," *Information and Management*, vol. 45, no. 3, pp. 143–152, 2008.

[3] J. Sangki, "Vision of future e-government via new e-government maturity model: Based on Korea's e-government practices," *Telecommunications Policy*, vol. 42, no. 10, pp. 860–871, 2018. [Online]. Available: https://doi.org/10.1016/j.telpol.2017.12.002

[4] H. Zhang, "Analysis of the impact of cloud computing technology to e-government performance evaluation," *Proceedings - 2nd IEEE International Conference on Mobile Cloud Computing, Services, and Engineering, MobileCloud 2014*, pp. 295–298, 2014.

[5] A. M. Al Khouri, "An Innovative Approach for E-Government Transformation," *International Journal of Managing Value and Supply Chains*, vol. 2, no. 1, pp. 22–43, 2011.

[6] P. L. Sun, C. Y. Ku, and D. H. Shih, "An implementation framework for E-Government 2.0," *Telematics and Informatics*, vol. 32, no. 3, pp. 504–520, 2015. [Online]. Available: http://dx.doi.org/10.1016/j.tele.2014.12.003

[7] E. P. Purnomo and K. Hubacek, "Management of commons with a proper way: A critical review Hardin's essay on the tragedy of commons," *ICEEA 2010 - 2010 International Conference on Environmental Engineering and Applications, Proceedings*, no. Iceea, pp. 4–7, 2010.

[8] M. J. Ahn and S. Bretschneider, "Politics of E-Government: E-Government and the Political Control of Bureaucracy," *Public Administration Review*, vol. 71, no. 3, pp. 414–424, 2011.

[9] M. Mansouri and A. Mostashari, "A systemic approach to governance in extended enterprise systems," *2010 IEEE International Systems Conference Proceedings, SysCon 2010*, pp. 311–316, 2010.

[10] R. Cloutier, B. Sauser, M. Bone, and A. Taylor, "Transitioning systems thinking to model-based systems engineering: Systemigrams to SysML models," *IEEE Transactions on Systems, Man, and Cybernetics: Systems*, vol. 45, no. 4, pp. 662–674, 2015.

[11] S. D. Ryan, X. Zhang, V. R. Prybutok, and J. H. Sharp, "Leadership and Knowledge Management in an E-Government Environment," *Administrative Sciences*, vol. 2, no. 1, pp. 63–81, 2012.

[12] W. Zhang and Q. Chen, "From E-government to C-government via cloud computing," *Proceedings of the International Conference on E-Business and E-Government, ICEE 2010*, pp. 679–682, 2010.

[13] A. A. Memon, C. Wang, M. R. Naeem, M. Aamir, and M. Ayoob, "Cloud government-a proposed solution to better serve the nation," *Proceedings of 2014 International Conference on Cloud Computing and Internet of Things, CCIOT 2014*, no. Cciot, pp. 39–44, 2014.

[14] T. McDermott, M. Nadolski, and L. Sheppard, "Use of systemigrams to identify emergence in complex adaptive systems," *9th Annual IEEE International Systems Conference, SysCon 2015 - Proceedings*, pp. 778–784, 2015.

[15] B. Sauser, M. Mansouri, and M. Omer, "Using Systemigrams in Problem Definition: A Case Study in Maritime Resilience for Homeland Security," *Journal of Homeland Security and Emergency Management*, vol. 8, no. 1, pp. 1–10, 2020.

[16] Y. Alghofaili, A. Albattah, N. Alrajeh, M. A. Rassam, and B. A. S. Al-Rimy, "Secure cloud infrastructure: A survey on issues, current solutions, and open challenges," *Applied Sciences (Switzerland)*, vol. 11, no. 19, 2021.

[17] D. Sagarik, P. Chansukree, W. Cho, and E. Berman, "E-government 4.0 in Thailand: The role of central agencies," *Information Polity*, vol. 23, no. 3, pp. 343–353, 2018.

[18] S. Woodruff, T. K. BenDor, and A. L. Strong, "Fighting the inevitable: infrastructure investment and coastal community adaptation to sea level rise," *System Dynamics Review*, vol. 34, no. 1-2, pp. 48–77, 2018.

[19] E. J. Ng'Eno, "Embracing e-Government in service delivery and business to people through libraries: A case for Kenya," *2010 IST-Africa*, pp. 1–9, 2010.

[20] J. Homer, "Best practices in system dynamics modeling, revisited: a practitioner's view," *System Dynamics Review*, vol. 35, no. 2, pp. 177–181, 2019.

[21] M. Saeri, M. M. Lotfi, and M. R. Mazidi, "A Causal Loop Diagram to Analyze Various Long-Term Effects of PV Integration into Power Systems," *ICEE 2019 - 27th Iranian Conference on Electrical Engineering*, pp. 852–855, 2019.

[22] G. Haghighat and N. Hosseinichimeh, "Why Organizations Fail to Reflect on Experiences: Insights from a Causal Loop Diagram of Reflection on Experience," *IEEE Engineering Management Review*, vol. 49, no. 1, pp. 81–96, 2021.

[23] N. Ghaffarzadegan and R. C. Larson, "SD meets OR: a new synergy to address policy problems," *System Dynamics Review*, vol. 34, no. 1-2, pp. 327–353, 2018.

[24] M. Mansouri, B. Sauser, and J. Boardman Dr., "Applications of systems thinking for resilience study in maritime transportation system of systems," *2009 IEEE International Systems Conference Proceedings*, pp. 211–217, 2009.

User-centered Data Driven Approach to Enhance Information Exploration, Communication and Traceability in a Complex Systems Engineering Environment

Fahim A. Salim
Department of Science and Industry Systems
University of South-Eastern Norway
email: fahim.a.salim@usn.no

Haytham B. Ali
Department of Science and Industry Systems
University of South-Eastern Norway
email: haytham.ali@usn.no

Gerrit Muller
Department of Science and Industry Systems
University of South-Eastern Norway
email: gerrit.muller@gmail.com

Kristin Falk
Department of Science and Industry Systems
University of South-Eastern Norway
email: kristin.falk@usn.no

***Abstract*—Organizations working on complex engineering projects have data scattered across many different systems. The data is often disconnected, and its potential remain largely untapped. Enterprises large and small find it difficult to explore the information cluttered around different systems. A major factor in this difficulty is a lack of the user perspective in complex engineering environments. The presented research focused on a case study of information exploration needs of engineers testing sub-sea equipment. The case study observed that enterprise software tools in complex systems engineering environment are often designed for the content producer and not the consumer. Which makes these tools difficult, and time consuming to use and discourage their adoption. By utilizing user-centered design and co-creation, the experience and needs of users is identified to design, a data driven approach for enhance information exploration. The proposed design has the potential to make modifications to existing information systems, that would create a large impact in information exploration, data utilization and would provide a better experience for engineers, management and other stakeholders and enhance the productivity of teams, equipment testing and design.**

***Index Terms*—User-centred Design; Participatory Design; Big data; Early Phase Decisions;**

I. Introduction

Most organizations working on complex engineering projects, generate a large amount of document centred data during the project's life cycle [1] [2]. The data is usually scattered around many different often disconnected systems where it is not easily explorable [1] [3]. Organizations understand the need of getting more value out of their data to improve their routine operations. However, its potential remains largely untapped [4].

There are many factors identified by researchers, which limits the utilization of available data in a complex systems engineering environment to enhance operations. These includes among others, a lack of common language among engineers and interdisciplinary teams, ineffective knowledge sharing, finding system information and ineffective communication among stakeholders [1] [5]–[8].

The presented work focuses on the issue of data dispersed around different systems and is not easily searchable by users. As a case study, we focused on test engineers testing sub-sea oil drilling equipment at our partner organization, which is a multinational corporation that provides complete project life cycle services for the energy industry.

The problem is not exclusive for our case study. Organization such as enterprises large and small find it difficult to explore the information cluttered around different system which may or may not be connected to each other [4] [7] [9]. One solution to this problem is to use a model base system engineering approaches and store data in central repository [2], [10]. However, it is not very likely as complex engineering projects involve different companies such as vendors, other contractors, separate subsidiaries, and different departments geographically dispersed with their own workflows and Standard Operating Procedures (SOP). Therefore, the data is bound to end up in silos and would require exploration through multiple systems.

A major factor in this difficulty is a lack of the user perspective in complex systems engineering environments [1] [3] [11]. In a recent survey, Qlik and Accenture [4] found that only 21% engineers reported to have access to dashboard style exploration system suitable for their job roles while 18% said that the systems were appropriate for their skill level.

Researchers have found that while employees are regarded as crucial in utilizing big data systems, they are very often neglected in the design process [12]. The needs of user control is important in the data exploration process [13] [14] and also there is a need to take in multiple perspectives in a soft systems context [11].

Building upon previous work [3], It is our contention that designing a data driven methodology to enable end users to explore the content in an efficient manner in a complex systems engineering environment would help users in utilizing the available data in efficient manner to enhance operations and make data driven early phase decisions.

The remainder of the paper is as follows: Section II describes the related work. The case study and proposed approach is described in Section III. Which is followed by a discussion in Section IV and finally Section V contains the concluding remarks and some plans for the future.

II. Related Work

Dashboard style systems are used extensively to explore data [15]. They often use semantic and video data [16]–[18]. Dashboard style systems often follow a familiar pattern of providing detail on demand access to multimodal information based on an issued query. Research is also done on novel visualization to give quick insights for further exploration [19] [20], and on new ways of querying large data sets [21].

In their recent survey regarding the utilization of big data in enterprise environments, Qlik and Accenture [4] found that about 21% of engineers have access to dashboard style exploration systems which are designed to be suitable for their needs and 18% believe that the tools are designed in accordance to their skill level. Disparate data silos across multiple systems and technical capabilities are regarded as major obstacles [9].

Researchers have long identified the need for more user control in exploration of data [13] and need for taking multiple perspective when designing data exploration in a soft systems context [11]. General purpose commercially available data exploration and document retrieval tools have limitations [2] [7] [22].

Co-creation [23] and user centred design (UCD) [24]–[26] are often utilized to understand the user techniques to design systems which are suitable for evolving user needs. Haesen et al. use a user centred design approach and semi-structured interviews to perform a qualitative analysis of the information exploration needs of professional video searchers [25]. Similar approach is utilized by Gravier et al. [24] in which authors utilized mockups and non-functional prototypes to understand the information exploration needs of different users to come up with design solutions. Their analysis concluded that different users may have different needs in terms of desired features in exploration systems. Salim et al. [26] extend this approach and use semi-functional prototypes, screen capturing, think out loud and questionnaires to understand the user journeys in engaging exploration of content. Similar techniques with additional semi-structured interviews is used by Koesten et al. [27] to understand users sense making with data-sets for recommending design of tools and documentation practices to allow data reuse.

To allow engineers to explore content beyond simple document retrieval, researchers have proposed solutions like social network systems specifically designed for engineering design communication and project management [22] model based system engineering (MBSE) approaches to model central repositories to allow engineers and other stakeholders access to relevant information [2].

Currently, there is a lack of taking in the user perspective in designing exploration systems [12]. There exist a need for considering the multiple user perspectives and user needs while designing exploration systems [3] [11] [28].

III. Case Study and Proposed Design

The presented research is utilizing Industry as a Laboratory [29] , user-centered design [28] and Human Media Interaction [14] [26] methodologies to focus on the issue of data dispersed around different systems and is not easily searchable by users.

As a case study we focused on test engineers at our partner organization. The partner organization is a multinational corporation that provides life cycle services for the energy industry. We conducted multiple workshops, observation sessions and semi-structure interviews to understand the real-life context of the company(team) of interest in a complex engineering project. While the sessions overall focused on the holistic view of the early phase activities of company of interest in acquiring and developing/executing projects (subject of future publications). The current paper is focused on the information needs of test engineers.

A. Information Needs of Test Engineers

Test engineers need to access information during their routine operations. The current case study focuses on test engineers running different test on sub-sea oil drilling equipment at their workshop. They require access to information about the equipment they are testing. The information they require about different parts may include:

- The project specification.
- The design specification of parts.
- The provider or designer of the part (i.e., the supplier).
- Product responsible department or person at that department or supplier organization.
- The maintenance history of the part.
- The information about any modification done to the part and its history.

During the different tests they run, e.g., System Integration Test (SIT) where a combination of different part is tested to see if the parts are performing as per the specifications. In case of an unexpected event such as equipment not performing as expected or has a fault or have a part missing or have any other problem. It is logged in an event log. The event contains information such as data about the equipment and its serial number, etc. along with the description of the problem. The log also contains information about the project such as work package and product responsible department or supplier and other project specific information. Currently those logs are kept in excel sheets files which are project specific, and the company does not do any analysis on the logs. They have logs going back more than 10 years.

The test engineers at SIT, do know the value of data analysis in terms adding value to their operations. They require the following:

- Ability to log information centrally and follow up (can be achieved by any online system).
- Traceability (of the equipment and reports):
  - Keep track of reported errors.
  - Keep track of equipment and its maintenance history.
- Trends: see what patterns or lack of them appears in the event logs. Natural Language Processing (NLP) analysis of the event logs shared with us has similarities with other partners case studies [5]).

B. Proposed Approach Design

Figure 1 shows the component diagrams of the current environment with our proposed components. In the first step a prototype system is developed for them to log the unexpected events and related data in a convenient manner i.e., enhance their ability to log information centrally.

In terms of trends, basic NLP analysis of the event logs is performed, and the functionality is added to the prototype.

In terms of traceability, the testing engineers need to be able to keep track of the progress on the reported problems by product responsible departments or suppliers. For this, the researchers suggest a semantic ontology driven equipment register based on the Digital Design Basis initiative to quickly search the product related information and to update the event log with relevant data, instead of current manual look up at different systems, which is time consuming and cumbersome.

Testing engineers and other departments require traceability of their equipment. The problem is that the equipment may be at different departments or at different subsidiaries which are dispersed all over the globe. Apart from that, the equipment may have gone through maintenance-based changes and may have alter in specification as the years have gone by. The ontology base register has the potential to streamline the process of crawling through different systems and find a match of equipment based on the ontology properties [30]–[32]. Connected to the event log system it could also help test engineers in quickly finding the specification and functionality of the different equipment and see product relevant information in a dynamic manner, i.e., due to the machine-readable nature of the data it can be used to transform the information to be curated in any UI design, e.g., an excel style sheet or a graphical representation of the equipment with overlapping information i.e. (digital twins of various fidelities).

C. Description of prototype and interviews with test engineers

To facilitate the understanding of the information needs of maintenance engineers. We developed a semi-functional prototype and use this to conduct interviews with SIT test engineering team. During our sessions we identified three basic requirements of SIT engineers namely logging, traceability and identifying trends (see Section III-A for details).

For event logging we propose an online system which shows the event logs in a grid (see Figure 2). The reason behind is that it is similar to an excel file so that, the engineers are comfortable using it as they are very used to, using excel files. In addition to centrally log all the events the users have functionalities like sorting and filtering. They can also have additional controls on updating the values of certain fields so, for example, only a test manager could edit certain values (see Figure 2).

For identifying trends, the prototype allows users to perform analytics on the event logs, e.g., identify what equipment or tag number is appearing most in the logs indicating a trend of equipment which causes errors. Additionally, it also lets user do NLP analysis of the event logs, e.g., to identify repeatedly appearing phrases such as "need to be calibrated" to identify trends and to communicate them with product designers and other responsible parties (see Figure 3). Details of the NLP analysis of the event logs are the subject of another publication.

For traceability, the test engineers require information from different systems. The information they usually require are product specification, and equipment maintenance history and location etc. currently engineers have to search for this information in several different systems and it is a very time consuming and a tedious task. In the prototype we suggested connections with those systems and to allow the engineers to get that information from within the prototype.

The prototype also showed some alternative ways of representing information to engineers, e.g., graphical representation of the equipment with equipment specific information overlayed in a detailed-on demand manner. The idea is that user could switch between excel like list and other representations to better suite their exploration and communication needs. E.g., communicating an error with equipment image and overlayed information to provide a richer experience when communicating events with different departments and stakeholders (see Figure 4).

The prototype was well received. Participants really liked the concept. During our sessions and discussions, users wanted to centrally view the events and the required information. They really liked the simplicity of the concept. Interview participants also liked the analytics features and saw a lot of potential in the NLP analysis of the logs and the ability to identify the trends and patterns occurring during different equipment testing.

Participants reiterated our observations from our co-creation sessions and observation of the team meetings, that looking for information in different systems is indeed a very time-consuming task and a drag to their productivity and user experience. They really liked the idea of linking the different information and presenting it in one interface. They also saw the potential of using digital twin representation of different fidelity and product specific information overlayed, instead of simply linking to the product documentation.

When asked about what is missing in the prototype and what functionality would further enhance their experience: the reply

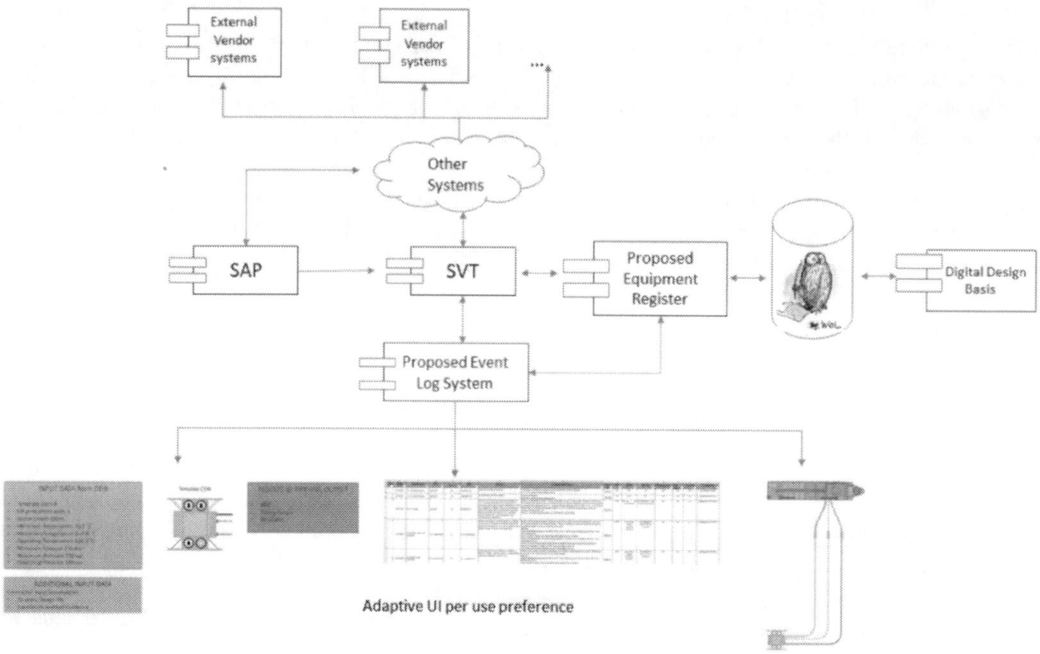

Figure. 1: Components Diagram overall approach (proposed).

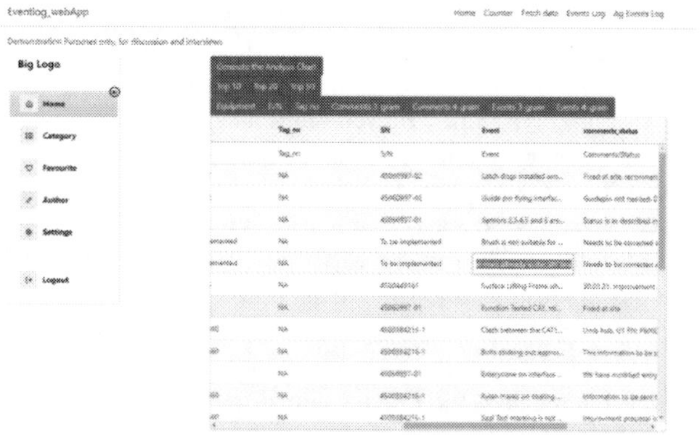

Figure. 2: Viewing and updating event logs prototype.

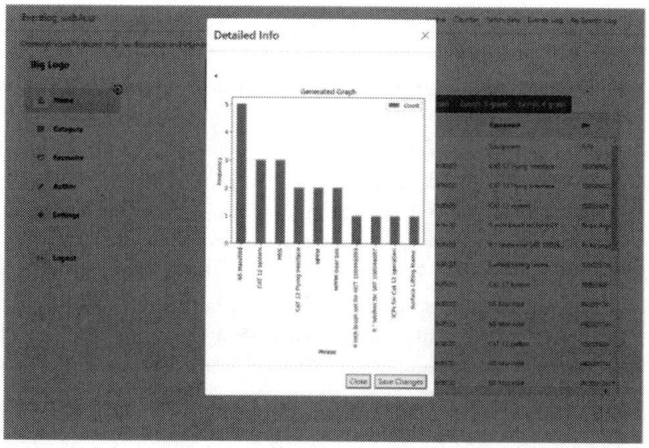

Figure. 3: Trend identification by NLP analysis.

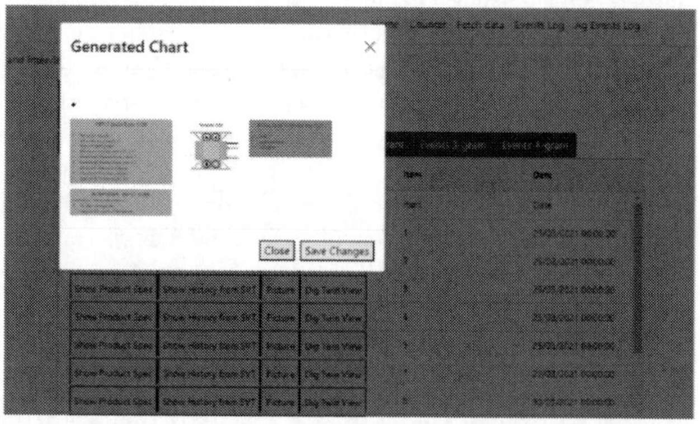

Figure. 4: alternative representation of equipment information.

was that they would prefer to have the information in different layers i.e., they wanted better control on the amount of detail they get about the equipment. It was also mentioned that different stakeholder may need access to different information and the need to control who can edit and view the information. Finally, the need to have easy to use system was reiterated and a need to standardized way to enter and edit the logs consistently across different teams and projects.

IV. Discussion

The co-creation sessions and interviews demonstrated the need for considering the user perspective to allow users to easily explore the information in a complex systems engineering environments. The case study shows that in large organizations despite having most of the infrastructure in place, users in certain functions still end up using sub-optimal exploration tools during their routine operations. This creates a big drag on their productivity. It is the sentiment expressed by the test engineers during our sessions.

Test engineers require a central place to search for the required information and the ability to make changes in a user-friendly manner. They also desire more control in viewing and editing of certain data and the amount of detail they get when looking at information i.e., detail on demand representation. Linking information from different systems and representing to them in easy to view manner is helpful for them. They also require standardized way to log information that can be achieve by implementing controlled vocabularies in the input interfaces.

The key takeaway from our sessions is that in complex systems engineering environments; the software tools are often designed for the content producers and not for the different users (consumers) of that information. There are also not easy to user for non-daily users to explore the available information. It makes it difficult for them to use, as it becomes time consuming for them to perform their routine tasks. It leads users to stick to old tools like excel files and not being able to utilize the benefits of technological developments.

V. Conclusion

The presented case study demonstrated that while large enterprises have many different systems to collect information and generate documentation and they may also have the necessary infrastructure to allow efficient use of the data. Users still end up not having a good experience with such tools and it creates hurdles in accessing the required information in an efficient manner. It discourages the adaptation of new systems and causes lost opportunities in terms of learning insights from the available information which could enhance daily operation or allow design decisions to avoid problems occurring in the future.

The case study demonstrates that by understanding the user needs, minor modifications to existing infrastructure can create a large impact in information exploration and utilization and a better experience for engineers, management and other stakeholders and enhance the productivity of teams, equipment testing and design.

In the future, we aim to extend the study to other teams at the partner organization to understand the similarities in information needs of different users in a complex systems engineering environment. We also aim to extend this to other partner organizations of the H-SEIF2[1]. consortium to come up with a design specification which could help in creating better interactive systems for enterprise users.

Acknowledgement

This research is part of the H-SEIF 2 project and is funded by the Research Council of Norway through the innovation project (IPN project no.: 317862).

[1]https://www.usn.no/hseif last accessed on 20-06-2022

References

[1] S. Engen, K. Falk, and G. Muller, "The need for systems awareness to support early-phase decision-making—a study from the norwegian energy industry," *Systems*, vol. 9, no. 3, 2021.

[2] H. Kannan, "Formal reasoning of knowledge in systems engineering through epistemic modal logic," *Systems Engineering*, vol. 24, no. 1, pp. 3–16, 2021.

[3] F. A. Salim, H. B. Ali, and K. Falk, "Towards a Data Processing Framework for Enhanced User Centric System Engineering ," in *PROCEEDINGS OF The Society for Design and Process Science, Workshop on Smart Pervasive Computing*, 2021, pp. 15–18.

[4] Qlik and Accenture, "The Human Impact of Data Literacy," Tech. Rep., 2020. [Online]. Available: https://thedataliteracyproject.org/humanimpact

[5] H. B. Ali and F. A. Salim, "Transferring Tacit Knowledge into Explicit: A Case Study in a Fully (Semi) Automated Parking Garage," in *PROCEEDINGS OF The Society for Design and Process Science*, 2021, pp. 11–14.

[6] B. A. Delicado, A. Salado, and R. Mompó, "Conceptualization of a T-Shaped engineering competency model in collaborative organizational settings: Problem and status in the Spanish aircraft industry," *Systems Engineering*, vol. 21, no. 6, pp. 534–554, 2018.

[7] K. Falk, A. K. Kamara, E. P. Brathen, K. Helle, P. T. Moe, and S. Kokkula, "Digitizing the Maintenance Documentation: A System of Systems in Oil and Gas Industry," *SOSE 2020 - IEEE 15th International Conference of System of Systems Engineering, Proceedings*, pp. 493–499, 2020.

[8] Juzgado P.D. Borches, "A3 Architecture overviews. A tool for effective communication in product evolution," Ph.D. dissertation, University of Twente, 2010.

[9] R. Technology, "AI / ML Annual Research Report 2022," 2022.

[10] J. Bickford, D. L. Van Bossuyt, P. Beery, and A. Pollman, "Operationalizing digital twins through model-based systems engineering methods," *Systems Engineering*, vol. 23, no. 6, pp. 724–750, 2020.

[11] M. Kjørstad, K. Falk, and G. Muller, "Exploring a Co-Creative Problem Solving Toolbox in the Context of Norwegian High-Tech Industry," *IEEE Systems*, pp. 1–11, 2020.

[12] D. H. Shin, "Demystifying big data: Anatomy of big data developmental process," *Telecommunications Policy*, vol. 40, no. 9, pp. 837–854, 2016. [Online]. Available: http://dx.doi.org/10.1016/j.telpol.2015.03.007

[13] C. Cobârzan, K. Schoeffmann, W. Bailer, W. Hürst, A. Blažek, J. Lokoč, S. Vrochidis, K. U. Barthel, and L. Rossetto, "Interactive video search tools: a detailed analysis of the video browser showdown 2015," *Multimedia Tools and Applications*, vol. 76, no. 4, pp. 5539–5571, 2017.

[14] F. A. Salim, F. Haider, S. Luz, and O. Conlan, "Automatic transformation of a video using multimodal information for an engaging exploration experience," *Applied Sciences (Switzerland)*, vol. 10, no. 9, 2020.

[15] A. Jackson, J. Lin, I. Milligan, and N. Ruest, "Desiderata for exploratory search interfaces to Web archives in support of scholarly activities," *Proceedings of the ACM/IEEE Joint Conference on Digital Libraries*, vol. 2016-Septe, pp. 103–106, 2016.

[16] J. Moreno-Schneider, A. Srivastava, P. Bourgonje, D. Wabnitz, and G. Rehm, "Semantic Storytelling, Cross-lingual Event Detection and other Semantic Services for a Newsroom Content Curation Dashboard," *Association for Computational Linguistics (ACL).*, pp. 68–73, 2018.

[17] F. A. Salim, F. Haider, D. Postma, R. van Delden, D. Reidsma, S. Luz, and B.-J. van Beijnum, "Towards Automatic Modeling of Volleyball Players' Behavior for Analysis, Feedback, and Hybrid Training," *Journal for the Measurement of Physical Behaviour*, vol. 3, no. 4, pp. 323–330, 2020.

[18] B. Yousuf and O. Conlan, "VisEN: Motivating learner engagement through explorable visual narratives," *Lecture Notes in Computer Science (including subseries Lecture Notes in Artificial Intelligence and Lecture Notes in Bioinformatics)*, vol. 9307, pp. 367–380, 2015.

[19] C. Perin, R. Vuillemot, C. D. Stolper, J. T. Stasko, J. Wood, and S. Carpendale, "State of the Art of Sports Data Visualization," *Computer Graphics Forum*, vol. 37, no. 3, pp. 663–686, 2018.

[20] T. Polk, J. Yang, Y. Hu, and Y. Zhao, "TenniVis: Visualization for tennis match analysis," *IEEE Transactions on Visualization and Computer Graphics*, vol. 20, no. 12, pp. 2339–2348, 2014.

[21] L. Shao, D. Sacha, B. Neldner, M. Stein, and T. Schreck, "Visual-interactive search for soccer trajectories to identify interesting game

situations," *IS and T International Symposium on Electronic Imaging Science and Technology*, vol. 0, pp. 1–10, 2016.

[22] J. A. Gopsill, H. C. McAlpine, and B. J. Hicks, "Supporting engineering design communication using a custom-built social media tool - PartBook," *Advanced Engineering Informatics*, vol. 29, no. 3, pp. 523–548, 2015. [Online]. Available: http://dx.doi.org/10.1016/j.aei.2015.04.008

[23] M. Guntveit, M. Kjrstad, and B. Sevaldson, "Early Validation of Stakeholder Needs by Applying Co-creation Sessions," *INCOSE International Symposium*, vol. 30, no. 1, pp. 1398–1415, 2020.

[24] G. Gravier, M. Ragot, A. Laurent, R. Bois, G. Jadi, E. Jamet, and L. Monceaux, "Shaping-Up Multimedia Analytics: Needs and Expectations of Media Professionals," in *The 22nd International Conference on Multimedia Modelling*, vol. 9516, Miami, 2016, pp. 303–314. [Online]. Available: http://link.springer.com/10.1007/978-3-319-27671-7

[25] M. Haesen, J. Meskens, K. Luyten, K. Coninx, J. H. Becker, T. Tuytelaars, G. J. Poulisse, P. T. Pham, and M. F. Moens, "Finding a needle in a haystack: An interactive video archive explorer for professional video searchers," *Multimedia Tools and Applications*, vol. 63, no. 2, pp. 331–356, 2013.

[26] F. A. Salim, F. Haider, O. Conlan, and S. Luz, "An approach for exploring a video via multimodal feature extraction and user interactions," *Journal on Multimodal User Interfaces*, no. October 2017, 2018. [Online]. Available: http://link.springer.com/10.1007/s12193-018-0268-0

[27] L. Koesten, K. Gregory, P. Groth, and E. Simperl, "Talking datasets – Understanding data sensemaking behaviours," *International Journal of Human Computer Studies*, vol. 146, no. October 2020, p. 102562, 2021. [Online]. Available: https://doi.org/10.1016/j.ijhcs.2020.102562

[28] J. Pinto, K. Falk, and M. Kjørstad, "Inclusion of human values in the specification of systems: bridging design and systems engineering," *INCOSE International Symposium*, vol. 29, no. 1, pp. 284–300, 2019.

[29] C. Potts, "Software-engineering research revisited," *IEEE Software*, vol. 10, pp. 19–28, 1993.

[30] Y. A. Akter and M. A. Rahman, "Extracting RDF Triples from Raw Text," *1st International Conference on Advances in Science, Engineering and Robotics Technology 2019, ICASERT 2019*, vol. 2019, no. Icasert, pp. 31–34, 2019.

[31] W. Baes, F. Portet, H. Mirisaee, and C. Labbé, "RDF triples extraction from company web pages: Comparison of state-of-the-art deep models," *CEUR Workshop Proceedings*, vol. 2708, 2020.

[32] P. Exner and P. Nugues, "Entity extraction: From unstructured text to dbpedia rdf triples," *CEUR Workshop Proceedings*, vol. 906, pp. 58–69, 2012.

State of Affair in Terms of Big Data Utilization in Complex System Engineering Organizations

Fahim A. Salim
Dept. of Science and Industry Systems
University of South-Eastern Norway
email: fahim.a.salim@usn.no

Haytham B. Ali
Dept. of Science and Industry Systems
University of South-Eastern Norway
email: haytham.ali@usn.no

Tommy Langen
Dept. of Science and Industry Systems
University of South-Eastern Norway
email: tommy.langen@usn.no

Andreas Wettre
Centre for Design Research
Oslo School of Architecture and Design
email: andreas.wettre@aho.no

Gerrit Muller
Dept. of Science and Industry Systems
University of South-Eastern Norway
email: gerrit.muller@gmail.com

Kristin Falk
Dept. of Science and Industry Systems
University of South-Eastern Norway
email: kristin.falk@usn.no

***Abstract*—The primary goal of this ongoing questionnaire is understanding the state of affairs in terms of big data utilization in Norwegian high-tech enterprises. Employees at partner organizations were asked 24 questions. The questions comprised of categories such as Data Availability, Usability, Integrity, Competency and Organizational behavior. The survey attempted to get a nuanced understanding of the current processes at partner organizations of the H-SEIF2 [1] consortium, or lack thereof to systematically utilize big data in their projects from the perspective of employee's perception. For example, the survey found that the Project Managers have a more optimistic perception of their usage of big data while upper management has a more modest opinion of their current state. In addition to providing insights, the results will act as a baseline for making recommendations and propose adaptive digitalization solutions for each partner organization.**

***Index Terms*—Questionnaire; Big data; Early Phase Decisions;**

I. Introduction

The benefits of using big data in enhancing operations in general and in project life cycle management are well understood by organizations of all types and sizes [2]–[5]. However, how to do so effectively is still an open questions for most organizations [3] [6] [7]. For example, a study conducted by Qlik and Accenture states that over 74% of employees feel anxiety with working with data [8], while a recent study by Rackspace Technology [2] reported that organizations perceived a rise in difficulty in terms of utilizing Big Data Analytics (BDA) and specifically Artificial Intelligence (AI) and Machine Learning (ML).

Researchers have identified multiple challenges which limits organizations ability for enhance utilization of big data. This includes, a lack of common language among engineers, ineffective knowledge sharing and difficulty in finding system information to name of few [9]–[12]. The presented paper will focus on the users of big data, specifically the internal users such as employees working on projects.

The primary goal of the ongoing survey is to understand the current state of affairs in terms of big data utilization at the partner organizations in the H-SEIF2 [1] project. The H-SEIF 2 project aims to harvest the value of big-data to enhance the experience of stakeholders during complex system engineering project by collaborating with industry partners to improve their digitalization efforts. The goal is to design data driven frameworks and methodologies to allow the industry partners in data supported early phase decisions.

Employees at partner organizations were asked 24 questions. The questions were comprised of categories such as Data Availability, Usability, Integrity, Competency and Organizational behavior. In doing so, the survey attempted to get a nuanced understanding of the current processes at partner organizations or lack thereof, to systematically utilize big data in their projects from the perspective of employee's perception. It aims to provide deeper insights at gaps and differences at different organizations or at different department within a large organization. This will act as a baseline for making recommendations and propose adaptive digitalization solutions for each partner organization.

There are few other surveys which analyse the state of affairs at organizations [2] [6] [8]. They have only focused on Chief Information Officers (CIOs) or high level decision makers. The presented paper takes a deeper dive and took the perspective of a cross section of employees to get a better understanding of the current state at each company.

The remainder of the paper is as follows: Section II describes the related work. Details about the questionnaire are described in Section III. Which is followed by a discussion in Section IV and finally Section V contains the concluding remarks and some plans for the future.

II. Related Work

Questionnaires and surveys are widely used for different purposes e.g., comparing two products and/or services [7] [13]. They are often used to understand the needs of perspective users of future products and services or as part of user-centric design [14] [15], or to collect data on customer, employee and/or student satisfaction, [16]–[18].

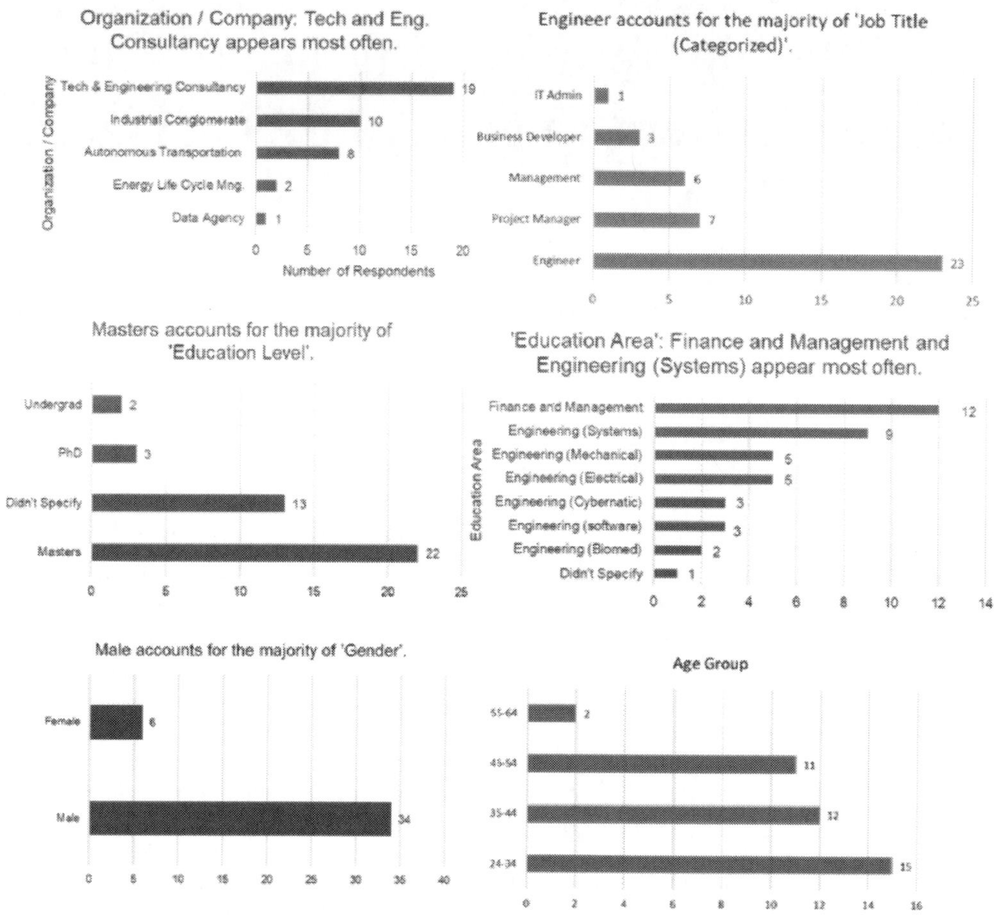

Figure. 1: Respondents Profile: information about respondents

Regarding the utilization of big data in operations of organizations, Qlik and Accenture [8] conducted a survey to have an understanding of big data utilization in enterprises . They found that 60 to 70% of the collected data in enterprise is never used and a vast majority of about 74% of employees feel overwhelmed or simply unhappy working with data. They also found that only 37% of employees trust their decisions more when they are based on data while 48% preferred gut feeling over data driven decision making [8].

Focusing on high level decision makers, a survey by Rackspace Technology [2] found that employees perceived difficulty with ML and big data has actually been increasing. The survey [2] also found that employees considered data dispersed across many different systems to be one of the biggest barrier in drawing insights from it. Lack of skillset and talented employees is perceived as a great concern and limitation in fully utilizing big data in enterprise decision making [2] [8] [19].

Raguseo [6] focused on the CIOs of French medium and large enterprises to understand differences if any, across industry and the size of organizations. Analysis of the questionnaire found that investments in technologies like machine learning software tools are influenced by the size of the organization and the author did not find any statistical differences across different industries.

While employees appear often in the discourse and considered a crucial element in utilizing big data systems, they are often the ones most neglected [20]. Moreover, majority of the above mentioned research focused on high level decision makers and not a cross-section of employees, departments and job roles.

The presented survey is part of the H-SEIF2 [1] research project that aims to develop human centered framework for the utilization of big data during early phase decision making. The presented work, by focusing on Norwegian industry partners extends the related work by focusing on a cross-section of employees to get a more nuance understanding of any differences among different departments, employee profiles and across different industries.

III. Survey Questionnaire

The survey questionnaire consists of 24 questions in 5 categories. The categories were selected by a combination of

TABLE I: THE QUESTIONNAIRE.

Information About You
Organization / Company Job title Department Job Description
Educational Background Gender Age group
In what Life-cycle phase(s) is your current work activities?
Idea Generation and Analysis, Concept Development, Detailed Engineering,
Fabrication Testing and Integration, Operations, Maintenance and Modification
Data Availability
1. In my current project, team spent a significant effort to gather relevant data for decision making.
2. In my current project we gather data of high relevance to end-user values.
3. When I do my work, I have easy access to all relevant data that I need to do my work.
4. I am familiar with tools and methods that can help me to better explore and analyze data that include AI and ML?
5. In my work, I have easy access to useful data-analysis tools and methodologies that help to better understand the task at hand.
6. I have available all the data-analysis tools and methods that I need to do my work effectively.
7. Pertinent data and information that is being held back from me in due to confidentiality.
Data Usability
8. Getting access to and analyzing big amount of data is an important part of the early-phase development-process in my company.
9. In my organization, we have a history of bashing out new ideas and products on data and information rather than on "gut-feeling".
10. In My company, we make disruptive innovations rather than incremental product improvements.
11. In my company we use data from previous systems/projects to improve the performance of the current system/project.
12. In my company we have a consistent and effective procedure for storing/sharing data.
13. The procedure for storing/sharing data in my company is sufficient for our purposes?
14. I always use the existing stored data from old projects as "lessons learned" in new projects.
Data Integrity
15. In my work, I fully trust the data presented and developed by others.
Competency
16. I am fully confident about how to best use data to improve products, services and/or systems.
17. In early-phases of product-development, I am fully confident that my team has sufficient knowledge to effectively use all available data.
18. My managers always understand the data and simulations I present to him/her.
19. I always have enough context when I use data in my work.
20. My company encourage competency-development digital skills such as big data and digitalization.
Organizational Behavior
21. My company fully take advantage of operational data as feedback in the early development.
22. We spend sufficient time to collect and analyze all available data in the early phase.
23. My company has a process that helps us make use of big-data for early validation of system solutions.
24. Decisions in my company are made based on reliable data rather than gut feeling

literature review [2] [3] [6] [8] [20] and our initial co-creation sessions with industry partners, in order to understand the issues faced by the H-SEIF2 [1] industry partners in fully utilizing big data in early phase decision making in their projects.

Table I lists the questions asked in the questionnaire. The participants were asked to rate the extent to which they agree or disagree with the statements on a 7-point Likert scale. In the initial phase, we have collected 40 responses from employees at partner organizations. Figure 1 shows the basic information about the survey respondents. Most respondents are from the Tech and Engineering Consultancy firm that works on a diverse range of innovative projects for their clients, followed by an industrial conglomerate with division in shipping and digital technology and startup incubation. More than half of the respondents are engineers i.e., 23, while 7 are project managers and 6 belong to top management positions.

In terms of educational background, 22 of the respondents reported having a Masters degree. Engineering was the most common reported educational background, while Finance and Management the other. The age distribution of the respondents is quite balanced as well (see Figure 1(f)), however our current data have a gender imbalance, as 34 out of the 40 respondents are male. We will make efforts to address that in future versions.

IV. Results and Discussion

The questionnaire results (see Figure 2) show that internal stakeholders (employees) feel dissatisfied by the utilization of big data in their projects, especially in early phase decision making as the Net Promoter Score (NPS) is negative across the board. It is not surprising, as it is not only the finding of our initial conversations with industry partners but other surveys reached the same conclusion [2] [8].

One notable surprise however is question# 7 which asks the respondents if data is being held back from them for confidentiality reasons; to which the respondents disagreed. In this case it is a positive outcome and runs counter to our earlier assumptions [21]. However, it may change when in the next phase we collect data from additional respondents belonging to industry partners involved with defense and aerospace industries.

Another interesting outcome is that engineers and personnel involved with technical aspect of projects gave lower scores than project managers and upper management. Project managers seem to have a rosier perception compared to others (see Figure 3). There is a need for greater communication among project managers and other non-technical stakeholder, engineers and technical personnel. While the more positive responses are somewhat in line with [8], there are notable differences compared to [8]. For example, in our survey the

Q #	1	2	3	4	5	6	7	8	9	10	11	12	13	14	15	16	17	18	19	20	21	22	23	24
NPS	-19	-17	-23	-28	-32	-27	-27	-29	-23	-27	-18	-20	-26	-23	-14	-14	-20	-15	-19	-21	-21	-29	-20	-24

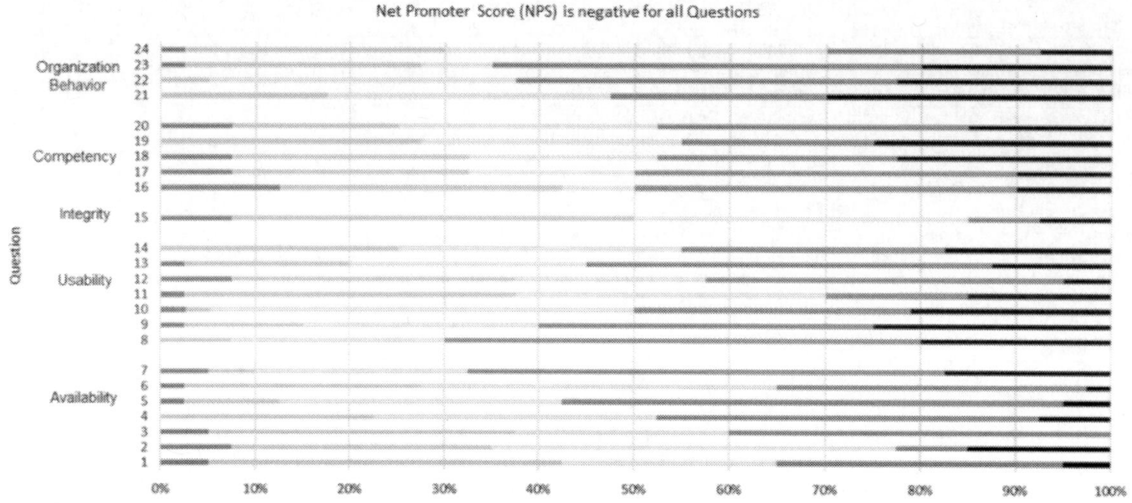

	1	2	3	4	5	6	7	8	9	10	11	12	13	14	15	16	17	18	19	20	21	22	23	24
Strongly Agree	2	3	2	0	1	1	2	0	1	1	1	3	1	0	3	5	3	3	0	3	0	0	1	1
Agree	15	11	13	9	4	10	2	3	5	1	14	12	7	10	17	12	10	10	11	7	7	2	10	11
Partially Agree / Neutral	9	17	9	12	12	15	9	9	10	17	13	8	10	12	14	3	7	8	11	11	12	13	3	16
Disagree	10	3	15	7	13	10	10	10	11	8	3	10	14	6	3	14	13	10	8	10	8	12	14	8
Strongly Disagree	2	0	1	9	8	3	10	10	3	3	3	5	3	5	0	2	3	0	0	3	1	4	4	1
Don't know/not app	2	6	0	3	2	1	7	8	10	8	6	2	5	7	3	4	4	9	10	6	12	9	8	3

Strongly Agree · Agree · Partially Agree / Neutral · Disagree · Strongly Disagree · Don't know/not app

Figure. 2: Overall responses

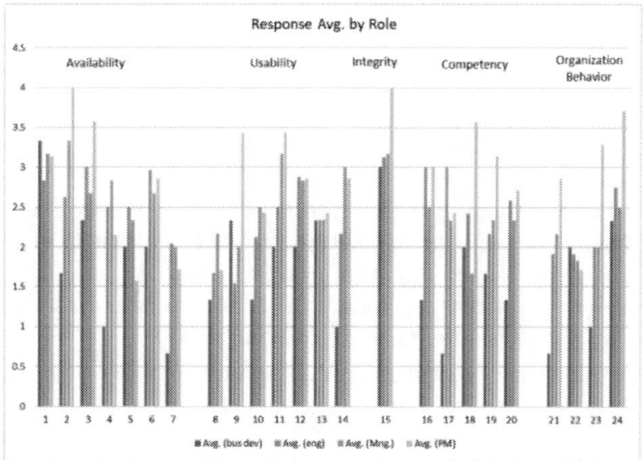

Figure. 3: Average responses per job roles.

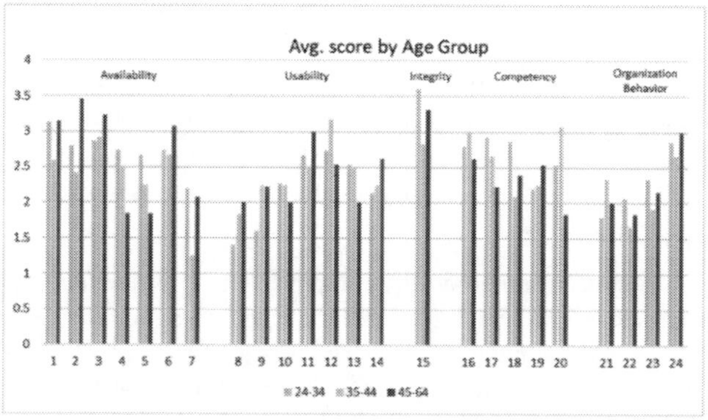

Figure. 4: Average responses per age group.

upper management seems less optimistic compared to the project managers.

Another notable exception is the "Competency" section of the questionnaire. For example, the report [8] stated that business leaders overestimate the capabilities of their workforce, while our survey showed that both engineers and project managers gave higher responses compared to the upper management (see Figure 3).

In terms of age groups, employees in younger and older age groups overall gave higher scores compared to middle (35-44) age group, while the middle age group reported the most confidence in their competency compared to the others (see Figure 4). Also, in terms of the organization behavior category, younger and senior employees express greater optimism compared to the 35-44 age group. Question# 21 was an exception, which asks about taking full advantage of operational data in early phase decision making, to which the 35-44 age group gave higher score compared to the others.

V. Conclusion

The current version of the survey gave us a deeper understanding of the state of affairs as perceived by the internal stakeholder at some of the industry partners. It provided a glimpse at the disparity of different stakeholders in terms of their perception of their utilization of big data in their operations and decision-making process. Overall, the survey concluded that employees at the H-SEIF2 industry partners understand the need of using big data in their project to enhance their operations as the NPS is negative across the board. Another conclusion that can be drawn is that the project managers need more communication with engineers and other technical personnel to get a better calibration of their big data needs.

In the future, we plan to extend the survey by gathering responses from all the industry partners in the H-SEIF 2 consortium to allow us an even deeper understanding of the perception of employees and the state of affairs. For future versions, we will target different departments within larger organizations to get a more balanced dataset for our analysis and we also plan to conduct semi-structure interviews with some employees to get further insights.

Acknowledgement

This research is part of the H-SEIF 2 project and is funded by the Research Council of Norway through the innovation project (IPN project no.: 317862).

References

[1] U. NISE, "H-SEIF 2 Project." [Online]. Available: https://www.usn.no/hseif last accessed on 20-06-2022

[2] R. Technology, "AI / ML Annual Research Report 2022," 2022.

[3] K. Falk, A. K. Kamara, E. P. Brathen, K. Helle, P. T. Moe, and S. Kokkula, "Digitizing the Maintenance Documentation; A System of Systems in Oil and Gas Industry," *SOSE 2020 - IEEE 15th International Conference of System of Systems Engineering, Proceedings*, pp. 493–499, 2020.

[4] H. B. Ali and F. A. Salim, "Transferring Tacit Knowledge into Explicit: A Case Study in a Fully (Semi) Automated Parking Garage," in *PROCEEDINGS OF The Society for Design and Process Science*, 2021.

[5] F. A. Salim, H. B. Ali, and K. Falk, "Towards a Data Processing Framework for Enhanced User Centric System Engineering," in *PROCEEDINGS OF The Society for Design and Process Science, Workshop on Smart Pervasive Computing*, 2021.

[6] E. Raguseo, "Big data technologies: An empirical investigation on their adoption, benefits and risks for companies," *International Journal of Information Management*, vol. 38, no. 1, pp. 187–195, 2018.

[7] F. A. Salim, F. Haider, S. Luz, and O. Conlan, "Automatic transformation of a video using multimodal information for an engaging exploration experience," *Applied Sciences (Switzerland)*, vol. 10, no. 9, 2020.

[8] Qlik and Accenture, "The Human Impact of Data Literacy," Tech. Rep., 2020. [Online]. Available: https://thedataliteracyproject.org/humanimpact last accessed on 20-06-2022

[9] B. A. Delicado, A. Salado, and R. Mompó, "Conceptualization of a T-Shaped engineering competency model in collaborative organizational settings: Problem and status in the Spanish aircraft industry," *Systems Engineering*, vol. 21, no. 6, pp. 534–554, 2018.

[10] S. Engen, K. Falk, and G. Muller, "The need for systems awareness to support early-phase decision-making—a study from the norwegian energy industry," *Systems*, vol. 9, no. 3, 2021.

[11] Juzgado P.D. Borches, "A3 Architecture overviews. A tool for effective communication in product evolution," Ph.D. dissertation, University of Twente, 2010.

[12] T. Tomiyama, V. D'Amelio, J. Urbanic, and W. Eimaraghy, "Complexity of multi-disciplinary design," *CIRP Annals - Manufacturing Technology*, vol. 56, no. 1, pp. 185–188, 2007.

[13] B. Laugwitz, T. Held, and M. Schrepp, "Construction and Evaluation of a User Experience Questionnaire," *HCI and Usability for Education and Work*, pp. 63–76, 2008.

[14] F. A. Salim, F. Haider, O. Conlan, and S. Luz, "An approach for exploring a video via multimodal feature extraction and user interactions," *Journal on Multimodal User Interfaces*, no. October 2017, 2018.

[15] G. Gravier, M. Ragot, A. Laurent, R. Bois, G. Jadi, E. Jamet, and L. Monceaux, "Shaping-Up Multimedia Analytics: Needs and Expectations of Media Professionals," in *The 22nd International Conference on Multimedia Modelling*, vol. 9516, Miami, 2016, pp. 303–314.

[16] G. Nicolini and L. D. Valle, "Errors in Customer Satisfaction Surveys and Methods to Correct Self-Selection Bias," *Quality Technology Quantitative Management*, vol. 8, no. 2, pp. 167–181, 2011.

[17] B. Popovic, R. Maletic, and T. Paunovic, "Employee Satisfaction Survey in Function of Business Improvement," *Management - Journal for theory and practice of management*, vol. 20, no. 76, pp. 31–40, 2015.

[18] L. She, L. Ma, A. Jan, H. Sharif Nia, and P. Rahmatpour, "Online Learning Satisfaction During COVID-19 Pandemic Among Chinese University Students: The Serial Mediation Model," *Frontiers in Psychology*, vol. 12, no. October, 2021.

[19] B. Dudley, "Digital Transformation Initiative: Oil and Gas Industry In collaboration with Accenture," *World Economic Forum*, no. January, p. 32, 2017. [Online]. Available: www.weforum.org last accessed on 20-06-2022

[20] D. H. Shin, "Demystifying big data: Anatomy of big data developmental process," *Telecommunications Policy*, vol. 40, no. 9, pp. 837–854, 2016.

[21] N. M. Sjøkvist and M. Kjørstad, "Eliciting Human Values by Applying Design Thinking Techniques in Systems Engineering," *INCOSE International Symposium*, vol. 29, no. 1, pp. 478–499, 2019.

AutoDrone - Use of Autonomously Operated Drone Technology in Forest Inventory

An Approach Realized on Wireless Sensor Networks

Robert Richter, Christopher Dunkel, Oliver Michler
Technische Universität Dresden, "Friedrich List" Faculty of Transport and Traffic Sciences, Chair of Transport Systems Information Technology
Dresden, Germany
email: robert.richter@tu-dresden.de
email: christopher.dunkel@tu-dresden.de
email: oliver.michler@tu-dresden.de

Abstract— **This paper describes the engineering solution of a system control technology for drones with the goal of autonomous drone flight on or over machine trails, skid trails, forest roads and similar line-like path in forest stands. The overall non-functional requirement here is for non-satellite positioning of the drone in real time based on a radio sensor network. The available open space above the line structures under the canopy of trees is used as the flight envelope. The problems of inaccurate satellite-based positioning inside the forestry environment are compensated primarily by the use of Wireless Sensor Networks for positioning. The goal is a valid recording of tree parameters and the creation of a digital map within the tree population. The control system of the drone is based on fused data from Wireless Sensor Networks, intertial sensors, satellite-based systems and visual position estimation. Our drone is thus able to automatically fly over freely selectable areas within the path without satellite-based positioning and thus fulfills the prerequisite for recording the tree parameters using suitable sensors. The practical application of this approach in the forest is presented and discussed.**

Keywords-Forest Inventory Monitoring; Wireless Sensor Network; Ultrawideband; GNSS Independent Localization; Drone

I. Introduction

For sustainable forest management, a solid data basis on the current stocking is absolutely necessary. In today's standard sampling method, trees in defined sampling circles are measured by terrestrial walking on the basis of a homogeneous, usually permanently established sampling grid. These data are stratified according to statistical procedures, aggregated and further processed for the calculation of forestry-relevant indicators. The current work process is becoming increasingly difficult for the following reasons:

- In the course of ecological forest conversion, mixed forests are aimed at that are rich in structure. This is associated with a highly developed vegetation layer near the ground, which makes accessibility and visibility extremely difficult for terrestrial methods.
- The sampling method used today is based on a personnel-intensive, time-consuming work process with a high cost burden for the forest enterprises. Although it is possible to reduce the costs associated with the surveys by means of the grids of the survey network, this is at the expense of the validity or statistical reliability of the results.
- With regard to accuracy, it must also be taken into account that manual measurement methods have a, high measurement error. Here, the error rate and measurement inaccuracies can be significantly reduced with the help of modern recording technologies.
- The process chains in forest management are for the most part still very extensive and decoupled. Automated data acquisition and subsequent automated data preparation allow the personnel and technical focus to be placed on data analysis and evaluations in the subsequent processing steps. Thus, the expertise is directed to the central tasks of silvicultural and forestry planning for the forest enterprise.

Against this background, the approach realized the use of an autonomously moving drone technology in forest inventory and operational planning is to be the basis for a later practicable, technologically mature procedure for the automated recording of individual tree parameters and the generation of population parameters relevant to planning and management. The focus of the work is on the technological innovation and implementation, the development of a control technology for drones with the goal of autonomous drone flight on or above machine trails, skid trails, forest roads and similar line structures within forest stands. Thereby, the available free space profile above the line structures is used as flight space. An appropriate flight altitude neglects the edges of the paths near the ground, which are covered by structures and which prevent a valid recording of the tree parameters inside the stand due to the obstructed view in terrestrial methods. The control system of the drone is based on fused data from radio sensor networks, inertial sensors, satellite-based systems and visual position estimation. A Light Detection and Ranging (LiDAR) sensor performs object avoidance. Our Drone is thus able to automatically fly over freely selectable areas within the path without global satellite-based (GNSS) positioning and thus fulfills the prerequisite for recording the tree parameters using suitable sensors. The specific tasks for this implementation were:

- Compensation of weak or non-existent GNSS signals in a forest environment through the use of range-capable Wireless Sensor Networks (WSN).
- Automatic flight stabilization with respect to altitude and required lateral positioning over the forest floor
- Multisensor data fusion and position filtering algorithms for autonomous flight primarily based on a WSN and secondarily based on an imaging (visioning) position module
- Application of a Wireless Sensor System for communication, localization and environment detection of drones
- Adaptation / further development of visioning position modules for the forest environment with regard to obstacle detection of trees, branches, bushes and segmentation of the forest floor as well as a constant flight altitude
- Implementation of a Simultaneous Localization And Mapping (SLAM) algorithm for autonomous flight within a geofender of the back alley

Figure 1 shows the system approach in this respect.

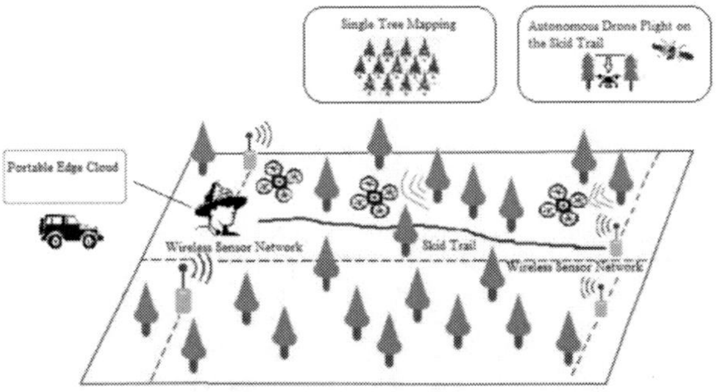

Figure 1. System approach for the use of drones in a forest environment.

The paper is structured as follows. After this introduction to the topic, which describes the problems and the boundary conditions for the use of autonomous drones in a forest environment, the state of the art in science and technology regarding drones and position technologies described in Section II. Section III gives an overview about the technological process flow for realizing a GNSS independent drone flight on the back alley in the forest. The test of the whole system setup and first flights on a test field are shown in Section IV. Section V addresses the evaluation of recorded measurement results of the performed test flights in a forest environment. In this regard, the results and resulting problems are discussed. The paper ends with a summary and an outlook on further work to solve the problems presented before.

II. State of the Art

Smaller drones or multicopters are relevant for the intended use in the forest on skid trails under the leaf canopy at a height of about 2 to 3 meters. This is due to the intended area of application of the drones, which are to fly autonomously under the treetops up to three meters above the forest floor, specifically in the area of skid trails. This eliminates large and heavy devices from the selection. Nowadays, drones can be used for very many disciplines in science and research due to their small design, improved control technology and falling prices. They open up entirely new perspectives for ecological research and environmental protection. For example, drones are already being used to map landscapes that are difficult to access or to take stock of endangered animal species. Today, drones already offer an efficient way to collect, aggregate and store or transmit data for scientific purposes using appropriately equipped sensor technology.

A. *Overview of relevant Drone Technologies*

A special focus is navigation in visual flight or with difficult or no GNSS reception. In principle, GNSS-based systems (mostly GPS and GLONASS) can currently achieve resolutions of barely more than three meters [1], which is sufficient for uninhabited landscapes - but not for urban areas or use inside buildings or in the forest on skid trails. In this regard, heavily attenuated or scattered GNSS signals under the treetops make autonomous drone flight enormously difficult to the point of impossible feasibility. Furthermore, they have to permanently avoid smaller and larger tree trunks, branches, smaller trees from the tree regeneration and shrubs. This requires a complex camera system, gyroscopes, accelerometers and ultrasonic sensors. This is the only way the aircraft can find out where it is and if there are any obstacles in its way. The state of the art is far advanced in this respect. Using so-called intelligent flight modes, the visual, inertial, ultrasonic and GNSS data are combined in a multi-sensor data fusion. This enables an assisted flight depending on the environment.

B. *Introduction of Wireless Sensor Networks for Drone Positioning and Navigation in a Forestry Environment*

In order to ensure autonomous flight in the forest environment, a WSN is adapted for positioning and applied to drones. Technical basis for this was the recent increased miniaturization as well as the advancing development of microsystem technology for the design of highly complex sensor nodes, which are combined as individual systems in an infrastructure-free and self-configuring WSN. In contrast to wired configurations, particular importance is attached to the radio-based transmission of information within the WSN and to a central coordination unit. The main task of these networks is the monitoring of extensive and usually difficult to access areas or extensive process chains, which can only be monitored by conventional systems with disproportionately high and uneconomical effort. The totality of all sensor nodes thus forms an information source with significant spatial extent, high flexibility and an almost unrestricted scaling behavior. Sensor nodes are generally highly complex individual systems consisting of a microcontroller, sensors or actuators, a memory, the communication unit and a power source. Thus, sensor nodes are basically capable of describing relationships with the environment, such as topological and geometrical information. The measured distance of sensor nodes to each other is, besides angular or simple presence information, the most commonly used form of neighborhood information and forms the data basis required for positioning and environment recognition methods. Broadband radio systems are used, which provide the required distance relations in the form of distance and angle measurements in corresponding real-time performance on the basis of the licensed Ultra-Wideband Spectrum (UWB). Within a WSN with a minimum of four fixed anchor nodes, a suitably equipped drone can fly autonomously along path on a forestry skid trail. The anchor nodes are static fixed in pairs on the trees. In principle, the anchor nodes can be attached to forestry vehicles, trees and other "static" points. The mobile nodes can be integrated, for example, in the clothing of forest workers or directly on mobile devices such as drones, chainsaws. Operationally and algorithmically, static and mobile nodes can switch properties [2].

III. Overview of the Technological Process Flow of the Radio Sensor Network Based Drone Flight in the Forest Environment

First of all, the realized process flow is described. At least four anchor nodes are placed in the forest along the skid alley for Wireless Sensor Network-based tracking by a forestry employee. The anchor nodes are attached to trees at a height of 1 to 2 m with the antenna pointing towards the skid alley (see Figure 2)

Figure 2. Pinned anchor node on a tree [3].

This focuses the radio channel on the area of interest for the positioning within the skid alley (see red marked area in Figure 3).

Figure 3. Skidding trail for wood harvesting (a), area of interest for autonomous drone flight marked in red (b).

A. *Technologies Used on the Drone*

The corresponding wireless sensor for positioning determination is additionally attached and integrated as a so-called node on the drone control unit. In this regard, the connection was realized via different interfaces like Universal Asynchronous Receiver / Transmitter (UART) and Controller Area Network (CAN). By calibrating the initial anchor into a geodetic reference system, especially a World Geodetic System 1984 (WGS84) coordinate and determining the angular offset to the north, the coordinate transformation into global coordinates then takes place. The novelty now is that the drone's determined relative position within the WSN is converted to a global coordinate and provided to the drone controller as a fake National Marine Electronics Association standardized position data exchange (NMEA) message. Missing NMEA parameters are simulated or replaced. The drone does not recognize any difference between converted or simulated and real GNSS environment. In this context, the interconnection of the system components required for this purpose is shown in the following Figure 4.

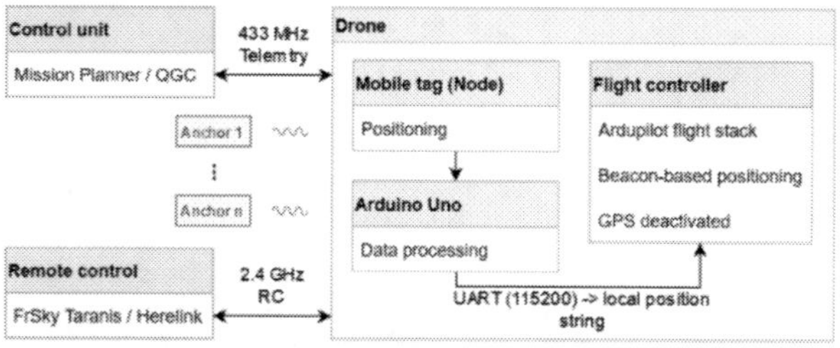

Figure 4. Interconnection between system components regarding the WSN and the drone, especially the flight controller and the integrated mobile node.

In the left part of the figure, the possibilities for drone control are shown. The control unit with the Mission Planner is a software for planning flight missions. It is used to plan the flight trajectory on the skid trail in prior, which the drone will then fly autonomously with the help of the WSN. Physically, the control unit is part of the so-called Ground Station (GS) and is equipped with a 433 MHz transceiver and connected to a computer running the planning software (see Figure 5). The trajectory planned on the computer is finally transferred via the telemetry channel to the drone and saved as a flight mission. Until now, the GS software used has been Mission Planner (MP) and QGroundControl (QGC).

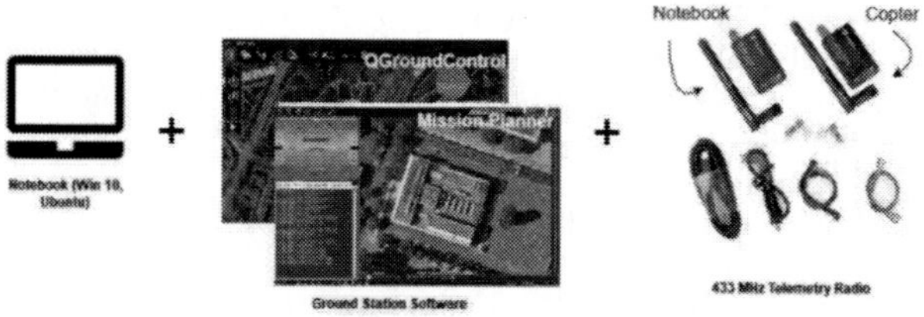

Figure 5. Ground Station system architecture.

The other remote control shown in Figure 4 serves as a fallback level to switch from autonomous flight to manual control. This is a commercially available programmable remote control (FrSky Taranis / Herelink Transceiver), which is connected to the drone with 2.4 GHz for pure flight control. This is only used in an emergency if problems are detected in autonomous flight.

The heart of the drone is the flight controller. This is where all sensor data ultimately converge. From this, the flight parameters are calculated and the corresponding rotors are controlled, for example, to execute the uploaded mission plan. The flight controller in this case is based on ArduPilot, an open source software for unmanned vehicles and the de facto standard for autonomous control of multicopters, fixed wing/Vertical Take Off and Landing (VTOL) gliders, helicopters, submarines and land vehicles. The FW variant for multicopters is called ArduCopter and is customizable. The configuration of the Firmware to the respective properties of the copter as well as its sensors is done via parameters. If changes to the FW are necessary, or if new modules not previously available, but have to be added such as positioning by using an extended Kalman filter (version 2 or 3), this can be implemented using the corresponding environment dependencies. To clarify this, the system architecture of the FW shown in Figure 6 is used with examples of the connection of further components. Via a companion computer (e.g., Arduino or Raspberry Pi on the drone) with the ground station, data of the copter can be retrieved, configured or changed. MAVLink (Micro Air Vehicle Link) is the protocol for communication between the components. The actual ArduPilot firmware is described in the Flight Code part. In this regard the flight controller, is a Cube Orange. It works according to the open Pixhawk standard, which defines guidelines for the implementation of the hardware (e.g., interfaces, voltage levels, etc.). The superordinate operating system is the RTOS (Real Time Operating System) ChibiOS. In normal operation, access to a large part of these components is not possible or not necessary, since the entire configuration of the system is done via the parameters [4].

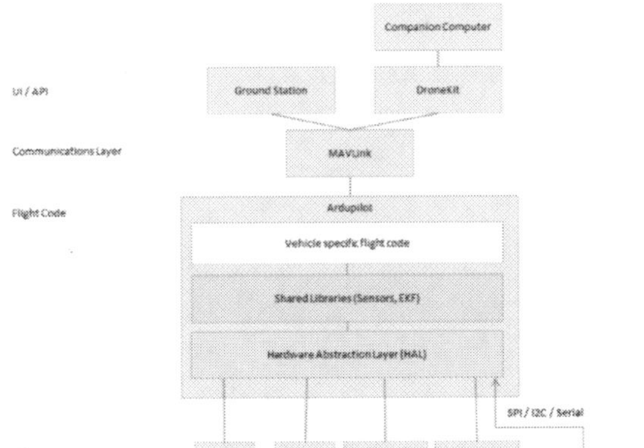

Figure 6. ArduPilot system architecture [4].

Finally, this section will look at the drone as itself. The drone is an PM Q685 Quadcopter and has the following technologies relevant to this particular system approach:

- Real Time Kinematic GNSS Positioning Modul
- Cube Orange Flight Controller
- HereLink Transceiver
- ArduPilot flight stack
- Ultrawideband sensor node (Pozyx) with Arduino Uno

The following Figure 7 illustrates the connection of the UWB sensor to the flight control of the drone. The Arduino Uno is responsible for the calculation of the positions to the individual anchors (PA1...PA4) as well as for the coordinate transformation.

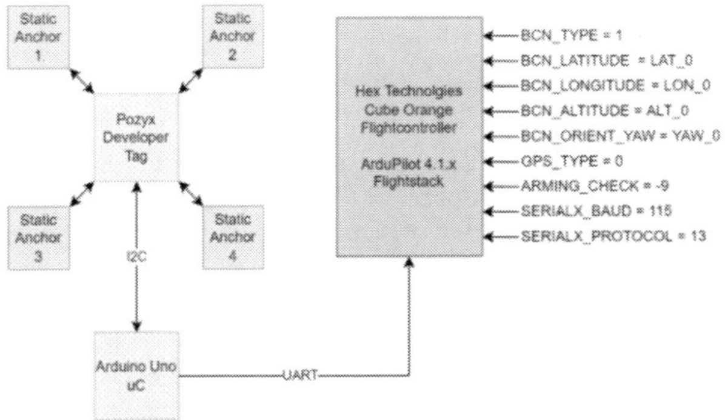

Figure 7. Integration of the UWB-based sensor node into the flight controller [4].

Finally, Figure 8 shows the operational drone modified for the goal of autonomous flight over a skid trail under the leaf canopy of trees in a forest environment. This fulfills the requirements for GNSS independent and sufficiently precise positioning with the use of a WSN distributed within the forest.

Figure 8. Operational ready drone at the launch point in the forestry environment at the skid trail.

B. Flight Mission Procedure

The preparation of the flight mission, i.e., the trajectory to be flying on the skid trails follows the sequence diagram below (Figure 9). As a result, the flight trajectory is transferred to the drone as a flight mission. At this point, in principle the drone is ready itself for fly.

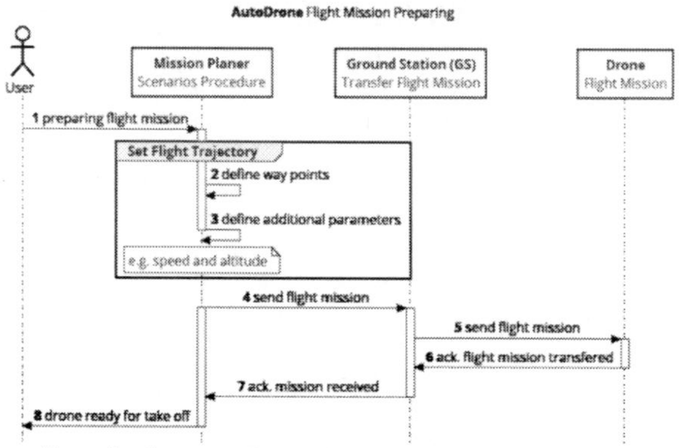

Figure 9. Sequence diagram for flight mission preparing.

In order for the drone to fly the trajectory autonomously in the forest environment, the following preparations must be fulfilled on site (see sequence diagram Figure 10).

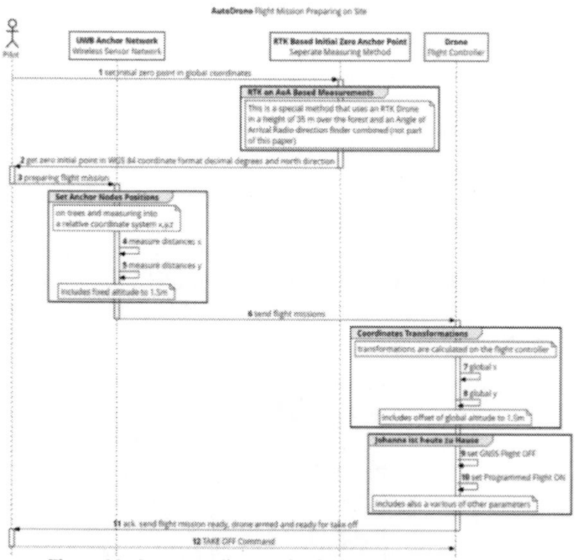

Figure 10. Sequence diagram for flight mission on site.

After this sequence diagram is completed, GNSS is deactivated and the drone flies the programmed route from the start and back again. During the flight all sensor data arriving at the flight controller are logged.

IV. TEST OF THE WHOLE SYSTEM SETUP AND FIRST FLIGHTS ON A TEST FIELD

The first flight tests and measurements were carried out on a test field. Here, the pilot still retained control of the drone. All process sequences were optimized and an artificial return path created on the test field was successfully flown autonomously in the end. For this purpose, a best-case scenario was designed and implemented. This included no sources of interference from the real environment such as trees, i.e., no or hardly any signal attenuation and multipath. The following figure 11 shows the test field and the flight area equipped with a WSN (marked in red).

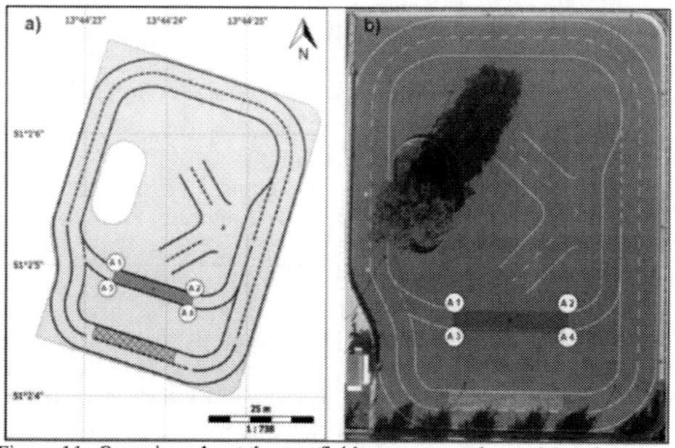

Figure 11. Overview about the test field as a surveyed map (a) and a satellite based view (b). The WSN area for flights is marked in red in each case.

The first interesting measurements are related to the distances between the anchors and the mobile node on the drone (see Figure 12). The symmetrical overlap of the distance measurements of all anchors at two points (outbound and return flight to the starting point) can be seen. There are minimal deviations in the 10 cm range of the distances during the entire flight. In summary, the distances are not very noisy and without detected outliers for this case. A comparison with the flight behavior confirmed this measurement.

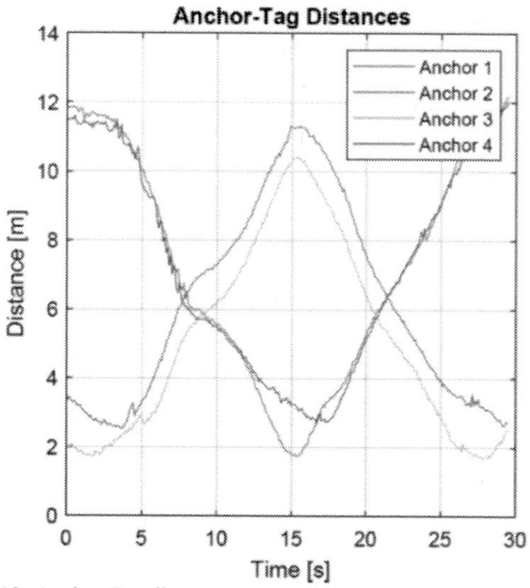

Figure 12. Anchor-Tag distance measurements during a flight in a radio sense optimal environment on a testfield.

Another important aspect of the investigation relates to the in-flight altitude measurement in the radio sensor network (see Figure 13). An optimization in terms of height measurement is the use of an ultrasonic sensor instead of the WSN. This type of sensor currently works more accurately due to the technical structure.

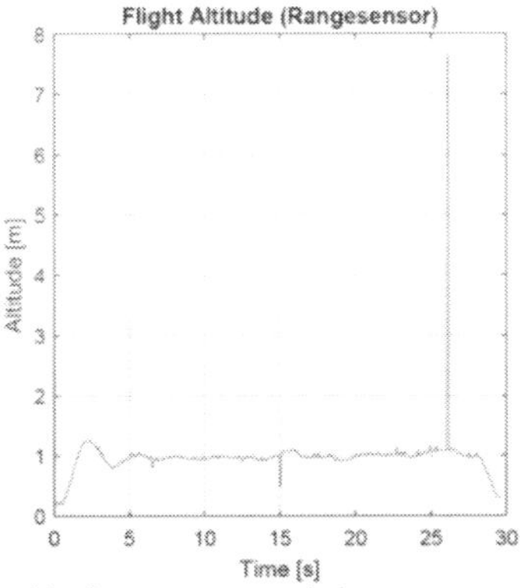

Figure 13. Flight altitude measurements during an autonomous flight on the test field.

The maximum height measurement ends at 7 meters, which is more than sufficient for our application. In the diagram you can see some outliers, which should not have been there due to a flight observation. A sudden drift of the drone in altitude could not be observed with the deviating altitude measurements (deviations at 15 s and 26 s). Since these deviations were short-lived, the Extended Kalman filter used compensated for them.

V. EVALUATION OF RECORDED MEASUREMENT RESULTS OF THE PERFORMED TEST FLIGHTS IN A FOREST ENVIRONMENT

The extensive test flights carried out in the forest confirmed the measurements on the test field. As results its presented here two interesting figures. Figure 14 shows the positioning of the drone with the mobile node/tag during the flight along the back road in the forest based only on the distance measurements of the WSN.

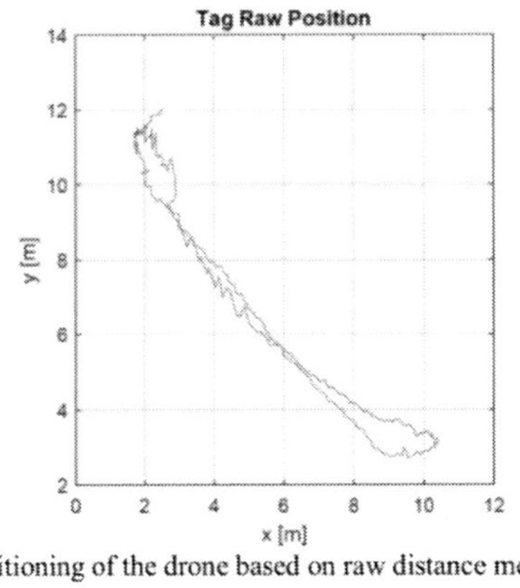

Figure 14. Positioning of the drone based on raw distance measurements.

It can be clearly seen that the positioning based on the raw data measurement of the distances varies with a deviation in the decimeter range. Thus, theoretically, no continuous smooth flight trajectory is possible on the sole basis of positioning in a WSN. Only by using the other onboard drone sensors, a smooth continuous flight trajectory becomes possible through a multi-sensor data fusion in the used Extended Kalman Filter (see Figure 15).

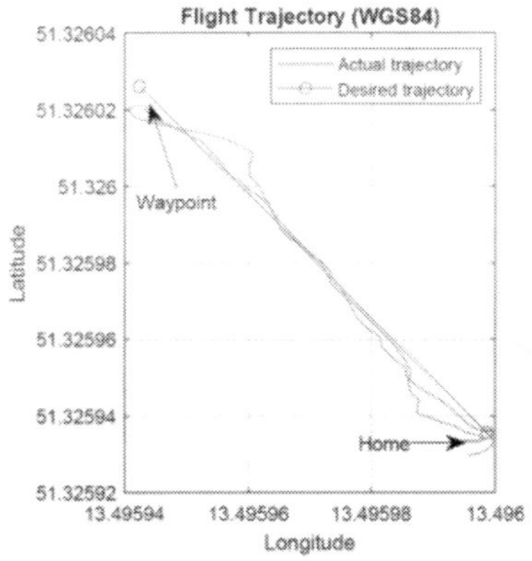

Figure 15. Data fused global positioning of the drone in the forestry environment.

VI. CONCLUSION AND FURTHER WORK

In this paper we have shown, that a GNSS-based positioning of a drone can be substituted by a local WSN for positioning. In this context, an already implemented solution of an autonomous drone flight within a skid trail was presented and discussed regarding its results (e.g., position accuracy, measurement setup). Further work relates to the objectives described in the introduction with respect to individual tree-to-tree mapping and radar-based tree condition detection.

ACKNOWLEDGMENT

We would like to thank the Agency for Renewable Resources (Fachagentur Nachwachsende Rohstoffe e. V. - FNR) as project sponsor of the Federal Ministry of Food and Agriculture (BMEL) [5].

REFERENCES

[1] W. Mansfeld, Werner, satellite positioning and navigation - basics and application of global satellite navigation systems. vol. 2, Wiesbaden, 2004

[2] A. Born, Algorithms for position determination and their accuracies in Wireless Sensor Networks, PhD thesis, München 2011

[3] Pozyx. 2021, Pozyx.io. [Online] Available from: https://pozyx.io/products-and-services/creator 2022.06.25

[4] Ardupilot, 2022, ardupilot.org. [Online] Available from: https://ardupilot.org/dev/docs/apmcopter-code-overview.html 2022.06.25

[5] BMEL 2022, fnr.org. [Online] Available from: https://www.fnr.de/fnr-struktur-aufgaben-lage/fachagentur-nachwachsende-rohstoffe-fnr.html 2022.06.25

Implementation of the RAM Analyses into a Discrete Event Simulation of a Process in Early Stages of its Development

Martin Kubic, Maurice Pendola
Axone
Meyreuil, France
m.kubic@axonegroup.com

Abstract — **Modeling complex systems has become a common tool in many fields, especially in engineering, mathematics, military, and transport sciences. It provides a relatively inexpensive way to gather information for comprehensive and decision-making purposes. Since the size and complexity of real systems in these areas rarely allow analytical solutions to provide the information, simulation has become the method of choice. One difficulty in the engineering design processes of the designed system is to introduce this powerful tool in presence of all the design uncertainties that arise due to the early stage of the design knowing the fact that it will be useful for verification purposes and is to today widely used for that. This paper aims at given issues in order to introduce combined intention to use simulation tool for allocation purposed during the architecting process in order to help to perform decomposition and architecture tradeoffs during early stages of the design. Further, it illustrates the benefits of using simulation through an implementation of the aspects of Reliability, Availability, and Maintainability (RAM) into a Discrete Event Simulation (DES) tool in order to perform architecture tradeoffs and performances allocation based on both physical behavior and RAM considerations in the early design phase of a complex storage plant.**

Keywords - RAMS analyses, Discrete event simulation, Allocation process, System Engineering

I. Introduction

Recent studies have shown that engineers continue to spend an enormous amount of time researching information and assembling reports. This trend has only grown with the increase of scale and complexity of systems, resulting in a dramatic increase in system requirements. Thus, managing requirements using simplistic methods is no longer enough. With increasing system complexity, document-centric approaches have become increasingly difficult to manage due to the increased risk of overlooking critical information and key interfaces. This has given rise of the Model Based System Engineering (MBSE) in order to replace the document centered management by a management centered around the models all along the life cycle of a system starting early in the design phase up the verification and validation phases ([1]).

Although the modelling of complex system has recently become a common practice in many industrial projects, the simulation methods are used primary in the later phases of the projects as a verification tool (Figure 1) [2][3]. The absence of the application of the simulations methods from the very beginning of a system life leads often to unpredicted additional costs and delays of the projects [4]. Although, there exist attempts to implement the simulation in the decision-making stage [6], several challenges are faced including constant evolution of the system's design or input data uncertainties. Very often, especially in the French nuclear environment, these obstacles overweight the potential outcome the simulation at the large scale of a system can provide. The aim of this paper to provide an example of the implementation of a simulation method at the very beginning of the design-phase of an industrial process to support the decision-making at the highest architect level.

The paper is structured as follows. Firstly, an introduction to modeling from a system engineering point of view, particularly in the design phase, supplemented by the principles of discrete event modeling is provided with the emphasis on the SimEvents tool. The body of the paper is then devoted to the description of the implementation of the RAM elements into a case study model applied to a high-performance process installation. Finally, the study is put in context with the implementation of the RAM analysis in early stages of a project as a decision-making support at the overall architect level to aim to improve the system design, to perform RAM requirements allocation based on the sensitivity of the subsystems, in order to put the efforts on important subsystems and then minimizing the design and operational costs over the system's life cycle.

II. Modelling of a Complex System

As mentioned above, there are simulation methods, tools implementing these methods, but they are generally not applied correctly. Many system engineers start modeling with the goal of modeling, overdoing it, going too deep (with the focus more on using simulation to verify or validate performance) or simply to model the bad things. Model-based systems engineering is essential in the efforts to design increasingly complicated and complex systems in an era of unprecedented change. However, it is a tool and a technique in many systems engineering toolbox. Nevertheless, the focus should be on applying systems engineering to deliver the required value to the customer and stakeholders effectively and efficiently.

Detailed models are not always desirable, especially in the early phases of the life cycle (the pre-study phase and the descending phase of the V-cycle). At this stage, the systems are not yet fully defined. The contribution of the models should provide a broader insight into the behavior of the system, giving directions and insights. The interest is not to chase the precise values as the result of the model (which is already quite difficult given the complexity of the systems). In many cases, orders of magnitude are enough to understand it. At the same time, the models must be able to provide the flexibility to model various scenarios and possibilities of the system configuration.

The objective of this paper is to demonstrate whether it is possible to build a recursive development of modeling as it is done elsewhere in system engineering on design in general by building à Simulation Breakdown Structure (SBS) and a corresponding Simulation Architecture in such way

- From the most general (system performance) to the specific (component performance) while changing the paradigm on precision. To favor the approximately right at the general level in the upstream phase to the detriment of the precisely wrong.
- Use this approximative modeling to develop and enrich the system engineering requirements model.

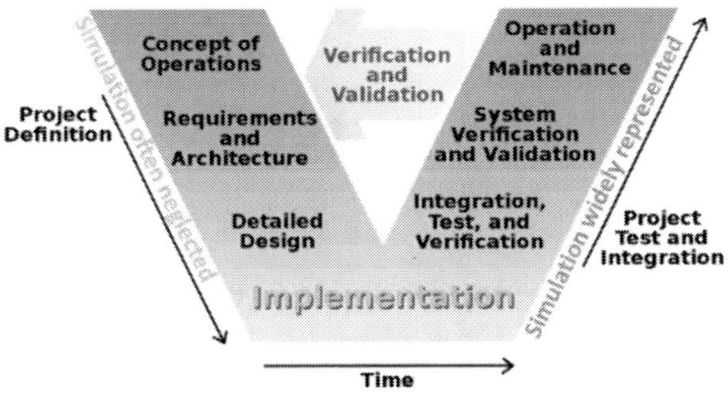

Figure 1. Example of a V cycle. Very often there is a lack of simulation methods in the decision-making phase.

In order to verify the above objectives, a simple test case is used consisting of a storage plant system which will be modeled as a discrete event system. The main principles of discrete event modeling are summarized in the following section.

III. DESCRETE EVENT SIMULATION

Discrete-event simulation is a method that allows to simulate the behavior and to quantify the performance of a process consisting of a series of ordered sequences. Unlike continuous systems whose state variable(s) change continuously over time, the state variable(s) of a discrete system varies only at a discrete set of points in time. A discrete system can be imagined as a set of entities that are connected and communicate when an event or activity occurs. Each entity is characterized by a set of properties (attributes) that describe their current state and affect their behavior. Entities representing components of the system under investigation must be explicitly modeled in order to capture the behavior of the system in relation to the simulation study. As the simulation time evolves, entities can change their state in consequence of activities that happened during a given simulation period. The time in the simulation at which such a state change occurs is called an event. The relationship between events and activities are defined by user and are based on the objectives of the studied system [5]-[9]. This includes in particular the specification of activity durations, which can be modeled as deterministic and based on stochastically influenced parameters (simulation of failures of the system's elements).

Discrete event simulation methods can be used in different fields of application. In this paper, the focus area is related a logistics process. The history of discrete event simulations goes back into the early 1960's, but it was only towards the end of the last century the DES application has spread widely as the information technologies boomed [12]. Currently, there exist many discrete event simulation tools [10][11].

IV. MATLAB SIMEVENTS TOOL

For the case study presented in this paper, it was decided to use the SimEvents software of the MathWorks company, because the SimEvents provides a wide range of predefined tools for the DES and in combination with Matlab Simulink allows the user to develop and customize the model according to his needs.

From a practical point of view, while the SimEvents library contains all the crucial types of blocks needed for basic simulations, it is obvious that the development of add-on blocks might be unavoidable if the system becomes more complicated, for example, by adding the possibility of machinery breakdowns in a manufacturing/processing line. Matlab Simulink can be a tool for reliability calculations [14], but objective here was to model a process line, for which the SimEvents module is adopted to.

However, in addition to the SimEvents library, Matlab contains a few exemplary models that users can test. The Matlab 2019a release provides an example of a Machine block that attempts to incorporate principles of failures, reliability, and maintainability into SimEvents simulations.

The main downside to the native form of the Machine block is that it simply does not model properly the case of a failure. Firstly, the random failures are characterized by an exponential law rather than a gaussian law. Another problem was related to the management of the resources needed to maintain a failed block that were not use at all causing serious consequences for the optimization studies of the installation resources. The last limitation of the default version of the machine block was related to the preventive maintenance. The theory of dependability studies considers the components undertaken a maintenance task as new which translates in simulation by resetting the internal component clock to zero. The default block configuration omitted this fact yielding the maintenance as it has never happened. One by one, all these issues have been treated by authors and the associated problems eliminated as well as some additional features were added allowing to switch properly between the block's internal states.

V. ILLUSTRATION CASE STUDY

This section is devoted to a demonstration of how a real system (which is in the design phase) can be modeled using

SimEvents. The case study concerns the modeling of the flow of storage / removal of items of a future installation in order to be stored. For the policy reason, some details cannot be shared. However, the aim is to focus on the benefits of the simulation method as a decision-making support at the overall architect level in order to improve the design and minimize the operational costs over the system's life cycle.

The items storage process can be viewed as a manufacturing process that transforms an object into another object. To take this into account, and due to certain Matlab limitations (existing pre-programmed objects), a single type of entity is used to represent the different objects appearing in the process (convoys with full or empty items, wagons, the secondary elements to be stored, or waste products. The entities themselves have no graphical representation. Their flow is represented by arrows connecting the blocks. On the other hand, entities can transport data in the form of attributes.

The installation is composed of several systems (that are denoted for simplicity as System1, System2 etc.) and some auxiliary systems to support the main systems (Figure 2). As the items advance through the storage line, each item undergoes a process of manipulation and transformation until it is temporary stored in the System3 (red lines).

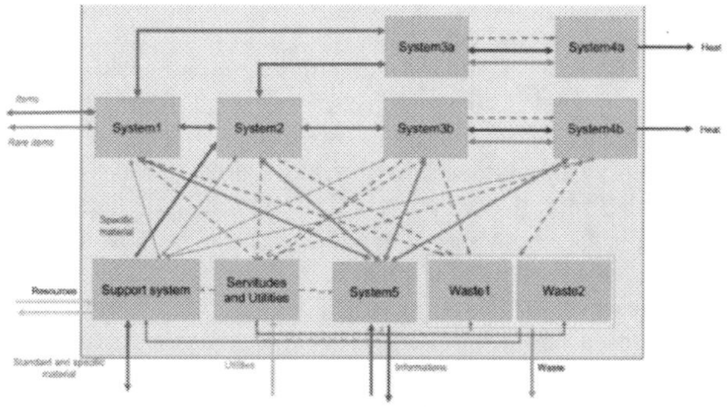

Figure 2. Illustration of the main elements of the storage facility.

Each of the system is composed of several subsystems (workstations). At the design phase, the composition of the subsystems is not yet defined, and the performance allocations are made at the subsystems and system levels (level 0 and level 1 of a traditional Product Breakdown Structure, PBS). The items to be stored arrive to System1 by a convoy at a predefined rate and are processed through the installation line. Inversely, the stored items can be also evacuated as the new ones arrive. The requirements impose a certain number of items to be stored over a given period. As can be seen, no detailed input data are provided and in fact there are not needed at this stage to model the system and its capabilities as is described next.

A. *Model Description*

In the model, each of the subsystem is represented by the improved block Machine which can transition between three predefined states that are defined in the operational phase of the considered system lifecycle

- Operation state
- Maintenance
- Breakdown

In the regular operation state, the machine acquires a working resource and processes a given task. In the scheduled maintenance state, the machine switches to service mode and the processing of a task is interrupted. After a fixed service time, the machine resumes regular operation. The machine can also break down sporadically following an exponential probability law and enter a breakdown state. The time to repair faults is defined through a mean time to repair and the machine resumes regular operation once the repair is completed.

The main structure of the flow model in the SimEvents interface is shown in Figure 3. As can be seen, the model contains several distinct blocks. The blocks are built according to the principle of Russian dolls which has the advantage of being able to look at and analyze the model at different scales. It also allows building a progressive validation.

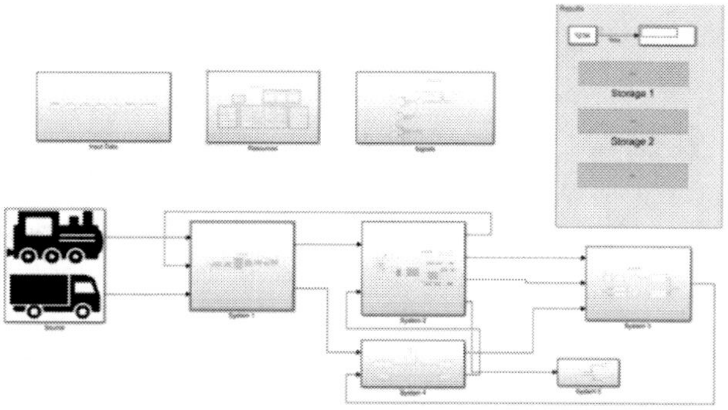

Figure 3. Main structure of the model in the SimEvents interface.

As the entity representing the treated object advance in the process, different events occur and trigger another subsystems and elements like resources.

B. *Model Validation*

The good performance of the model was systematically and incrementally validated. In addition, non-regression checks were carried out each time the model was upgraded (implementation of a new block, a control function, etc.): an immediate check in the simulation data inspector was performed in order to check if the behavior of the model was correct.

To demonstrate that the flow inside the installation is correct, the case of a convoy transporting three objects arriving at the installation was considered. The Gantt chart representing the progress of the transformation of the arriving items into its stored location is shown on the Figure 4.

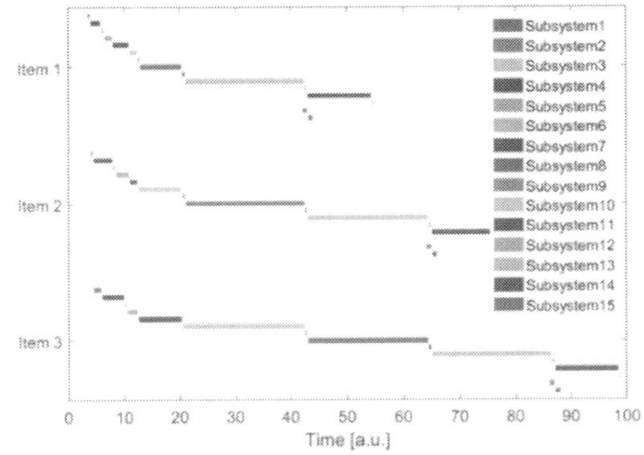

Figure 4. Gantt diagram of the flow of three items.

Figure 4 shows that the flow of the objects inside the installation is continuous and in order. This shows that the flow is controlled meaning that the entity (object) cannot advance if the next position is occupied by treating another object.

In principle such a simple case can be modelled manually if some average values were considered reinforcing the model validation. However, if the random failures are considered, the situation changes dramatically. Figure 5 gives an example of the delay necessary to treat one convoy. As can be seen, that the delays are now becoming irregular as some subsystems break down and processing is delayed due to the time required for repair.

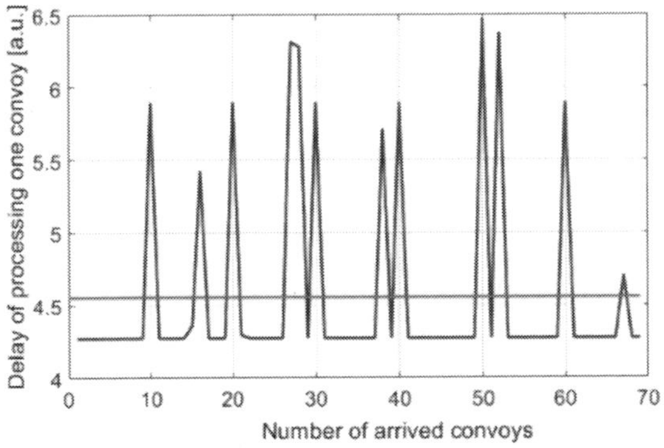

Figure 5. Example of the delays necessary to treat the content of one convoy. Red line represents the mean delay.

In addition to possibility to model the random breakdown of the various subsystems, the model allows to manage and to size the need of the resources. With regard to the resources involved in the operation of the installation, their rate of use is shown in Figure 6. Information on the rate of use of the resources allows to optimize the pace of work. For example, it does not appear necessary for the teams to be always present at the installation. In addition, their presence must be carefully planned, because some subsystems may break down, which would delay the flow. The model as it stands assumes that resources are available when needed.

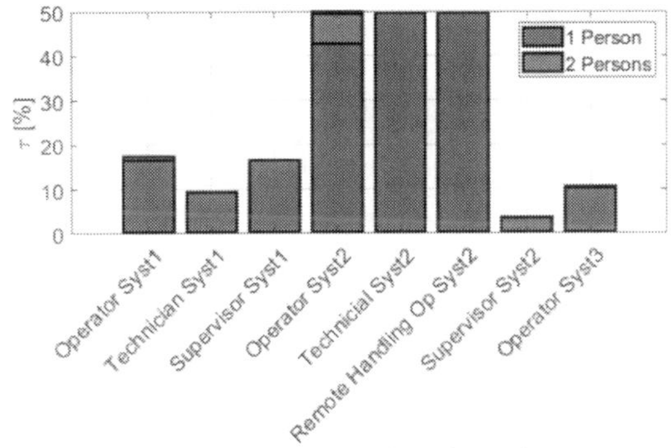

Figure 6. Resources use rate for various subsystems.

VI. Summary

The model presented here was developed to simulate the storage process of a future installation. Model validity was performed systematically and incrementally. Non-regression checks were carried out at each evolution of the model in order to check whether the behavior of the model was correct. The model is based on decision parameters and model version for a given configuration state of the design with its associated definition artefacts (functional architecture, physical architecture, etc.)

The line process is not difficult to imagine for simple cases, but the model becomes very useful when the introduction of workstations availability is applied. The model clearly shows that it can be considered as a reliable source for predictions of various scenarios.

The results obtained with the model show that the installation is able to meet the requirement of receiving a given number of objects even if considering the availability of workstations. Failure modeling is completely random, which makes each simulation unique from the standpoint of workstation availability. The impact of the reliability of workstations on the flow can be visible over longer periods (mitigated by regular maintenance).

The paper presents only certain scenario, but due to the wide variety of model parameters, the model allows the study of other scenarios as well. The modeling strategy adopted (starting from the most general or more specific) will allow to refine the model and gradually allocate performances /objectives to lower-level subsystems / components in the physical breakdown structure as the progress of the design advances and thus be able to simulate more precisely and progressively what is happening inside each subsystem up to the desired level of detail.

VII. Conclusion

Although models are not a perfect representation of a system, MBSE can provide insight and feedback earlier and at lower cost than implementation alone. This approach tested in this case study has clearly shown that the use of the simulation method is suitable for managing the development of the system by showing the weak points of the system and therefore the points for its improvement and adaptation. It has been shown that there is not always a need to go into deep detail when modeling a system. Parameters describing performance could be sufficient and subsystems could be treated as black boxes. In addition, when such a model is deployed early in the design phase, it can always be updated as the design studies progressively refine the physical breakdown structure and can finally serve as a validation / verification tool in the ascending phase of the V-cycle.

Regarding the perspectives, it would be interesting to find out how accurately SimEvents can manage the management of human resources, especially if the pace of work is not continuous. Currently, the "Resource Pool" block does not offer the option to specify whether resources will only be available for a fraction of the time. On the other hand, it allows the use of a fraction of a resource. However, further investigation would be required to answer this question.

REFERENCES

[1] INCOSE, "Systems Engineering Handbook, A Guide for System Life Cycle Processes and Activities", 4th edn. Wiley, New York, 2015.

[2] A. Hazle and J. Towers, "Good Practice in MBSE Model Verification and Validation", INCOSE UK Annual Systems Engineering Conference (ASEC), 2020.

[3] D. Cook and W. Schindel, "Utilizing MBSE Patterns to Accelerate System Verification", Insightm vol. 20m pp. 32-41, 2017.

[4] M. J. Simões-Marques, "Modeling and Simulation in system life cycle", Procedia Manufacturing, vol. 3, pp. 785 – 792, 2015.

[5] O. Ullrich and D. Lückerath, "An Introduction to Discrete-Event Modeling and Simulation", Simulation Notes Europe SNE 27(1), pp. 9-16, 2017.

[6] T. Han, Q. Huang, A. Zhang, and Q. Zhang, "Simulation-Based Decision Support Tools in the Early Design Stages of a Green Building", Sustainability, vol. 10(10), pp. 3696, 2018.

[7] D. Antonelli, P. Litwin, and D. Stadnicka, "Multiple System Dynamics and Discrete Event Simulation for manufacturing system performance evaluation", Procedia CIRP, Volume 78, Pages 178-183, 2018.

[8] G. S. Fishman, "Discrete-Event Simulation: Modeling, Programming, and Analysis", Springers series in operations research, 2001.

[9] B. Babulak and M. Wang, "Discrete Event Simulation: State of the Art", Int. Journal Online Engineering (iJOE), vol. 4, No 2, 2008.

[10] L. Dias, A. Vieira, G. Pereira, and J. Oliveira, "Discrete Simulation Software Ranking – A Top List of the Worldwide Most Popular and Used Tools", Proceedings of the 2016 Winter Simulation Conference, 2016.

[11] J. J. Swain, "Simulation Software Survey", OR/MS Today magazine from Institute for Operations Research and the Management Sciences (INFORMS). Lionheart Publishing. 1991-2009.

[12] R. E. Nance, "A history of discrete event simulation programming languages", In: Proceedings of the 2nd ACM SIGPLAN conference on History of programming languages, pp. 149-175,1993.

[13] R. F. Stapelberg, "Handbook of reliability, availability, maintainability and safety in engineering design", Springer-Verlag London Limited, 2009.

[14] S. Kadwane, J. Kumbharem and D. Mohanta, "A Matlab/Simulink modeling for reliability analysis of inverter applied to MPPT based PV system", 2015 Annual IEEE India Conference (INDICON), pp. 1-6, 2015.

VR-SysML: SysML Model Visualization and Immersion in Virtual Reality

Roy Oberhauser[0000-0002-7606-8226]
Computer Science Dept.
Aalen University
Aalen, Germany
e-mail: roy.oberhauser@hs-aalen.de

Abstract - **As systems grow in complexity, the interdisciplinary nature of systems engineering makes the visualization and comprehension of the underlying system models challenging for the various stakeholders. This, in turn, can affect validation and realization correctness. Furthermore, stakeholder collaboration is often hindered due to the lack of a common medium to access and convey these models, which are often partitioned across multiple 2D diagrams. This paper contributes VR-SysML, a solution concept for visualizing and interacting with SysML models in Virtual Reality (VR). Our prototype realization shows its feasibility, and our evaluation results based on a case study shows its support for the various SysML diagram types in VR, cross-diagram element recognition via our backplane followers concept, and depicting further related (SysML and non-SysML) models side-by-side in VR.**

Keywords - Systems Modeling Language (SysML); virtual reality; systems modeling; systems engineering.

I. INTRODUCTION

Systems engineering (SysE) is an interdisciplinary collaborative engineering field dealing with the design, integration, and management of complex system solutions over their lifecycle. The field faces a continuous challenge of growing system complexity, an increasing share of functionality shifted to software, system resource constraints, while coping with compressed development timeframes and project budget and resource constraints. Furthermore, the interdisciplinary nature of SysE means that diverse stakeholder types and groups with their specialty competencies and concerns are involved and who may not be readily acquainted with the model types and modeling languages involved. Any models may be digitally isolated or practically inaccessible to all stakeholder types, "hidden" within "cryptic" modeling tools that certain modeling specialists may understand. Due to the interdisciplinary nature of SysE, the inaccessibility and lack of model comprehension can hamper collaboration and affect overall system validity and correctness with regard to requirements.

While SysE can involve various models including physical, mechanical, electrical, thermodynamic, and electronic, the focus of this paper is on the Systems Modeling Language (SysML®) [1]. SysML is a dialect of the Unified Modeling Language (UML®) and defined as a UML 2 Profile. Views and their associated diagrams can help reduce cognitive overload, yet their divided nature also risks overlooking a relation or element and comprehending the overall model. Ideally, a model should be whole and complete to the appropriate degree for the reality it is depicting and simplifying. Yet the modeling languages and associated tooling typically assumes a 2D display and portrays portions of models sliced onto 2D diagrams. Although 3D models can be portrayed on 2D displays, they lack an immersion quality.

VR is a mediated visual environment which is created and then experienced as telepresence by the perceiver. VR provides an unlimited immersive space for visualizing and analyzing a growing and complex set of system models and their interrelationships simultaneously in a 3D spatial structure viewable from different perspectives. Lacking a proper 3D system modeling notation, in the interim we propose retaining the well-known SysML notation and interconnecting 2D SysML diagrams in VR, which can suffice for depicting the relations between elements across diagrams and assist with navigating and validating complex models. As system models grow in complexity and reflect the deeper integration and portrayal of their system reality and environment, an immersive digital environment provides an additional visualization capability to comprehend the "big picture" model for structurally and hierarchically complex system models via interconnected diagrams and associated digital elements.

As to our prior work, VR-UML [2] provides VR-based visualization of UML diagrams. VR-BPMN [3] visualizes BPMN-based business process models in VR, while VR-EA [4] visualizes Enterprise Architecture (EA) ArchiMate® models in VR. This paper contributes VR-SysML, a solution concept for visualizing and interacting with SysML results in VR. Our prototype realization shows its feasibility, and a case-based evaluation provides insights into its capabilities.

The remainder of this paper is structured as follows: Section 2 discusses related work. In Section 3, the solution concept is described. Section 4 provides details about the realization. The evaluation is described in Section 5 and is followed by a conclusion.

II. RELATED WORK

As to visualization approaches with SysML, Nigischer and Gerhard [5] proposed a lightweight 3D visualization for SysML models in Product Data Management. They describe an approach and concept, but no prototype is shown. Sanvordenker [6] describes a 3D SysML digital-twin-in-loop virtual simulation environment of a distribution center for truck driving test scenarios integrating IBM Rhapsody with Unity3D; VR and immersion are not considered. Mahboob et al. [7] describe a model-based approach to generate VR object collision simulation scenes from SysML behavior models.

Besides our own VR-UML [2], VR features are not yet commonplace in UML tools: Ozkaya [19] analyzed 58 different UML tools without any mention of VR, and Ozkaya and Erata [20] surveyed 109 practitioners to determine their UML preferences without any mention of VR. Non-VR 3D-based UML visualization includes X3D-UML [6], VisAr3D [8], and the case study by Krolovitsch and Nilsson [7].

In contrast, VR-SysML provides a VR-centric visualization and immersive experience with SysML models, providing automatic layout of views as stacked 3D hyperplanes, visualizing the reality of inter-view relations and recurrence of elements, and enabling interactive modeling in VR. Hypermodeling enables SysML, UML, and other models to be simultaneously visualized in the same virtual space, supporting cross-model analysis across various diagram types and stakeholder concerns.

III. Solution Concept

Our solution concept is based on VR. In support of our view that an immersive VR experience can be beneficial for model analysis, Müller et al. [10] compared VR vs. 2D for a software analysis task, finding that VR does not significantly decrease comprehension and analysis time nor significantly improve correctness (although fewer errors were made). While interaction time was less efficient, VR improved the user experience, was more motivating, less demanding, more inventive/innovative, and more clearly structured.

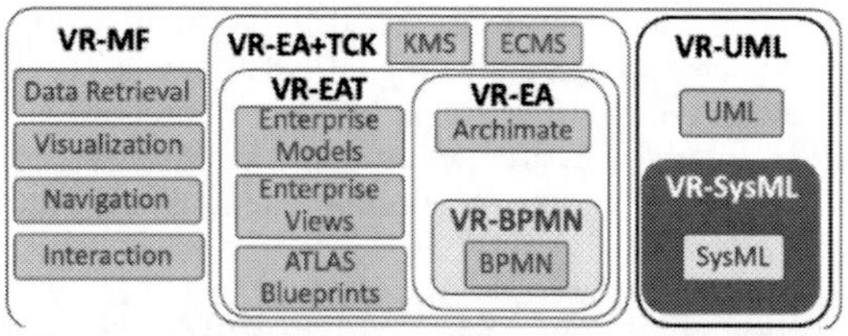

Figure 1. Conceptual map of our various VR solution concepts.

SysML is a general-purpose architecture modeling language for systems and systems-of-systems, supporting their specification, analysis, design, verification, and validation. Out of UML 2's diagrams, it reuses seven (modifying four of these) while adding two additional ones. Thus, for VR-SysML (Figure 1) we chose to extend our VR-UML [2] solution concept, which is based on our generalized VR Modeling Framework (VR-MF) (detailed in [4]). VR-MF provides a VR-based domain-independent hypermodeling framework addressing four aspects requiring special attention when modeling in VR: visualization, navigation, interaction, and data retrieval. Our other VR modeling solutions include VR-BPMN [3], VR-EA [4], and VR-EAT, which integrates the EA tool Atlas to provide dynamically-generated EA diagrams in VR. VR-EA+TCK adds additional capabilities, integrating enterprise Tool, Content, and Knowledge such as a Knowledge Management Systems (KMS) and/or Enterprise Content Management Systems (ECMS). While SysML is popular for embedded and model-based systems, it is also applicable to domains such as EA.

A. *Visualization in VR*

Our concept attempts to leverage the best of 2D and VR: to support diagram comprehension, we chose not to diverge significantly from the SysML notation. Yet placing 2D SysML images like flat screens in front of users would provide little added value in the 3D VR space. A plane is used to intuitively represent a diagram. Stacked hyperplanes are used to support viewing multiple diagrams at once, while permitting a user to readily have an overview of the number and types of diagrams. Furthermore, hyperplanes serve a grouping function and allow us to utilize the concept of a common transparent or invisible backplane to indicate common elements across diagrams via multi-colored inter-diagram followers. Versus side-by-side, stacked diagrams are a scalable approach for larger projects since the distance to the VR camera is shorter. Multiple stacks can be used to group diagrams or delineate heterogeneous models. Diagrams of interest can still be viewed side-by-side by moving them from the stack via an anchor sphere affordance on a diagram corner, which is also used to hide or collapse diagrams to reduce visual clutter. To distinguish SysML elements types, 2D icon images can be placed on generic (e.g., block) model elements, in order to reduce the effort of modeling each SysML element type as a separate 3D form for VR.

B. *Navigation in VR*

One navigation challenge arising from the immersion VR offers is supporting intuitive spatial navigation while reducing potential VR sickness symptoms. Thus, we incorporate two navigation modes in our solution concept: the default uses gliding controls for fly-through VR, while teleporting instantly places the camera at a selected position. Although potentially disconcerting, it may reduce the likelihood of VR sickness induced by fly-through for those prone to it.

C. *Interaction in VR*

As VR interaction has not yet become standardized, in our concept user-element interaction is supported primarily through VR controllers and a *Virtual Tablet*. The Virtual Tablet provides detailed element information with context-specific Create, Retrieve, Update, Delete (CRUD) capabilities including a *virtual keyboard* for text entry via laser pointer key selection. The aforementioned corner *anchor sphere* affordance supports moving / hiding / displaying diagrams. Inter-diagram element *followers* can be displayed, hidden, or selected (emphasized).

IV. Realization

The logical architecture for our VR-SysML prototype realization is shown in Figure 2.

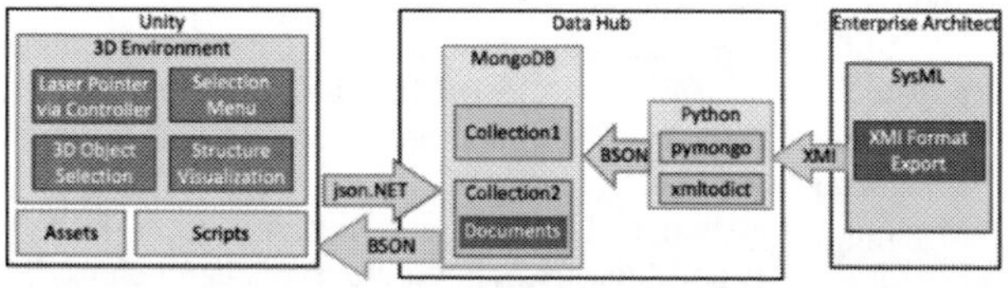

Figure 2. VR-SysML logical architecture.

SysML models are imported in XMI format to our Data Hub that is implemented in Python. Xmitodict is used to convert the XMI to a key-value dictionary and the built-in json package is used for JSON conversion. Pymongo is used to store the JSON (as BSON) in the NoSQL document database MongoDB. The scripts in the Unity environment utilize json.NET. SysML XMI files produced from SparxSystems Enterprise Architect were used. Our prototype currently does not consider the Allocation Table (relationship matrices).

V. EVALUATION

We base the evaluation of our solution concept on design science method and principles [1], in particular, a viable artifact, problem relevance, and design evaluation (utility, quality, efficacy). A case study is used with an emphasis on SysML diagram type support, how these are visualized in VR, and additional capabilities in VR. A sample SysML project with all 9 SysML diagram types is used to compare the visualization in Enterprise Architect to that in VR-SysML, grouped as requirement, behavior, or structure diagram types.

As shown in Figure 3, the various diagrams of the SysML model are mapped to stacked hyperplanes that provide an anchor affordance (black sphere) with which to expand, collapse, or move a diagram. Planes and elements have a shallow 3D depth with labeled edges to support recognition from different viewing angles. The colors of the planes can be configured to help with differentiation or grouping. Furthermore, our backplane concept creates followers that allow one to quickly find the same element across different diagrams in the same model, to readily see in which diagrams that element participates, or to determine that the element is only shown on one diagram (it not having a follower). The colored followers can be selected (made bold) and the other followers can be hidden if desired to reduce visual clutter for larger models.

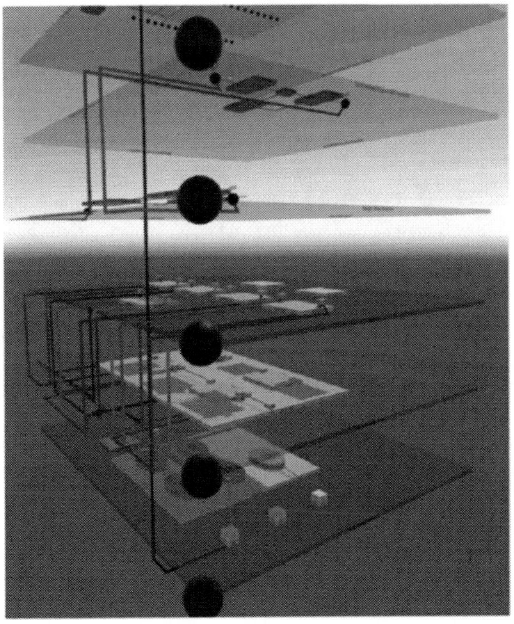

Figure 3. Backplane with inter-diagram followers.

A. *SysML Requirement Diagram*

SysML extends UML with an additional diagram type, the Requirement diagram. It can be used to specify functional and non-functional requirements for the model. An example viewed in EA and in VR is shown in Figure 4. In VR, elements are labeled on edges to support reading from different angles. The VR Tablet can provide more details or interaction capabilities for a selected element, and while support for modeling capabilities is shown on the interface, these are currently placeholders and have not yet been fully implemented in the prototype (create, modify, delete, export).

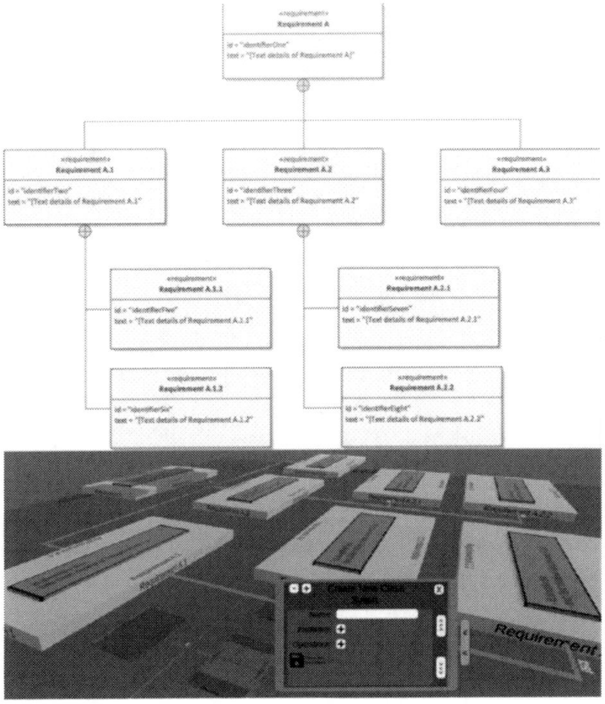

Figure 4. Requirement Diagram in EA (top) and in VR (bottom).

B. *SysML Use Case Diagram*

As a behavior diagram, SysML includes the Use Case Diagram from UML as shown in Figure 5. In order to more readily recognize and differentiate the diagram type, an oval shape was used for the use cases. However, the actors utilize our generic cube concept with notation symbols placed on the various sides. This provides a flexible mechanism for quickly supporting various notation element types and tailoring or extending model element types using any icons or images.

C. *SysML Activity Diagram*

Another dynamic behavior diagram type that can be used to specify dynamic system behaviors, such as control flow and object flows, is the Activity diagram in SysML (see Figure 6). It is slightly modified from that in UML, adding additional semantics for Continuous Flow and Probability.

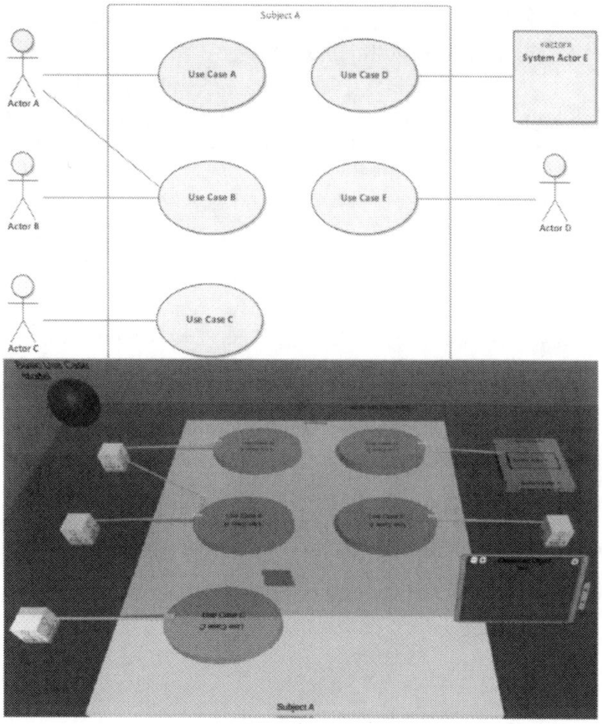

Figure 5. Use Case Diagram in EA (top) and in VR (bottom).

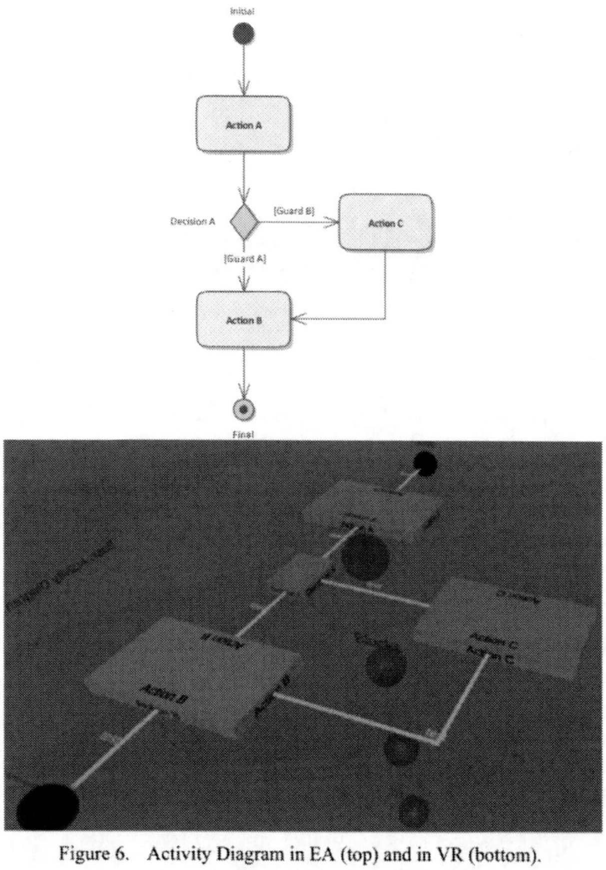

Figure 6. Activity Diagram in EA (top) and in VR (bottom).

D. SysML Sequence Diagram

Sequence diagrams (unmodified from UML) provide a further dynamic behavior diagram, showing interactions via message sequences (see Figure 7).

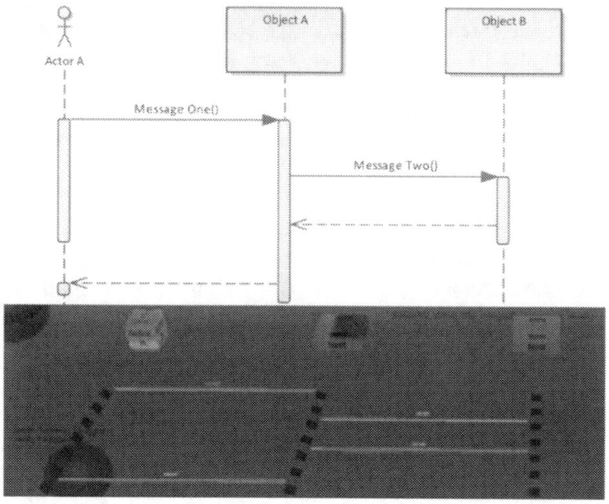

Figure 7. Sequence Diagram in EA (top) and in VR (bottom).

E. SysML State Machine Diagram

State machine diagrams (unmodified from UML) are a dynamic behavior diagram showing states transitions that occur in response to events (see Figure 8).

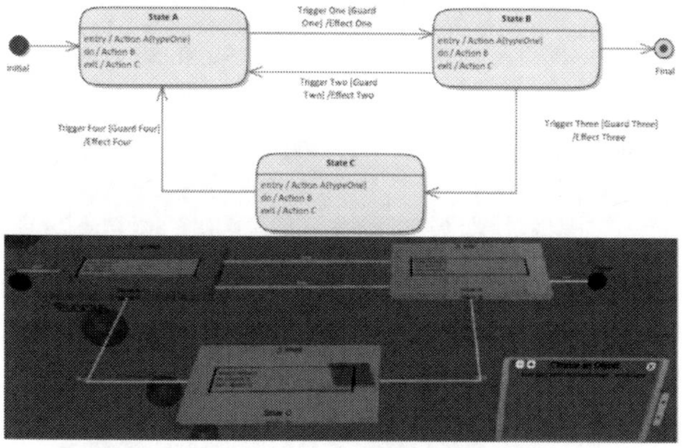

Figure 8. State Machine Diagram in EA (top) and in VR (bottom).

F. SysML Block Definition Diagram (BDD)

A BDD (see Figure 9) is a static structural diagram, analogous to the UML Class diagram type with certain modifications, and shows system components, their contents (as properties, behaviors, constraints), interfaces, and relationships. It can be used for describing the system structure as a hierarchy of relations between systems and subsystems typically consisting of "black-box" blocks. As a possible specialization, it can be useful to explicitly model constraints separately, referred to as Constraint Block diagrams (see Figure 10), which can be referenced by Parametric diagrams.

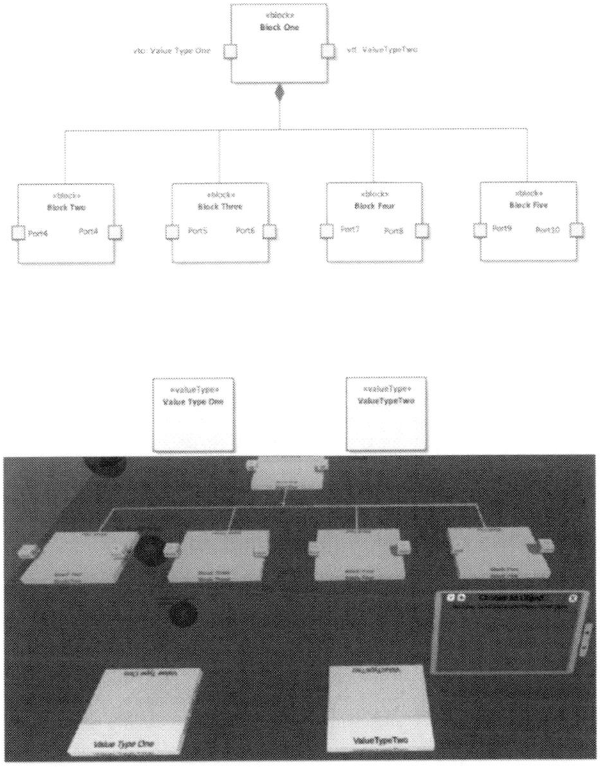

Figure 9. BDD in EA (top) and in VR (bottom).

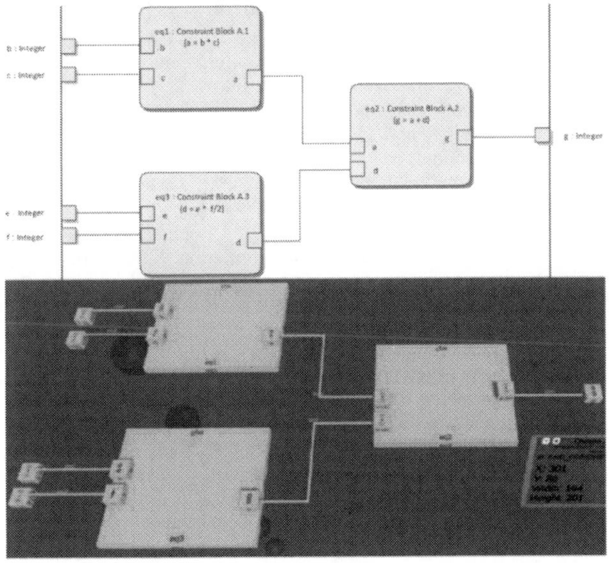

Figure 10. Constraint Block Diagram in EA (top) and in VR (bottom).

G. SysML Internal Block Diagram (IBD)

An IBD is a static structural diagram that depicts the internal (encapsulated) composition (structural contents) of a Block in a BDD, i.e., a "white-box" view. This includes properties, parts, interfaces, connectors, and ports, and can be used to depict the flow of inputs and outputs between them.

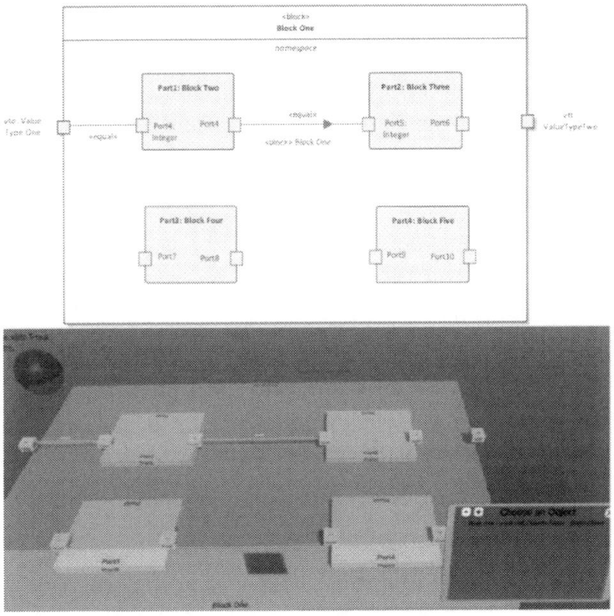

Figure 11. IBD in EA (top) and in VR (bottom).

H. SysML Parametric Diagram

A static structural diagram type, Parametric diagrams (see Figure 12) are a specialization of IBD to model equations with parameters and can be used to enforce mathematical rules or constraints defined via Constraint Blocks.

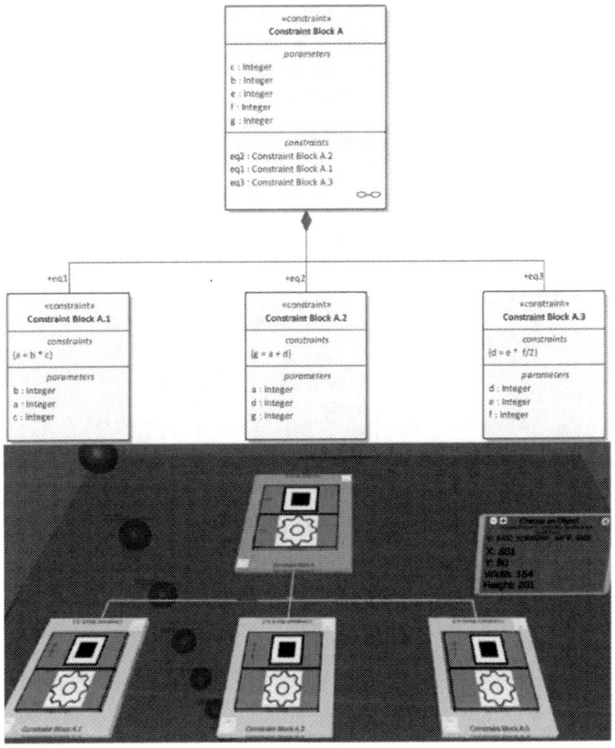

Figure 12. Constraint Parametric Diagram in EA (top) and in VR (bottom).

I. SysML Package Diagram

A SysML Package diagram (see Figure 13) is further static structural diagram based on the equivalent UML type (with minor modifications). Packages provide a general-purpose mechanism for grouping model elements and diagrams, and the diagram can be used to show their contents and the relationship between them.

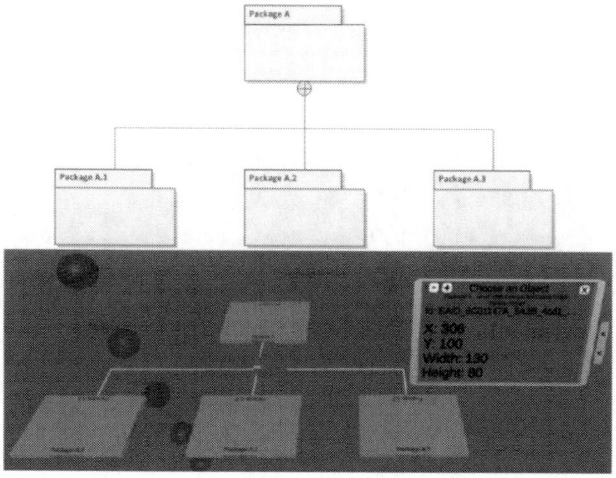

Figure 13. Package Diagram in EA (top) and in VR (bottom).

J. Multi- and Heterogeneous Model Depiction in VR

VR's unlimited virtual space provides the potential to view, compare, and analyze multiple SysML (left and center models in Figure 14) or heterogeneous models side-by-side (exemplified with an ArchiMate enterprise architecture model on the right in Figure 14). For SysE, this immersive approach also has the potential to support interdisciplinary collaboration between specialization experts for complex systems.

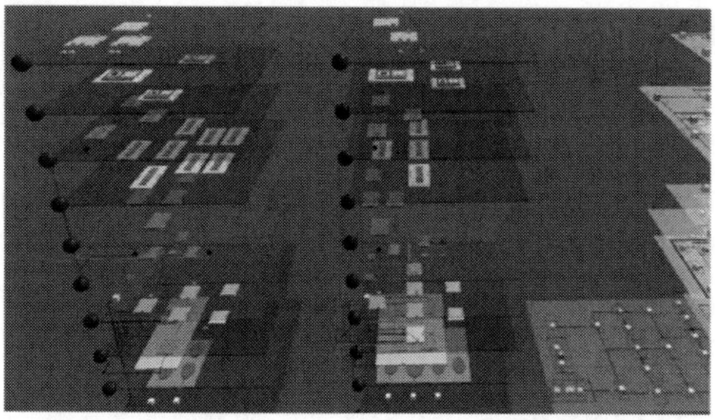

Figure 14. Multiple and heterogeneous side-by-side models in VR.

VI. Conclusion

VR-SysML contributes an immersive SysML model experience for visually depicting and navigating SysML diagrams of models in VR. The solution concept was described and a VR prototype demonstrated its feasibility using a case study. Based on our VR hyperplane principle, SysML diagrams are enhanced with 3D depth, color, and automatically-generated inter-diagram element followers based on our back-plane concept. Interaction is supported via a virtual tablet and keyboard. The unlimited space in VR facilitates the depiction and visual navigation of large models, while relations within and between elements, diagrams, and models can be analyzed. Furthermore, in VR additional related (SysML or non-SysML) models can be visualized and analyzed simultaneously and benefit complex systems-of-systems architectures or collaboration. The sensory immersion of VR can support task focus during model comprehension and increase modeling enjoyment, while limiting the visual distractions that typical 2D display surroundings incur. Future work includes support for modeling directly in VR, integrating further SysML tooling and simulation capabilities, supporting model verification and validation, and conducting a comprehensive empirical study.

Acknowledgment

The authors would like to thank Shadrach Arulrajah and Marie Bähre for their assistance with the design, implementation, evaluation, and diagrams.

References

[1] OMG, "OMG Systems Modeling Language Version 1.6", Object Management Group, 2019.

[2] R. Oberhauser, R., "VR-UML: The unified modeling language in virtual reality – an immersive modeling experience," International Symposium on Business Modeling and Software Design (BMSD 2021), Springer, Cham, 2021, pp. 40-58.

[3] R. Oberhauser, C. Pogolski, and A. Matic, "VR-BPMN: Visualizing BPMN models in Virtual Reality," In: Shishkov, B. (ed.) BMSD 2018. LNBIP, vol. 319, Springer, Cham, 2018, pp. 83–97. https://doi.org/10.1007/978-3-319-94214-8_6

[4] R. Oberhauser and C. Pogolski, "VR-EA: Virtual Reality Visualization of Enterprise Architecture Models with ArchiMate and BPMN," In: Shishkov, B. (ed.) BMSD 2019. LNBIP, vol. 356, Springer, Cham, 2019, pp. 170–187.

[5] C. Nigischer and D. Gerhard, "Lightweight visualization of SysML models in PDM systems," DS 87-3 Proc.eedings of the 21st International Conf. on Engineering Design (ICED 17) Vol 3: Product, Services and Systems Design, 2017, pp. 61-70.

[6] I. Barosan, A. Basmenj, S. Chouhan, D. Manrique, "Development of a Virtual Simulation Environment and a Digital Twin of an Autonomous Driving Truck for a Distribution Center," Software Architecture (ECSA 2020). CCIS, vol 1269, Springer, Cham, 2020, pp. 542–557.

[7] A. Mahboob, S. Husung, C. Weber, A. Liebal, and H. Krömker, "SYSML behaviour models for description of Virtual Reality environments for early evaluation of a product," In DS 92: Proc. 15th Int'l Design Conf. (DESIGN), 2018, pp. 2903-2912.

[8] M. Ozkaya, "Are the UML modelling tools powerful enough for practitioners? A literature review," IET Software, vol. 13, 2019, pp. 338-354. https://doi.org/10.1049/iet-sen.2018.5409

[9] M. Ozkaya and F. Erata, "A survey on the practical use of UML for different software architecture viewpoints," Information and Software Technology, Vol. 121, 106275, 2020.

[10] R. Müller, P. Kovacs, J. Schilbach, and D. Zeckzer, "How to master challenges in experimental evaluation of 2D versus 3D software visualizations," In: 2014 IEEE VIS International Workshop on 3Dvis (3Dvis), IEEE, 2014, pp. 33-36

[11] A.R. Hevner, S.T. March, J. Park, and S. Ram, "Design science in information systems research," MIS Quarterly, 28(1), 2004, pp. 75-105

A Systematic Mapping of Natural Gas Transportation Systems' Reliability and Risks Analysis

Yefeng Liang
School of Systems and Enterprises
Stevens Institute of Technology
Hoboken, NJ, USA
yliang32@stevens.edu

Mo Mansouri
School of Systems and Enterprises
Stevens Institute of Technology
Hoboken, NJ, USA
mmansour@stevens.edu

***Abstract*—This paper will analyze the challenges, profits, and risks that the gas transportation systems could face. As valuable economic and industrial systems, gas transportation systems are complicated, comprehensive, and elastic. However, gas transportation systems connect different levels of customers, and gas transportation systems rely heavily on the relationship loop between gas customers and gas producers, these factors make the gas transportation systems have to face comprehensive engineering and human-related challenges. In this paper, we will analyze the natural gas transportation system together with four parts of its interaction systems. First, we will list general gas transportation challenges. Second, we will analyze the risks and interactions between each part of the system. Finally, we will bring our conclusions about the system's construction risks.**

***Index Terms*—system engineering; natural gas transportation systems; system risks analysis; decision making; stakeholders.**

I. Introduction

The Gas Transportation Systems can transport gas and energy across the border, support thousands of residents, families, commercial agents, product institutes, as well as different industries. A natural gas transportation system is made up of compressor stations, pipelines, city gate stations, and storage facilities [9]. However, since this system has so many stakeholders and bring benefits to so many people, it is inevitable that the systems could face many transportation risks. How to target those risks and avoid these effects could be a important part to expand and maintain the system.

Current research put the concentrations on economic analysis for the transnational natural gas transportation system [12][13][15], technology assessment [2][3], and policy analysis of managing transnational natural gas transportation system [6][8][17]. One of the basic consideration is the risks and reliance of this high-level systems.

In this paper, we will list challenges and risks of transnational natural gas transportation systems' construction in section 2, 3, 4, 5, analyze the reasons that cause these challenges and potential consequences in section 6, 7, and bring the suggestions about how to maintain target sub-systems 8. Finally, in section 9, we explain our conclusions from the research. The research of this paper is expected to bring more risk analysis options, ideas, and methods on building transnational natural gas transportation systems.

II. Natural Gas Production and Transportation Overview

First, we need to take an example to explain how normal gas transportation systems work as a whole part.

The figure below shows the example of Malaysia Peninsula Gas production and transportation systems.

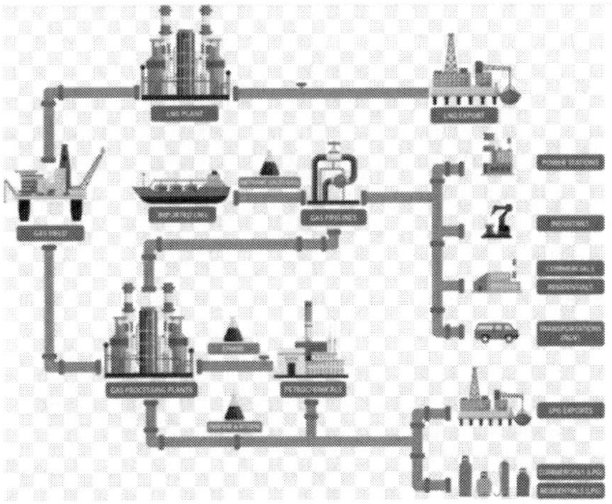

Fig. 1. Malaysia Peninsula Gas Utilisation Natural Gas Natural-gas Processing Pipeline Transportation [16]

As the figure shows here, there exits different commercial gas using, thus, there are many forms of the gas generated energy, this could cause the transportation systems to become complicated. The production, processing, transportation and selling processes make the whole systems full of uncertainty. Those uncertainty things in each step leading significant construction risks. In order to make the whole system works normally and resiliently, we have to be aware of the factors that cause those risks, how these factors work in the whole system and what decisions need to be made at the same time.

Since the whole systems is complicated and technique comprehensive, at the beginning, we should put the list of factors in the natural gas transportation system, in this project, we focus on these main factors: Pipelines constructions, gas distribution limitations, gas distribution system's stakeholders, and the system shaping forces.

Besides those key factors, there are other defining characteristics in constructing the system:

Local environment and residents' energy-using safety and health. Commercial monopoly. The system maintains' problems. Realigned infrastructures Challenges of constructions Local benefits of the gas supplement.

III. Natural gas transportation and pipelines construction

The natural gas transportation is a crucial activity performed by the gas industry in which the gas and other energy has to be moved from one location to another. Several types of transportation means might be applied to transport the gas, yet it is well known that pipelines represent the most economical means to transport large quantities of natural gas. In addition, the advent of metallurgical improvements and welding techniques, coupled with the exponential increase of pipeline networks during the last decades all over the world, have made the gas transportation via pipelines more economically attractive.

Currently, pipelines are used in constructions on both offshore and onshore energy transportation systems, with a remarkable difference in terms of security and construction prices. Building pipeline systems under the sea is highly costly and technically demanding, a lot more than onshore. For example, the Nord Stream2 pipeline project is expected to as long as 1,222km corresponds to the 965.7 km long onshore pipeline system on Russian and German territories, whereas the remaining is destined to the 259.4 km long offshore section of the project. However, as the consequence of Russia's recognition of the Donetsk and Luhansk republics, Nord Stream 2 AG, a consortium for construction and operation of the Nord Stream, filed for bankruptcy on 1 March 2022 and laid off all 106 employees from its headquarters in Zug, Switzerland [8]. Hence, when financial, political or environmental issues arise, gas transportation operators need to look for different alternatives to perform this task inevitably. Especially for onshore gas transportation, from which natural gas can be transported as liquefied natural gas (LNG), medium conditioned liquefied gas(MLG), or compressed natural gas(CNG), by using the tank of specially constructed seagoing vessels.

The scale of a gas network system be greatly different from one country to another. In the US, for example, a large gas network system may encompass several hundreds of pipelines (adding up to several hundreds of thousands of miles) and tens of compressors stations strategically distributed along the transmission lines. The US natural gas pipeline network has about three million miles of mainline and other pipelines that link natural gas production areas and storage facilities with consumers. This natural gas transportation network delivered more than 25 trillion cubic feet of natural gas in 2016 to about 74 million customers" (Natural Gas Pipelines, 2017). On the contrary, the natural gas transmission network in Belgium is composed of a relatively smaller number of pipelines (20–40) and compressor stations (4–8) when compared to those found in the US and Russia [10].

While the size of a gas pipeline system definitely plays an important role when solving natural gas network flow problems, it is the network topology that really defines the complexity of the model, e.g., cyclic networks are extremely more difficult to solve than its (gun-barrel and tree-shaped) network counterparts [2]. The current state of the art on natural gas transmission network problems in steady-state can efficiently handle large gas systems by applying network reduction and decomposition techniques, or hybrid-heuristic algorithms, most of them, however, with no guarantee of optimality, which enforces the scientific community to enhance the existing methods [2].

IV. Stakeholders

We list the main stakeholders that rely on the natural gas transportation systems.

1. Technical engineering institutes 2. Local residents 3. Natural gas customers' communities 4. Natural gas company and government

- 1. Technical engineering institutes
  1.1 Pipeline constructions 1.2 Pipeline operations
- 2. Safety and environment impact for residents
  2.1 Health
  2.2 Living environment
- 3. Impact on the natural gas customers' community 3.1 Stability 3.2 reliability
- 4. Economic benefits for natural gas company and government 4.1 Revenues to the government 4.2 Employment 4.3 Flexibility of transport increases industry profit margins; minimizes price instability

After listing the main stakeholders, We draw a relationship impact map and a interest map of stakeholders to discuss those stakeholders.

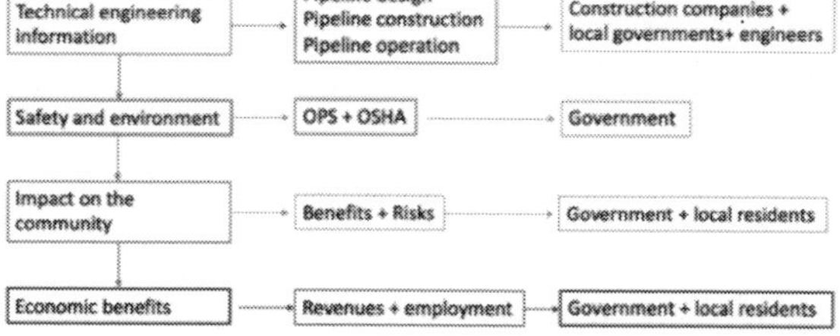

Fig. 2. Stakeholder Relationship

According to Figures 2 and 3, each of those stakeholders rely on the benefit of natural gas transportation systems. At the same time, they have interactions with each other. The negative impact between different stakeholders hurt the resilience of the whole natural gas transportation system.

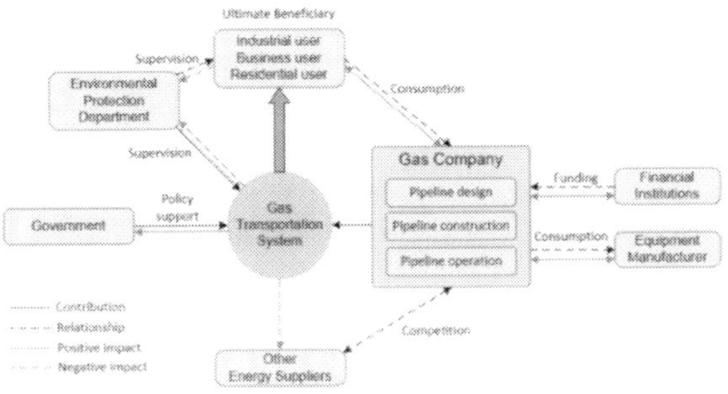

Fig. 3. Interest Map of Stakeholders

One of the general and significant case is the natural environment. The impact between natural gas providers and natural environment, as well as the impact different levels of natural gas customers and natural environment, both of those two groups have to face environment challenges and the value transformations brought by gas supply constitution. The government, as the potential stakeholder controller, have to consider some trade-off solutions and implement them as policy. This case of natural environment decides the reliability of the whole system. On the other hand, system's controllers have to face several specific and inevitable risks when they make construction decisions on different parts of gas providing facilities and gas consuming facilities.

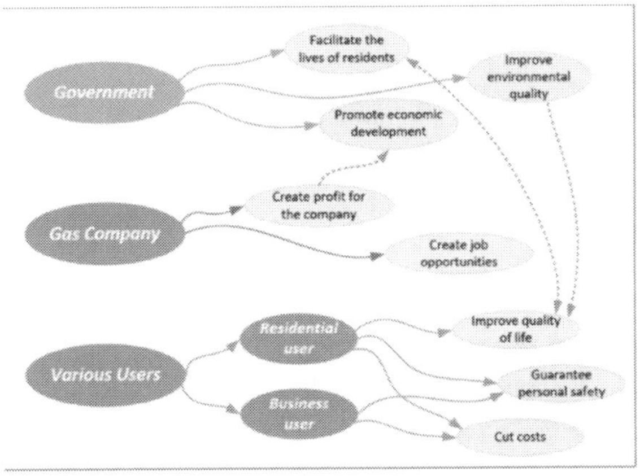

Fig. 4. Value adding process

After those construction decision settle down, as different parts of the natural gas transportation systems, those stakeholders wish to keep the values that brought by the system to be consistent, and expect to expand these values based on their needs.

V. Risks Analysis

The specific attributes of transportation and the complexity of gas pipeline networks both bring operation challenges. Natural gas producers and different levels of consumers are dominant stakeholders of the whole gas transportation system. Those parts could be the sub systems that rely on the gas transportation systems, even have inner reliance across sub systems. We have to be aware of the risks during these systems' interactions with gas transportation system, and strength the reliance in building gas transportation system.

We would first try to analyze and summarize short and long term risks exit on the natural transportation systems.

A. *Short-term risks*

The construction of gas transportation system require large investment. Investment costs in the natural gas transportation system would be higher due to the frequent need to invest not only in the pipelines itself, but also in the insulation of houses and additional supplementary infrastructure. Therefore, a change would often have negative financial consequences and hence potentially negative social consequences as well [5].

Natural gas transportation brings health risks aligned with natural gas producing system. Producing natural gas can contaminate air and drinking water, creating negative health impacts for citizens close to production sites. The gas-related accidents and the threat of earthquakes also named as additional threats. Studies also identified an increased human mortality rate due to shale gas (compared to conventional gas, nuclear, or renewables) [5].

B. *Long-term risks*

Long term risks of gas transportation systems always bring concerns about energy security. For the example from Russia, concerns from two main aspects: -The need for long-term shortage-free supply of consumers with the required energy resources, provided the energy sector operates under nominal conditions. -The creation of conditions for providing consumers with energy resources under emergency conditions [3]. For the example from Germany, the country is widely recognised as a climate leader with impressive progress in its energy transition and ambitious plans while at the same time offering strong state support to three new LNG terminals.

Consideration of the energy security calls for identification of critical facilities, i.e. energy transportation systems which, in case of partial or complete failure to operate, can cause severe damage to the country through the energy sector [3].

Some health risks, especially invisible ones (such as risks that occur underground such as the contamination of aquifers or seismic activity), are beyond the direct perception of lay people. Moreover, those risks are spatially diffuse, uncertainty exists about which region will be affected to what extent, and the effects are often temporally delayed [6].

VI. Shaping Forces

Compared with other systems that high related with natural transportation systems. Gas export system could be sensitive and sometimes vulnerable when facing shaping forces. In this project, it is the diplomatic situation.

In most cases, gas, oil, electricity, and other energy systems have huge transportation costs. The values that exist in these huge transportation systems could be a vital remedy and, probably benefits for these transportation systems.

But in general, those transportation systems cover huge areas, even across countries. When gas transportation work across the border, the export system could be the sub-component of this system. The export system of gas transportation systems could bring interests from political, commercial, and economic values to gas transportation systems. Sometimes, those benefits could be affected and even dominated by political forces.

In EU, many countries are small and failed to accomplish energy producing-consuming balance. They rely heavily on energy import from Russia. As the chart shows, some countries rely on almost totally energy import from Russia. Actually, until 2022, Russia supplies about 40% of the natural gas European Union overall [18].

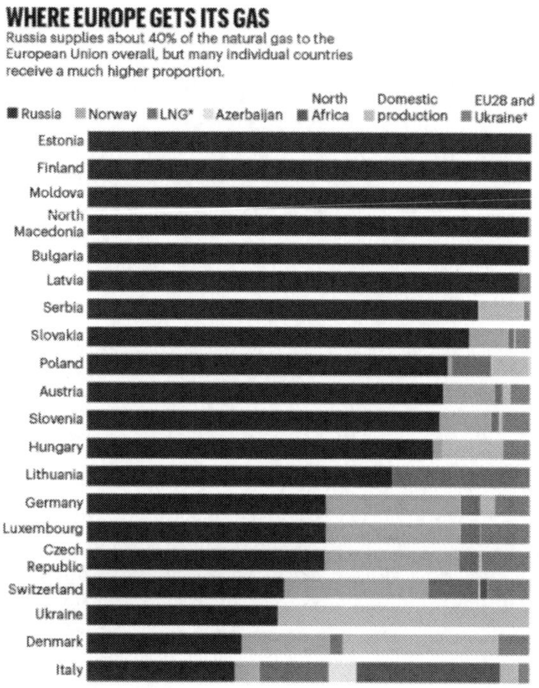

Fig. 5. Europe gas import percentage chart (Sources: Bruegel/European Network of Transmission System Operators for Gas/Eurostat/UK Government/Government of Ukraine)

The diplomatic relationship between many countries could shape and determine the export systems, transnational system constructions, international energy transportation, and different levels of stakeholders, as Figure 8 shows, all of these essential components can't work and add other values without stable diplomatic agreement. Considering current Ukraine War, the shaping force are definitely reshaping the energy map of the EU.

Besides, the diplomatic activities could force the gas providing and transportation in a economic way, the price fluctuations of energy market. This cause the stakeholders, such as energy company and the government may face deficits. This

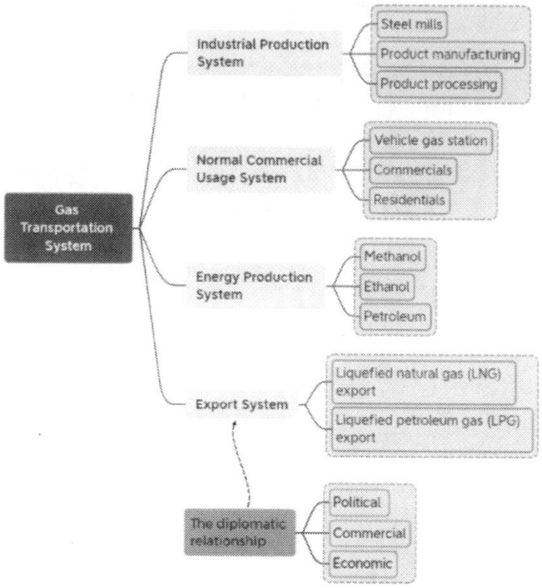

Fig. 6. Shaping Forces

deficits consequence, again, decrease the fund that used for transportation facilities and security remediations.

VII. Reliance Analysis

Many energy consumers rely on gas transportation systems. Figure 9 shows the reliance among gas transportation systems and other 4 main gas-using systems.

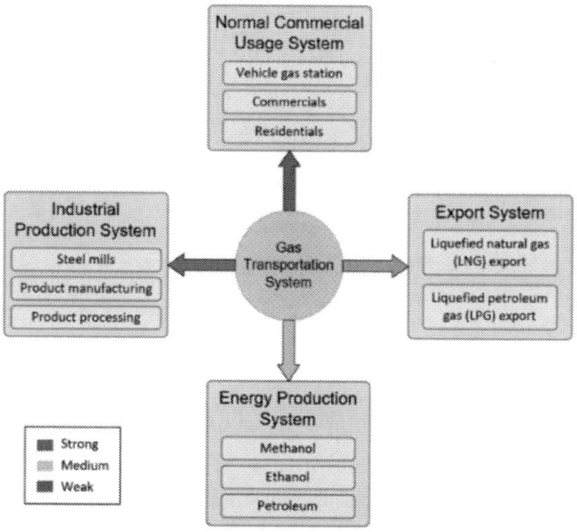

Fig. 7. Reliability between systems

Figure 10 shows the whole map of risks, reliance from stakeholders, related gas using subsystems to the gas transportation system, in most of cases, those different circle parts in this graph shows bi-direction relationship. Those relationship put risks, and the reliability of gas transportation could decrease and avoid these risks.

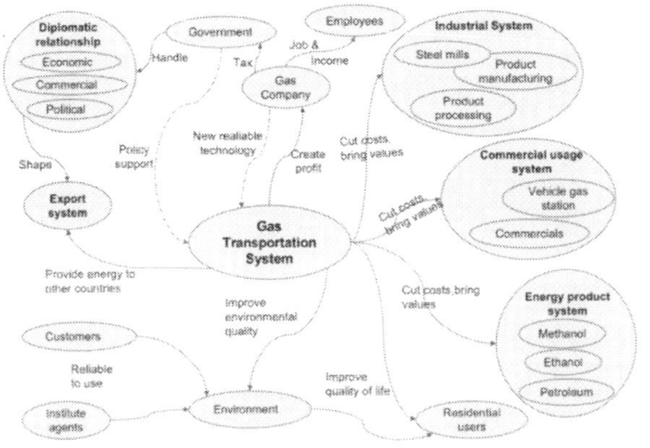

Fig. 8. Risk and reliance relationship graph of gas transportation system

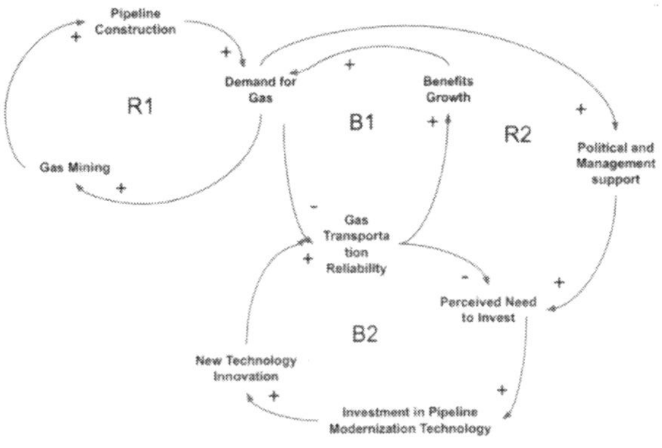

Fig. 9. Casual Loop analysis for gas providers

Those reliance above need a operational gas transportation system. They revealed how a stable gas transportation can link those consuming systems together tightly.

Consider the complex of gas transportation, such as Nord Stream1 and Nord Stream2 built though comprehensive geographic situations, offshore gas transportation and onshore gas transportation bring more options for gas transportation. For example, the onshore transportation can finish by using either vessel with tanks or undersea pipelines. The latter always face huge costs and uncertain risks, financial crisis, diplomatic shaping forces, geographic limitations and benefits for stakeholders could could the decision to be complicated. In order to minimize the technical uncertainty and stabilize the benefits, the gas transportation systems should be built to be reliable at the early time.

Transporting energy by pipeline is safe and environmentally friendly. Furthermore, pipeline transportation is safer than transportation by road, rail, or vessel, as measured by incidents, injuries, and fatalities even though more road and rail incidents go unreported [17]. This means the pipelines based gas transportation are more reliable compared to other transportation methods.

A. Cost saving and safety improvement for energy providers

In Figure 11, the causal loop of the natural gas providers shows the factors' relationship with reinforcement (R in Figure 11) and balance forces' explanations (B in Figure 11), positive (+) and negative consequent effects (-) among these factors. In this graph, one factor is among the causes of another factor.

According to this graph, the reliable gas provider could inform a positive feedback loop, the factors in this loop all receive potential benefits: The reliable gas transportation system decrease the perceived need to adding new investment. The gas company could use saved money to invest in the improvement of natural gas pipelines' modernization technology, this motivate would accelerate the new technology's innovation. All of these could reinhence the gas transportation reliability, strengthen the positive loop and keep benefits, and save cost for gas providers.

B. Price fluctuation and Monopoly

Figure 12 shows the natural gas price' fluctuation in these years. To avoid huge fluctuations, the whole gas transportation system have to be built in a control organization, this organization generally consists of several gas producers, they aim to stabilize the gas supply, to avoid the gas supply shortage when one of the gas producers halt its gas providing, and protect the reliable gas supply system.

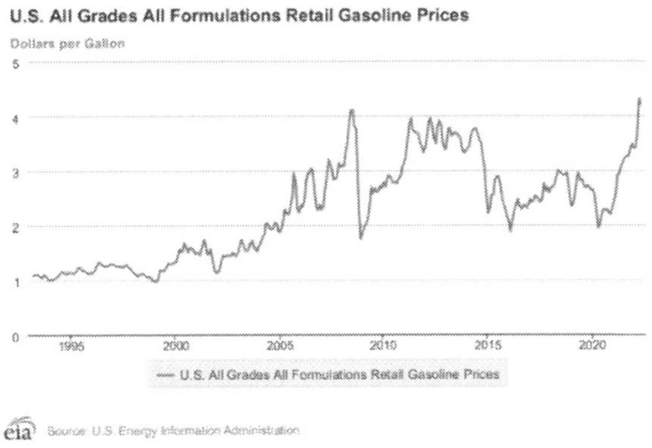

Fig. 10. Gas price fluctuation chart in U.S

After the year of 2021, in 2022, with the influence of Russia-Ukraine War, the U.S banned Russia energy, cause the significant price increase over past 25 years.

If one country's gas transportation systems not working for providing gas, especially for the main gas export country like Russia, this could cause chaois for the whole gas transportation network, even cause the transportation halting. To avoid this situation, the related stakeholders need a third party organization to guarantee the price of the gas. The organization, such as OPEC, could aim to stabilize the international energy supply and price could make decisions to avoid energy price's huge fluctuations. During Iraq War time, this measure could even flat the price fluctuations [5].

VIII. Conclusions

The transnational natural gas transportation systems brings benefits for thousands of consumers. Stakeholders of natural gas transportation systems rely heavily not on each other, but also the natural gas transportation systems.

At same time, the complicated benefits groups may face more specific risks from engineering challenges, making the trade-off between system construction and environment, customers living experience and gas benefits. Those considerations bring more implementation uncertainty and risks. Concerns from those challenges and issues need the natural gas transportation system to be built reliability and durable.

In the end, try to identify risks and avoid related severe consequences in early system-building stage, these measures would lead the whole system become more stable and robust, and the system could benefit more stakeholders in a very long term. The controllers and decision makers of the system could make the improvement of current system to be reality and with low economic and environment cost.

Acknowledgement

Thanks to my research teammates, Meng Jiao and Shiyu Yuan, they help draw those analysis graphs and contribute their ideas about how to list and plot analysis steps for each research section.

References

[1] Joaquín Navarro-Esbrí, Adrián Fernández-Moreno, Adrián Mota-Babiloni, "Modelling and evaluation of a high-temperature heat pump two-stage cascade with refrigerant mixtures as a fossil fuel boiler alternative for industry decarbonization," Energy, Volume 254, Part B, 2022.

[2] Roger Z. Ríos-Mercado and Conrado Borraz-Sánchez, "Optimization problems in natural gas transportation systems: A state-of-the-art review," Applied Energy,Volume 147,2015, pp.536-555.

[3] S.M. Senderov and A.V. Edelev, "Formation of a list of critical facilities in the gas transportation system of Russia in terms of energy security," Energy, Volume 184,2019, pp.105-112.

[4] Alvaro Silva-Calderón, "Short and long-term energy security in the UNECE region: trends and prospects Speech by Dr Alvaro Silva-Calderón, OPEC Secretary General to the Energy Security Forum, UN Economic Commission for Europe Committee on Sustainable Energy". Geneva, Switzerland, 20 November 2003.

[5] G.P. Hammond and Á. O'Grady, "Indicative energy technology assessment of UK shale gas extraction Application," Energy, 185 (2017), pp. 1907-1918.

[6] M. Cotton, I. Rattle, and J. Van Alstine, "Shale gas policy in the United Kingdom: an argumentative discourse analysis," Energy Policy, 73 (2014), pp. 427-438.

[7] Hanna Brauers, Isabell Braunger, and Jessica Jewell, "Liquefied natural gas expansion plans in Germany: The risk of gas lock-in under energy transitions," Energy Research Social Science, Volume 76, 2021.

[8] Valentin Jeutner, "Amendments, annexations, alternatives: Nord Stream 2's contemporary status under EU and international law," The Journal of World Energy Law Business, Volume 12, Issue 6, December 2019, pp. 502–512.

[9] Anna Mikulska, "Gazprom and Russian Natural Gas Policy in the First Two Decades of the 21st Century," Orbis, Volume 64, Issue 3, 2020, pp. 403-420.

[10] Rios-Mercado and Roger. Z. Borraz Sanchez, Conrado, "Optimization problems in natural gas transportation systems: A state-of-the-art review," Provided by the author(s) and the Los Alamos National Laboratory (2016-01-08). Applied Energy, Volume 147, 1 June 2015, pp.536-555.

[11] John A.P. Chandler, "Developing offshore petroleum to meet socio-economic objectives: Lessons from Australia, Norway and the United Kingdom," Energy Policy, Volume 144, 2020.

[12] Justyna Woźniak, Zbigniew Krysa, and Michał Dudek, "Concept of government-subsidized energy prices for a group of individual consumers in Poland as a means to reduce smog," Energy Policy, Volume 144, 2020.

[13] Balázs R.Sziklaiac, László Á.Kóczyab, and Dávid Csercsikd, "The impact of Nord Stream 2 on the European gas market bargaining positions," Energy Policy Volume 144, September 2020.

[14] Paulina Landry, "The EU strategy for gas security: Threats, vulnerabilities and processes," Energy Policy, Volume 144, 2020.

[15] James Conca, "Pick Your Poison For Crude – Pipeline, Rail, Truck Or Boat," Forbes, April 26 2014.

[16] V. Zapukhlyak, Yu. Melnychenko, . kipnyi, L. Poberezhny, Ya. Grudz, N. Drin, and M. Chernetskyy, "Reliability assurance of gas-hydrogen mixture transportation by gas pipeline system," Procedia Structural Integrity, Volume 36, 2022, pp. 378-385.

[17] Diana Furchtgott-Roth and Kenneth P. Green, "Intermodal safety in the transport of oil," Studies in ENERGY TRANSPORTATION. October, 2013.

[18] Jeff Tollefson, "What the war in Ukraine means for energy, climate and food Russia's invasion has caused a short-term spike in prices, but could prompt a long-term shift towards sustainability," NEWS FEATURE, Nature, April 05, 2022.

Multi-Protocol Interoperability Between Distributed Cyber-Physical Systems Towards Industry 4.0 Collaborative Optimization

Md Sabbir Bin Azad
Dept. of Mathematics and Industrial Engineering
Polytechnique Montreal
Montreal, Canada
e-mail: sabbirbinazad@gmail.com

Dr. Christophe Danjou
Dept. of Mathematics and Industrial Engineering
Polytechnique Montreal
Montreal, Canada
e-mail: christophe.danjou@polymtl.ca

Abstract— **Industry 4.0 has emerged as a potential strategy to providing extensive connectivity in the production environment, which is rapidly evolving combined with rising commercial demand, mass personalized manufacturing. Mass customization and complicated products necessitate more data and more adaptable Machine-to-Machine (M2M) communication that facilitates smooth data interchange and interaction between industrial components in smart manufacturing. Integrating industrial Internet of Things (IoT) devices to benefit different industry sectors simultaneously requires extensive network connectivity, interoperable communication, and collaboration among the networked machines. While critical technical issues with network connectivity have been properly addressed, the technology is not ready for flexible and seamless communication between disparate machines. One of the challenges that arises because of this development is the growing need for interoperable standards and protocols at various levels of the manufacturing ecosystem. Considering the interoperable infrastructure required for Industry 4.0, the paper provides a secure and cost-effective interoperable solution for multi-protocol translators. The key contribution of the paper is a method for mapping IoT multi-protocols into a low-cost gateway, as well as providing effective full-duplex interoperable M2M communication and cloud integration for compatible platforms.**

Keywords- IioT; Gateway; Interoperability; Protocols; M2M; Raspberry Pi.

I. INTRODUCTION

Industry 4.0, fourth industrial revolution brought about by introduction of Internet of Things(IoT) and Cyber Physical Systems (CPSs) [1], has emerged as a promising approach to provide extensive connectivity in manufacturing environment [2]. The development of smart manufacturing technologies is fast changing, and when it is coupled with increasing commercial demand, additive manufacturing shows numerous advantages in providing customized and specifically designed products [3]. Mass customized and complex products leads to a greater needs of information and more flexible automation solutions [4]. This flexibility and more advanced information handling requires more intelligence in the system [5]. One of the resulting challenges of this flexible information management is the increased need for interoperability at different levels of the manufacturing ecosystem [6]. Successful system integration requires good strategies to manage middleware connectivity.

However, integrating new devices to benefit different industry sectors simultaneously requires significant challenges as part of what is being called the Industrial Internet of Things (IIoT) [7]. IIoT devices have unique features, such as low processing and memory, low bandwidth for data download and upload, and limited battery life [8]. Given the ubiquity of these devices and facing such limitations, it is necessary to develop new types of communication protocols designed to deal with these limitations.

Generally, the used protocols are based on communication through cloud and between machines [9]. Semantic interoperability should be achieved in an interworking solution in order to provide a common meaning of the data exchanged by heterogeneous devices, even if they belong to different domains [10]. Different communication protocols are employed in IoT, e.g., Hyper Text Transfer Protocol (HTTP), Constrained Application Protocol (CoAP), MQ Telemetry Transport (MQTT), Modbus Transmission Control Protocol and Internet Protocol (TCP/IP), Web Sockets, Advanced Message Queuing Protocol (AMQP). The main driving force for the design of such protocols is the hardware limitations of embedded devices, which impede the use of traditional network protocols. The integration of communication protocols would cause interoperability among several devices and services, and a possible solution is the conception of a multiprotocol strategy [11]. Though existing standards, e.g., MTConnect, OPC Unified Architecture (OPC-UA) and AutomationML, allow for specifications of industrial objects and information-rich machine-to-machine (M2M) communications, the information models generated from these standards are not semantically defined, making the semantic understanding and intelligent decision-making a challenge [12]. In this regard, an IoT system interchanging between access protocols may overcome the said challenges in interconnected heterogenous systems.

The primary contributions of this research can be summarized as follows:

- Design protocol selection framework among HTTP, MQTT, CoAP, WebSocket Modbus TCP protocol based on the capabilities and requirements of the device and sensor data transmission.

- Design and Implement model of interoperable interpreter for effective M2M information exchange and action plan at a faster pace towards sustainable Industry 4.0 manufacturing

The remainder of the paper is organized as follows: in Section II, related work and interoperability standards are discussed; the strategy proposed, and its characteristics are defined in Section III; Section IV focuses on development model and strategy of proposed architecture; validation of the proposed system through case study is demonstrated in Section V; finally, in Section VI, we discussed conclusions and future work.

II. RELATED WORK

The popularity of the internet has led to the emergence of internet protocol-based communication standards, creating a unified infrastructure for the integration of disparate systems and devices. There are several solutions proposed or implemented with the aim of increasing IoT interoperability.

H. Derhamy et al. [13] developed a multi-protocol solution for IoT interoperability issue. The solution includes protocol implementation translators based on Service Oriented Architecture (SOA), intermediate format to reduce the number of translations necessary. The system also detects protocol incompatibilities and performs the translation.

Barros et al. [14] introduced Internet of Things Multiprotocol Message Broker (IoTM2B) strategy to integrate various communication protocols such as HTTP, MQTT and CoAP and their performance evaluation based on two scenarios, machine-to-machine (M2M) protocols Communication and cloud-based environment. This strategy extends IoT DSM to provide integration with embedded devices Via various protocols.

Derhamy et al. [15] proposed interoperability solution consists of a multi-protocol translator that is injected into the service exchange on demand. The main contribution of this research is to suggest ways to map OPC UAs to intermediate formats. Intermediate formats can be mapped to other standard IoT protocols such as CoAP, HTTP, and MQTT.

The main issue with current interoperable solutions is that there isn't a method that fits well with integration of IoT multi protocols in a gateway and effective full duplex interoperable communication to interconnect the sensors, IIoT devices, and machines and cloud integration for compatible platforms.

III. PROPOSED SOLUTION

To address this integration and interoperability challenges, we proposed a platform to develop an interoperable system which can connect heterogenous devices with different protocol, process and exchange the data with different machines and cloud platform. Fig. 1 illustrates the architecture of the proposed research framework. We defined the architecture of the gateway with four modules which are the key functions of the embedded communication.

A. *Protocol Selection Framework*

To facilitate safe and high-speed data transfer among end IoT devices, users set protocols among MQTT, CoAP, HTTP, WebSocket and Modbus TCP for the nodes and/or sensors to send data to the gateway. Each of these protocols have distinct features and capabilities, which add complexity to the identification of a protocol suitable for specific use cases.

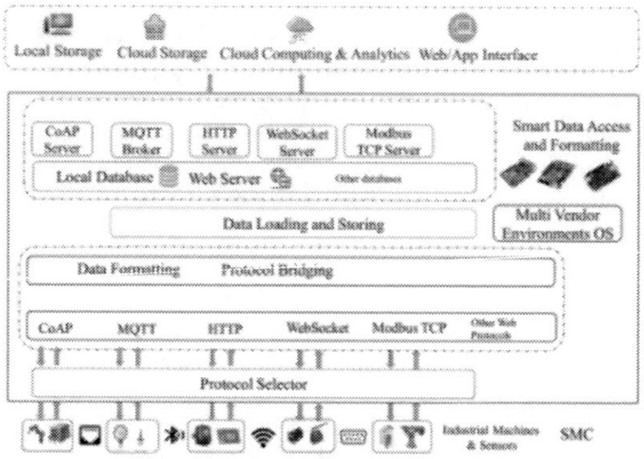

Figure 1. Architecture of the proposed research framework

For instance, MQTT is recommended in network scenarios where bandwidth consumption must be reduced and the devices involved in communication have low processing and memory capacity [16]. WebSocket protocol's standard connectivity helps simplify many of the complexities and difficulties involved in the operation of bi-direction communication.

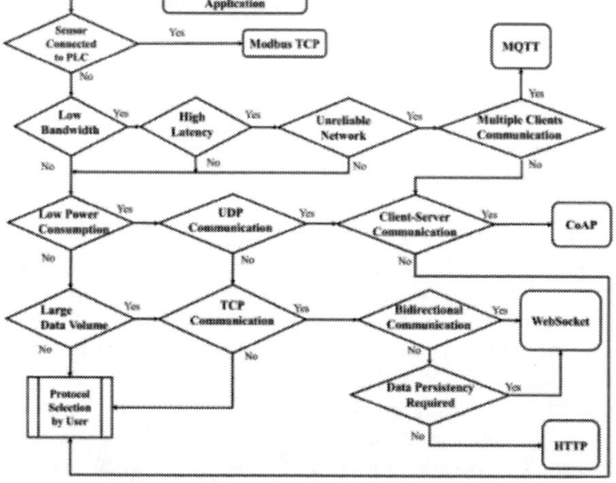

Figure 2. Protocol Selector for IoT Application

However, a difficulty is that the sensors in industries and shop floors are mainly connected to Programmable Logic Controllers (PLCs) to collect large amount of sensor data and to transfer it to a communication system [17]. To enable IoT connectivity for these sensors connected to PLCs, the controller needs to configure with Modbus TCP protocol. Fig. 2 demonstrates protocol selection framework based on the capabilities and requirements of the sensor data transmission to gateway. In addition to the protocol selection for the nodes, it is necessary for the processor unit to have the ability to run and execute a Web Server, on which services will be deployed.

B. *Connectivity with Heterogenous Nodes*

The First module of the IoT gateway system is to receive data from heterogenous nodes and/or sensor with multi-protocol communication. The gateway uses wireless communication protocol (e.g., Zigbee, Bluetooth, Wi-Fi) and Local Area Network (LAN) to acquire the packet from the heterogenous sensor nodes, and use the 3G/4G and, other network interfaces to read and parse the data and then send it to data format module for standardizing.

C. *Data Formatting*

Since heterogeneous nodes and sensors send data over different protocols, they send data with different data format. The gateway uses JavaScript Object Notation (JSON) format to systematize the representation of data coming from the nodes and sensors. An example of the representation of the data recorded by the temperature and humidity sensor, in JSON format, is shown in Fig. 3.

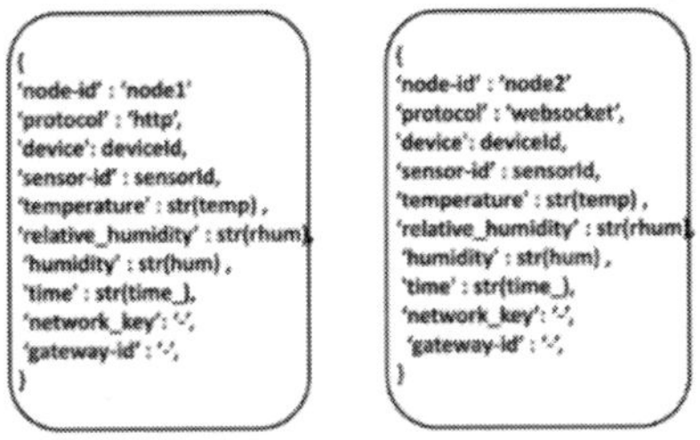

Figure 3. Example of systematized data format

This format has important advantages such as simplicity and low resource consumption [16].

D. *Protocol Bridging*

The proposed IoT gateway acts as a bridge between different protocols, mainly among HTTP, MQTT, CoAP, WebSocket and Modbus TCP. The gateway is continuously being ready for listening for these multiprotocol connection requests and message payload with the standardized format. An example is given in Fig. 4 to illustrate the interoperable protocol communication among the nodes and gateways in the proposed architecture.

The broker Mosquitto is a message broker that implements several versions of the MQTT protocol and it is relatively a lightweight software [18] and it has low power profile. The advantages of data transfer MQTT is good, reliable, easy to build and it uses less network resources even in conditions of unstable network [19]. In the gateway, WebSocket communication technology also is adopted in MQTT broker as WebSocket provides full-duplex communication channels over a single TCP/IP connection. Another most familiar protocol is HTTP which user can set for communication between nodes and gateway server. The data sent to the server with POST is stored in the request body of the HTTP request. Another high interoperability protocol for embedded devices with an increased level of security is CoAP.

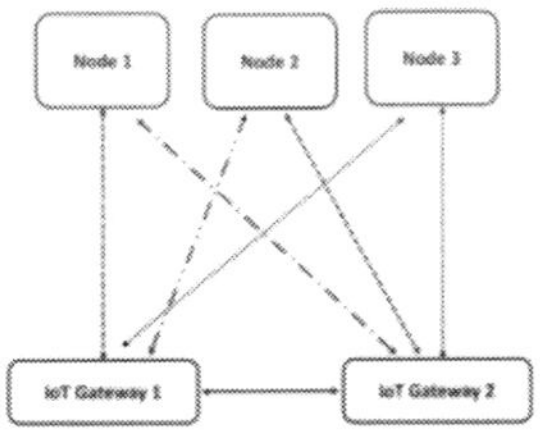

Figure 4. Interoperable communication among the nodes and gateways

The node which acts as CoAP Client could send data to the server on a particular port 5683 with the help of browser add-on Copper (Cu) CoAP user-agent. A relevant characteristic of Modbus TCP is that it is supported by both proprietary and open-source hardware/software, so different equipment can seamlessly share information enabled by this protocol [20].

IV. RESEARCH DEVELOPMENT

Key components and flows are described at a high level below.

A. *Proposed System Architecture*

The solution proposed in this research aims at enabling interoperable connectivity from heterogenous devices and data acquired from different communication protocols and extending these networks towards the IoT universe. To this purpose, we implemented 5 modules within the application: (i)Multi-protocol gateway development (ii)Multi-protocol server integration (iii)Node MCUs and Sensors Integration (iv)Nodes and gateway interoperable communication (v)Data storage to multiple databases. Fig. 5 illustrates the implementation phases of the architecture.

B. *Multi-Protocol Gateway Development*

For the development of the gateway, Raspberry Pi 4B was used which is illustrated in Fig. 5(f). At first, multiple single board computers were compared to find the cost efficient and complex task management compatible gateway. Table 1 is provided to show the comparison among the development boards.

TABLE I. COMPARISON OF SINGLE BOARDS

	Raspberry Pi 4	**Raspberry Pi 3**	**Beagle Bone**	**Intel Galileo**
Processor	Quad core 64-bit ARM-Cortex A72	Broadcom BCM2837 Quad Core	ARM Cortex-A8	Quark SoC X1000, 32-bit Intel
Frequency& RAM	1.5GHz, 4GB	1.2GHz, 1GB	1GHz, 512MB	400MH, 512 KB SRAM 256Mb DRAM
Operating System	Raspbian, Debian, Fedora, ARCH Linux ARM, Ubuntu etc.	Raspbian, Debian, Fedora, ARCH Linux, ARM etc.	Android, Debian, Angstrom, Yocto, Fedora, Ubuntu etc.	Arduino, Linux distribution for Galileo, Rocket etc.
Power	15.3W	10W	15W	15W
Cost	70 CAD	45 CAD	70 CAD	100 CAD

Raspberry Pi is proposed as gateway because of its lower cost, high processing capability, random-access memory (RAM), 40 general purpose input/output (GPIO) pins, RJ45 port and Wi-Fi connectivity. The Pi 4 is continuously being ready for listening for these multiprotocol connection requests and message payload with the standardized format through 802.11 b/g/n/ac Wireless LAN network.

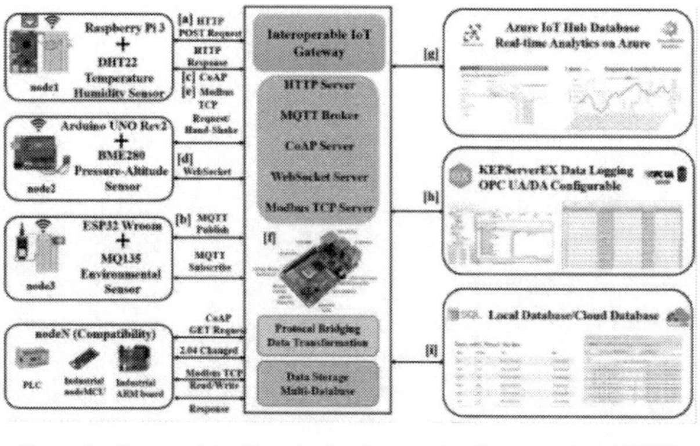

Figure 5. Proposed Architecture Implementation Framework, [a]HTTP, [b]MQTT, [c]CoAP, [d]WebSocket, [e]ModbusTCP, [f]Raspberry Pi 4 as Gateway, [g]Azure IoT Hub Database, [h]KepwareServer Data Logging, [i]Local/Cloud Database

C. *Multiple Server Configuration on the Gateway*

MQTT, HTTP, CoAP, Modbus TCP and WebSocket server are integrated in the gateway. Raspbian OS has been installed in the system to configure all the servers and install the required software and libraries.

1) MQTT Broker Configuration: The software that is being used here is Mosquitto. After installation series of packages, the gateway broker was ready to publish or subscribe the topic. Fig. 6 illustrates the start-up Mosquitto MQTT broker on the terminal.

Figure 6. Mosquitto MQTT Broker Running on Terminal

2) HTTP Server: The Apache web server (HTTP server) is installed on the Raspberry Pi 4 IoT gateway. Apache can communicate between nodes and the server over the HTTP. The Apache profile opens the port 80. Fig. 7 demonstrates apache2 Raspbian version running on the gateway.

Figure 7. Apache3 Raspbian Version Webserver Installed

3) CoAP Server Implementation: In this work, the aiocoap Python CoAP library was used to implement the CoAP protocol [21]. Two access methods are initiated here one is PUT which allows the node connected with the sensors transfer data to the gateway and, the other is GET which allows the nodes with actuators to register with the resource so that nodes can be notified when gateway initiates any feedback command and transfer data.

4) Modbus TCP Server: For Modbus TCP/IP communication, an open-source and full modbus protocol called "pyModbus" is used. It works as fully implemented modbus server and supports read/write on discrete and register. 30 registers are written initially for receiving read/write requests from the clients. More registers can be added for further development.

5) WebSocket Server Deployment: As WebSocket enables bidirectional communication in real time over the web, WebSocket server is deployed in the gateway for horizontal interoperable communication. After enabling Node.js html server, http does the handling requests and serving content and Uniform Resource Identifier (URL) helps to parse requested URLs.

D. *Communication between Node MCUs and Sensors*

For the development of the proposed design, sensors are connected through the GPIO pins and input/output (I/O) interface of the node MCUs. Three sensors DHT22 sensor, BME280 sensor, MQ-135 are connected to three node MCUs Raspberry Pi 3, Arduino Uno Rev2 and ESP32. These sensors collect the data from surroundings like temperature, humidity, pressure, altitude, and air quality.

E. *Communication between Node MCUs and Gateway*

In this development, node2 Arduino Uno with bme280 pressure sensor send data over WebSocket Protocol. Node3 ESP32 send data over MQTT protocol. Node1 is configured to communicate with HTTP, CoAP and Modbus TCP protocol.

In Fig. 5(d) node2 creates client socket and tries to establish a communication link to the gateway server using its IP address and port number 80. When the communication established between node2 and gateway, it received pressure and altitude from node2 Arduino Uno Wi-Fi and showed the data to the interface. Here, the gateway is also devising as MQTT broker which facilitates the communication from node3 transferring messages from publisher to subscriber and subscriber to publisher in Fig. 5[b]. Node3 ESP32 with environmental sensor provides air quality data in ppm unit. In regards, reading data from sensor and sending data to the gateway broker, PubSubClient MQTT library is used on the node3 end. Node1 will use the Adafruit DHT library to retrieve the DHT22 sensor's current temperature and humidity readings. After the gateway is configured to receive data from node1 over CoAP protocol shown in Fig. 5(c), CoAPthon Python library the script is activated to create a CoAP endpoint. Fig. 8 shows sensor data receiving in the gateway from node1, node2 and node3.

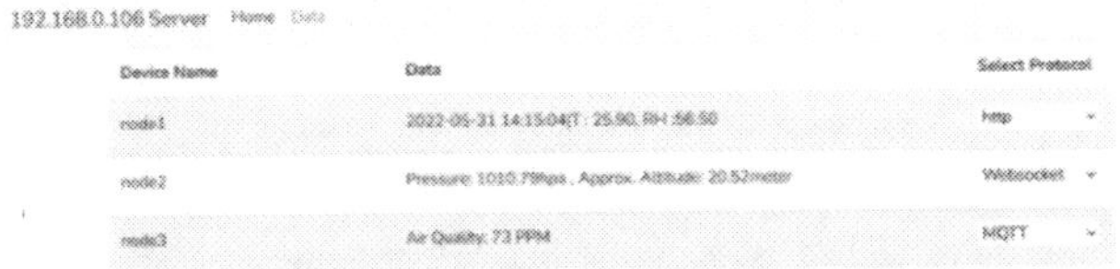

Figure 8. Node1, node2, node3 data collected from gateway

To demonstrate Modbus TCP communication between the client and gateway, in Fig. 5 (e) node1 was configured as Modbus client that transfers temperature and humidity data to gateway which works as Modbus TCP server. As the gateway had register map for all data types with desired size, these registers received read/write requests from the node. For the demonstration of http protocol communication, node1 was also configured as HTTP client.

F. Data Collection and Storage

Three databases are presented to visualize and process for server and device communications. We divided the databases into (i) local and cloud database (ii) KEPServerEX data logging and communication and (iii) Azure IoT hub databases.

After processing data received from the nodes, the gateway sends data to MariaDB which is shown in Fig. 5(i). In the experiment, the gateway receives data from the different nodes and edge devices and provides it to KEPServerEX OPC server MQTT client by Kepware. From the Fig. 5(h), we demonstrated Air Quality data with the corresponding timestamp that received from the MQTT client through the KepServerex and stored into Microsoft Access Databases. Azure IoT hub environment is deployed to connect the gateway with nodes to the cloud. After obtaining primary connection string, gateway establishes communication with the IoT hub and sends data over MQTT protocol to the hub. In Fig. 5(g) data ingestion is shown in Azure Data Explorer Database.

V. VALIDATION

This section contains a case study to analyze a workflow involving data collection from nodes with sensors, gateway integration to cloud with the goal of validating the interoperability concept of integrating any platforms with the developed multi-protocol gateway.

A. Case Study: Implementation on ThingsBoard

The case study refers to implementation communication between gateway and ThingsBoard IoT platform. ThingsBoard is an open-source IoT platform built on the Java 8 platform that functions as an IoT gateway between registered devices communicating via HTTP, CoAP, and MQTT protocols to collect, analyse, visualize, and manage data [22].

1) Configuration: ThingsBoard is configured to monitor and visualize data by creating IoT Dashboards and updating in real-time. The multi protocol gateway receives sensor data from three different nodes with different protocols Modbus TCP, WebSocket and MQTT and, process the data as JavaScript Object Notation (JSON) format before sending to ThingsBoard Platform. Fig. 9 illustrates the integration details between the gateway and the ThingsBoard platform.

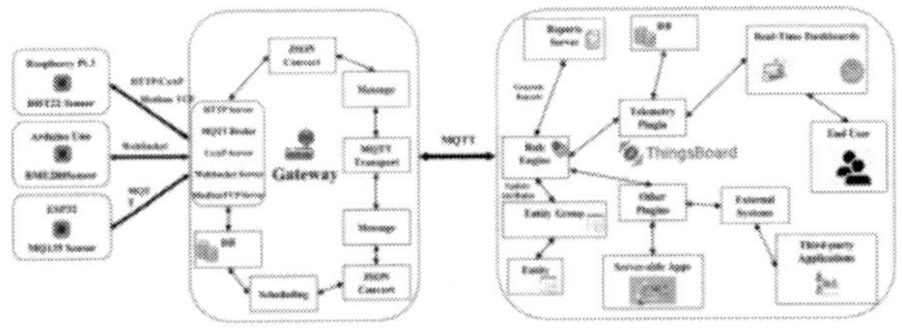

Figure 9: ThingsBoard platform integration with muti-protocol gateway

The gateway uses an access token to access the web interface of the ThingsBoard cloud server. Telemetry sent by the gateway for logging in the platform is inserted into the SQLite database table before being transferred to the ThingsBoard. To publish telemetry data to ThingsBoard, gateway publish message to the following topic: "v1/devices/me/telemetry". Finally, the telemetry data get uploaded to the ThingsBoard using the MQTT publishing feature.

2) Real-time Visualization on ThingsBoard: ThingsBoard's integration APIs allow custom applications to be built, and they use their own data visualisation tools.

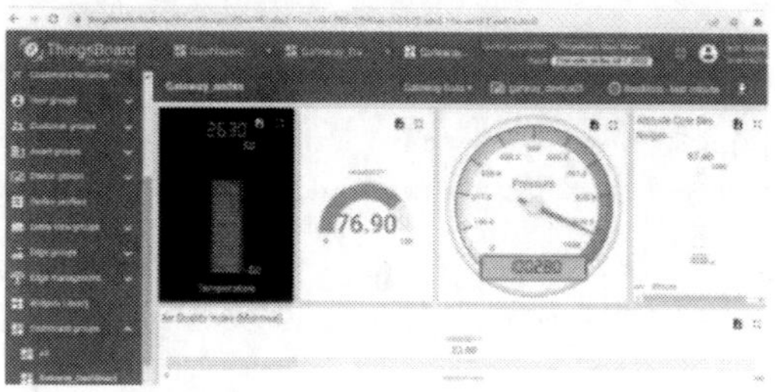

Figure 10: Real-time data visualization dashboard on ThingsBoard

Devices configured as Gateway_device01 in the ThingsBoard received telemetry data from the multi-protocol gateway. As seen in Fig. 10, gateway is sending all the sensor values received by ThingsBoard platform with timestamp.

B. Results

Successful integration of the multi protocol gateway to the open source IoT ThingsBoard platform validates interoperable data exchanges compatibility of the proposed gateway. The gateway receives data from three different embedded devices over three different protocols such as Modbus TCP, WebSocket and MQTT. The gateway receives the signal, processes, and transfers the sensors values real time into ThingsBoard IoT platform over MQTT protocol. To address the IoT Interoperability challenges, the gateway can provide the strategy of using different protocol integration, and data conversion, as well as integrating real-time data analysis with Kafka and Spark platforms on ThingsBoard platform for big data analytic applications. Thus, Integrating different protocol-enabled devices into each system enables the scalability, automation, and flexibility of Industry 4.0 manufacturing systems.

VI. CONCLUSION AND FUTURE WORK

For interoperable M2M communication between heterogenous devices, we proposed and developed an interoperable middleware gateway by enabling multi protocol integration. In Section V, we evaluated the potential gain of deploying the middleware gateway in a case study to provide a real-time cloud-based integration and visualization that facilitates sensor-based data collection, gateway integration and interoperability management, and to validate the interoperability concept of integrating any platforms via any of the industry standard protocols MQTT, CoAP, HTTP, Modbus TCP and WebSockeT. Future development can be expanding the supported OPC UA service and AMQP, CAN, CC-Link protocols implementation and PLC and other controllers bridging in the gateway. Future experimental tests will evaluate the performance of data analytics systems in terms of responsiveness, flexibility, and scalability in large, real-world scenarios.

REFERENCES

[1] H. Kagermann, J. Helbig, A. Hellinger, and W. Wahlster, Recommendations for implementing the strategic initiative INDUSTRIE 4.0: Securing the future of German manufacturing industry;report of Industrie 4.0 Working G. Forschungsunion, 2013.

[2] H. S. Li, L. F. Lai, and H. V. Poor, "Multicast Routing for Decentralized Control of Cyber Physical Systems with an Application in Smart Grid," IEEE J. Sel. Areas Commun., Article vol. 30, no. 6, pp. 1097-1107, 2012, doi: 10.1109/jsac.2012.120708.

[3] Y. Meng, Y. Yang, H. Chung, P.-H. Lee, and C. Shao, "Enhancing Sustainability and Energy Efficiency in Smart Factories: A Review," Sustainability, vol. 10, no. 12, 2018, doi: 10.3390/su10124779.

[4] H. A. ElMaraghy, "Flexible and reconfigurable manufacturing systems paradigms," Int. J. Flexible Manuf. Syst., Article; Proceedings Paper vol. 17, no. 4, pp. 261-276, 2005, doi: 10.1007/s10696-006-9028-7.

[5] D. Zuehlke, "SmartFactory – from Vision to Reality in Factory Technologies," IFAC Proceedings Volumes, vol. 41, no. 2, pp. 14101-14108,2008,doi:https://doi.org/10.3182/20080706-5-KR-1001.02391.

[6] A. Zeid, S. Sundaram, M. Moghaddam, S. Kamarthi, and T. Marion, "Interoperability in Smart Manufacturing: Research Challenges," Machines,Review vol. 7, no. 2, 2019, doi: 10.3390/machines7020021.

[7] D. Serpanos and M. Wolf, "Industrial Internet of Things," IoT Systems: Architectures, Algorithms, Methodologies. Cham: Springer International Publishing, 2018, pp. 37-54.

[8] E. Sisinni, A. Saifullah, S. Han, U. Jennehag, and M. Gidlund, "Industrial Internet of Things: Challenges, Opportunities, and Directions,"IEEE Trans. Ind. Inform., Article vol. 14, no. 11, pp. 4724-4734, 2018, doi: 10.1109/tii.2018.2852491.

[9] N. Kshetri, "Can Blockchain Strengthen the Internet of Things?," IT Prof.,vol.19,no.4, pp. 68-72, 2017, doi: 10.1109/MITP.2017.3051335.

[10] S. Cavalieri, "Semantic Interoperability between IEC 61850 and oneM2M for IoT-Enabled Smart Grids," Sensors, Article vol. 21, no. 7, 2021, doi: 10.3390/s21072571.

[11] P. Desai, A. Sheth, and P. Anantharam, "Semantic Gateway as a Service architecture for IoT Interoperability," IEEE Int. Conf. on Mob. S., NewYork, 2015, pp. 313-319, doi: 10.1109/ms.2015.51.

[12] I. Grangel-González, Semantic Data Integration for Industry 4.0 Standards. 2017, pp. 230-237.

[13] H. Derhamy, J. Eliasson, and J. Delsing, "IoT Interoperability—On-Demand and Low Latency Transparent Multiprotocol Translator," IEEE IoT Journal, vol.4, no.5, pp.1754-1763, 2017, doi: 10.1109/JIOT.2017.2697718.

[14] V. Barros, S. Junior, S. Bruschi, F. Monaco, and J. Estrella, "An IoT Multi-Protocol Strategy for the Interoperability of Distinct Communication Protocols applied to Web of Things," Brazillian Symposium on Multimedia and the Web, 2019.

[15] H. Derhamy, J. Rönnholm, J. Delsing, J. Eliasson, and J. v. Deventer, "Protocol interoperability of OPC UA in service oriented architectures," IEEE Int. Conf. on Ind. Inf. (INDIN), 2017.

[16] C. Wilder, M. Jose, P. Harold, and J. D. Alvarado, "Internet of things: a multiprotocol gateway as solution of the interoperability problem," in Mechatronics, Electronics and Telecommunications Advances Towards Industry 4.0, Bonaventuriana Ed., 2021, ch. 5, p. 24.

[17] T. John and M. Vorbröcker, "Enabling IoT connectivity for ModbusTCP sensors," IEEE Int. Conf. on Emerging Tech. and FactoryAutomation(ETFA),2020.Available:https://ieeexplore.ieee.org/document/9211999/.

[18] R. Light, "Mosquitto: server and client implementation of the MQTT protocol," The Journal of Open Source Software, vol. 2, 2017, doi: https://doi.org/10.21105/joss.00265.

[19] N. Q. Uy and V. H. Nam, "A comparison of AMQP and MQTT protocols for Internet of Things," NAFOSTED Conf. on Info. and C.

Science(NICS).2019.Available:https://ieeexplore.ieee.org/document/9023812/.

[20] I. González, A. J. Calderón, and J. M. Portalo, "Innovative Multi-Layered Architecture for Heterogeneous Automation and Monitoring Systems: Application Case of a Photovoltaic Smart Microgrid," Sustainability, vol. 13, no. 4, p. 2234, 2021, doi: https://doi.org/10.3390/su13042234.

[21] Maciej Wasilak and C. Amsüss. "chrysn/aiocoap.", 2014, http://github.com/chrysn/aiocoap/

[22] L. T. D. Paolis, V. D. Luca, and R. Paiano, "Sensor data collection and analytics with thingsboard and spark streaming," IEEE W. on Environmental, Energy, and Structural Monitoring Systems (EESMS),2018, pp. 1-6, doi: 10.1109/EESMS.2018.8405822.

Achieving City Intelligence - A Systems Engineering Approach

Yaw Adom-Mensah
School of Systems and Enterprises, Stevens Institute of Technology
e-mail: yawadom@gmail.com

Mo Mansouri
School of Systems and Enterprises, Stevens Institute of Technology
e-mail: mo.mansouri@stevens.edu

Abstract—**Intelligent systems sense and react to their environment. They are amenable to change, heterogeneous, sustainable and secure. By their nature, cities develop due to various preconditions affirmative to local sustenance of their inhabitants. They are complex systems that encounter ranging pressures stemming from urbanization to uncontrolled socio-technical effects. To control and manage these pressures, various suggestions, frameworks and concepts have been proposed including but not limited to transitioning into Smart Cities. It is relatively accurate that most cities will aspire to be Smart merely for the perceived benefits of such a state. Nonetheless, the research on attainability and progress measurement is varied and deferring in this regard. In this paper, cities are presented as complex sociotechnical systems such that their optimization is a function of people, social systems and network-technological systems. Five incremental levels of the city's intelligence journey are proposed: Insulation, Micro-Functional, Macro-Functional, Spatial Dominance, Self-Orchestration and Astute.**

Keywords-intelligent cities; systems thinking; smat cities.

I. INTRODUCTION

Cities happen to be problems in organized complexity, like the life sciences. They present "situations in which a half-dozen or even several dozen quantities are all varying simultaneously and in subtly interconnected ways." Like the life sciences, cities do not exhibit one problem in organized complexity, which, if understood explains all. They can be analyzed into many such problems or segments which, as in the case of the life sciences, are also related with one another. The variables are many, but they are not helter-skelter; they are "interrelated into an organic whole" [1].

The city is manifestly a complicated system and only partial control can be exercised over its growth and form. It is a product of growth rather than of instantaneous creation. [2] compared the city to a biological entity. That is, a single organism covering the entire landscape surface and showing signs of a vast intelligence [3]. Cities typically evolve spontaneously and subsequently governed into desired states. Thus, more often cities are self-organizing and evolve from local-actions. This spontaneity contains elements of spatial consciousness and random unique forms commonly called *fractals*. Understanding these interacting elements have taken precedence on research on city systems since the nascent stages of the 20th Century.

As systems, cities have existed no less than over 5000 years ago and changes in their form follows a randomized process that manifest simultaneously at different spatial levels. The need for a formal control mechanism to close the gap between fur-flung anarchy and sporadic orderliness inspired the development of disciplines such as City Planning, Urban Studies et al. These specialized disciplines engaged in atomistic and mechanistic approaches to *plan* communities. Urban studies and related, have exerted a great deal of effort in theoretical and practical techniques following this pursuit.

Cities generally are taken as a composition of discrete spatial nodes that perform separate functions at different points in time. This view has been prominent and promotes a vertical hierarchical-node structure where everything is controlled from a [city's] central core. A theoretical idea extended from 19th century German economist, von Thünen whose 1826 iconoclastic treatise, *The Isolated State,* a century later led to – the mono-centric city models – one of the fundamental insights in Urban Planning. The idea of location theory, as Thünen's views are known, has since the mid-19th century inspired a revolution of economists' and geographers who have extended location theory into mainstream economic models. The latter mainly were interested in economic consideration and physical analogies as a means to explain emerging city patterns.

The vertical elaboration of the city system has been dominant therein with notable applications in research on scaling patterns and in land use planning. However, this structure is changing into a horizontal one and spatial processes are no longer mainly controlled from a central core. Thus, relational linkages tend to be horizontal rather than hierarchical/vertical. At the same time, there is the shift from competitive cities to cooperative cities. The rest of this paper is organized as follows. Section II elaborates more on the traditional view. Section III describes the core problem. Section IV discusses what an intelligent city is and Section V introduces and proposes the five stages. Section VI connects the dots.

II. THE TRADITIONAL VIEW

In Figure 1, foundational view about the city is dominated by well-defined familiar structures, a central market place or core, distinct route structures that enable people to travel rapidly to the center from outlying places, suburban locations or neighborhoods or district centers that exist within a clearly structured hierarchy of places and segregated areas where industrial activities take place [4]. This view implicitly assumes that everything in space is homogenous and works as expected.

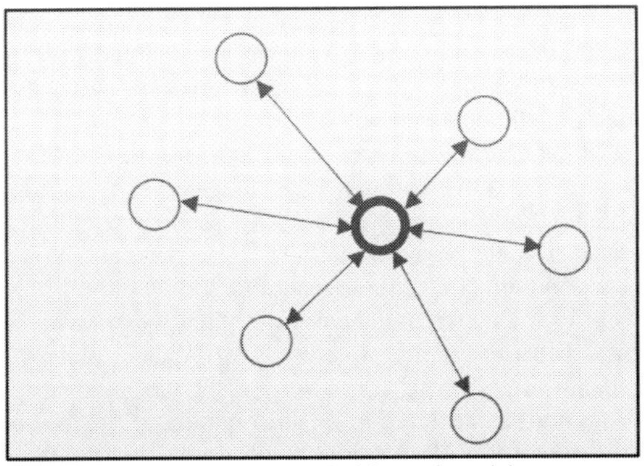

Figure. 1. Traditional view of Cities and spatial processes; akin to star networks exhibiting a one-to-one relationship

On the contrary, cities are open complex systems and exchange both mass and energy with their surroundings, and is a product many builders: Planners, Technologists, Architects, Scientists, Engineers and Policy Makers. They, [the] *builders,* constantly modify the structures of cities for reasons of their own. Regardless of the city exhibiting fundamental characteristics of open systems including the property of multiple builders, many theoretical propositions developed to explain and predict urban spatial structures typically describe the city as closed *static* system. That is, a system permitting the export of mass but not energy. Forrester [5] attempted to introduce the concept of the closed *dynamic* system in his well-received but controversial book: Urban Dynamics. By a closed dynamic system, Forrester, does not outright describe the city as a conventional open system. Instead, as a system that generates its own problems and should be capable of reinventing itself to meet internal demands given institutional, economic, governance and infrastructural structures – a common property of all-natural systems. And as an emergent property, the boundaries do not exist in isolation - in order words, cities only have imaginary boundaries. Forrester strengthened his supposition and stated that: *"it does mean cause and effect loops do not reach outside the boundary and return. For example, migration to the area [cities] has its effect by filling and thereby altering the area not by emptying the outside world".*

This position was fundamental in pioneering a complementing focus on the dynamics of urban systems as against only analyzing the current state and function of such cities. In Figure 2, we demonstrate the representation of the city as a mesh.

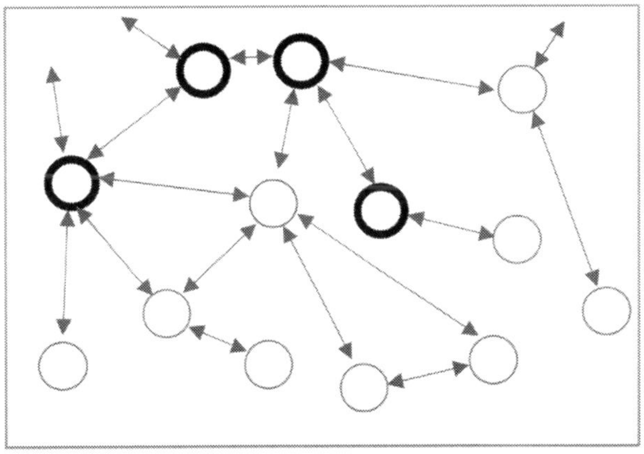

Figure. 2 The city as a mesh with many-to-many relationships

III. THE CORE PROBLEM

The governance of urban systems poses an enormous challenge to stakeholders and their community of decision makers; a challenge heighted by the increasing need for resilience, sophistication, durability and intelligence in urban instrumentation defined, embedded and utilized in cities. The city problem is getting more profound and complex. Since 2008 and for the first time in human history, the world became more urbanized than rural, with more than 50% of the human population residing in cities. Estimations predict this percentage to surpass 70% by 2050.

Attainment of this milestone ushered in a new era for which cities were opened to mega challenges and mega opportunities encapsulated in the complexities of sociotechnical systems – the fundamental goal for cities shifted. Cities seek to minimize problems and to maximize opportunities across systems and processes. Some cities by virtue of structures, processes and available infrastructure are better positioned to explore these opportunities, however, none is immune and many especially, most in the developing world are highly susceptible to the negative repercussions of urbanization. As cities continue to search for solutions in what is theoretically an infinite solution space, it is indispensable to implement and monitor systems, programs and policies that inform and enforce a set of key performance parameters. *Making-A-City-Think*; in order words, architecting an intelligent urban space has emerged as the indispensable strategy to cope with the problems generated by the changing dynamics – and there are many of such challenges. However, the success of such transformation depends on how it is done [6]

Smart or intelligent cities by definition and application imply an extended integration of new technologies, solutions, policies and decision making in the ontology of city existence comprising of mobility, living, governance, economy, environment, civic/people support [7]. It is primarily enabled by new computational power, open data availability and advanced problem synthesis and analysis.

The city system has become an experimental plot to test propositions and suppositions emanating from different academic disciplines. A new generation of city scientists and researchers employing multidisciplinary approaches to address many challenging city problems is relatively new [although actually old] and has doubled over the last decade due to rapid *urbanization*. Unlike any period in history, we observe an active desire of more and more people wanting to the move towards the cityscape in search of *city resurgence* – and not necessarily wanting to vacant the bucolic peripheries of the country side. We make this distinction, and to borrow from Forrester, such a movement is not intended to empty the country side [which will never happen] but rather to fill the cities.

It is intuitive and conceptually appropriate to describe the shift to cities – migration on bases of '*interpreted*' transaction cost theory. That is, we relate how people move as a set of transactions with the cost of the transaction split between: *perceived individual benefit(s)* and *perceived collective benefit(s)* of migrants [as agents]. That is, the decision maker(s) probabilistic outcomes of 'success' at their [intended] destination is/are larger than their origin. Assuming Occam Razor all individuals and groups – all things being equal –are greedy and rational and that tentatively, gain a cognitive [learning] ability to infer, approximate, distribute and map as a function of time their egoistic and collective goals relative to their current state. Where perceived state is greater than generated state, they seek a movement towards nearest (*Basic mobility ability, that is: distance travelled depends on distance to be travelled to reach the destination of choice*) destination for improvement, that is: ($P_s > P_g$). For instance, in developing countries, the decline of subsistence farming [favoring the masses] – the rise of mechanized large scale [favoring the few] coupled with the growing knowledge-based information centric technological age has generated a shift of form and a change in occupational dependents. When speaking with a 'Lagotian' (Somebody that has lived or preferably lives in Lagos, Nigeria – Africa's biggest megacity) recently, he remarked: "*In Lagos, you can sell anything and make money out of an*ything". In order words, whereas their *economic* choices in the bucolic regions are limited; opportunities are assumed to be abundant in cities – literally. Glaeser [8] sums this up: in reality, there is no such thing as a poor urbanized city or a rich rural region.

Succinctly, cities generate more interactions with more people than rural areas because they are central places of trade that benefit those who live there and so people moved to cities because they intuitively perceived the advantages of urban life [3]. While technically possible, the assumptions above are not intended for quantitative translations. In making the above logical constructs, we are only re-emphasizing a trait of *Homo sapiens* such that are learning creatures - we learn both voluntarily and involuntarily. And that in fact, our most valuable knowledge may be one acquired involuntarily – just like the seasoned power plant engineer who through acquired intelligent cognition can *think-ahead* of machine warnings and shut down generators before an inevitable power surge. As a pioneer, Skinner [9] was the first persuader in this direction when through a counter theory to [10] he stressed on the need to focus more on the productive behavior [of a system] itself rather than using it to make hypotheses about mental states. In Figure 3, we provide an implicit example of a pseudocode of a human agent program that may be used to explain the growth of the core problem.

The choices of many especially in the developing countries to move to urban areas underscore the high-level of attraction the city offers. In essence, people have elevated their expected value of city returns – partly economic, others technological and some cultural, others security, etc. Stereotypically, intelligence permeates our cities because we now live in a world where objects are capable of gathering, processing, displaying, transmitting or taking physical action on information all at the same time. The roles of cities are being gradually transformed into managers of these containers of intelligence - egocentric centers of innovation and cognition embedded in socio-technical complexities.

IV. WHAT IS AN INTELLIGENT CITY?

The city's problems are relatively similar everywhere, they just vary by the degree of sophistication, intensity and impact. Climate change affects all cities and megacities are not necessarily generating new kinds of problems but rather intensifying and exposing the inability of existing structures to cope with and or minimize negativities.

Due to its definitional impreciseness, numerous unspoken assumptions and a rather self-congratulatory tendency [11], a smart city can mean different things to different entities – there exist an inherent *stakeholder bias* that practitioners, civic leaders, technocrats and related must strive to. In most cases, where cities are using networked infrastructure. [sometimes mainly, 'plug and play'] solutions to gain a centralized view of information across certain city departments and agencies, they are sometimes referred as smart cities.

To the citizen, a smart city can mean automatically finding the fastest way to get to work; where smart meters control power usage and even to some [especially in developing countries], where drinking water that can be counted on, or perhaps, where they are safer streets due to increased closed circuit monitoring. To the city administrator, a smart city can mean optimization of process through the installation of city management systems, etc. To the environmentalist on the other hand, a smart city may mean a city that produces few carbon emissions or one whose citizens have a smaller ecological footprint.

Figure 4 is a *Systemigram*. Systemigrams are used to bring context to the meaning of *togetherness* that is, to unravel ambiguity in methodical system descriptions, parts and relationships. Through this approach Systemigrams are able to gather and clearly present the structure and behavior of systems diagrammatically as an emergent whole.

The mainstay [the diagonal, from left to right] is the principal stakeholder bias; this can also be termed as the dependent variable given that it acts as a centralized governance structure that depends on the perspectives of other interests/ agents in the urban system. Such a governed interplay is for purposes of good service delivery in urban systems. For instance, in the smart growth node, consider "*walkable neighborhood*" a citizen may not necessarily consider himself safe [his community walkable] on the street because business and convenient-shops are within his reach of < 10 minutes of walking but because the city has installed real-time communications technologies to monitor streets.

From above and by extension, an intelligent city is therefore a smart connected community capable of reinventing itself through appropriate and optimal communications between local nodes enabled by the network and in addition, it engages in interconnectedness with foreign entities relevant to local sustenance and/or evolution. Getting to this point is not guaranteed by the upgrade of a sub-system – *it helps*- but to achieve or work towards achieving intelligence, a city must navigate a systematic and holistic course comprising of Insulation, Micro-Functional, Macro-Functional, Spatial Dominance, Self-Orchestration and Astute. Therefore, where intelligence shall be a function of:

C (*intelligence*) = *f* (C*w1*, A*w2*, A*w3*, S*w4*...)

Function parameters: weighted rate of the 5 stages

V. THE STAGES

Below are the proposed incremental stages considering a city's intelligence journey.

A. Insulation

The main purpose of insulation is to limit the transfer of energy between the inside and outside of a system [12]. Cities [as we know] have been complex open systems since the evolution of the first of its kind. They have acted as centers of knowledge incubation, dissemination and transfer. They are the drivers of political, structural and economic growth of the national dynamic boundaries within which they are situated.

Cities need to articulate a complex insulation mechanism in the form of predictive models on people movement in and out of cities and to control the attraction and retention of talent, local education institutions and related. The above does not call for restrictive policies to constrain the mobility of people seeking social opportunities, as misguided interventions often divert resources to locations that are not profitable for local level growth [13]. One cannot design a system without understanding the boundaries of such a system.

B. Micro-Functional

Effective approximation of the simple functions of a city measured against a verification and validation mechanism contributed by the actors of each individual sub-system. This approach is intended to assess the optimal operation or lack there-off of the assets in a neighborhood. This approach is akin to a focus group intended to collect perceptions of a product performance, and/or to improve features. In theory, it is possible to account for all properties of any particular urban system; for instance, the Health care delivery system or the Energy system and so on if available data allowed for a comprehensive knowledge of all the characteristics of such and the relationships existing between them. Practically however, this is infeasible because, we will never be able to know or even approximate all the properties of these systems. Few reasons are because urban systems defer from city to city with multiple socio-technical interacting relationships that are varying, unpredictable and subject to multiple subjective interpretations.

C. Macro-Functional

This is the extrapolation and extension of a holistic representation of the state of a city. It is the assessment how micro-functional agents are working collectively and optimally. Given the whole is greater than the sum of the parts, Macro-functional states are distinct and poses a different set of challenges in complexity. From a far, there may not be direct link between mobility and education but the nuances in-between are the containers to the solution.

As a *satisficing* [14] solution to this complexity, the properties of the complex wholes – independent systems embedded in the city's system of system ecology – remain irreducible to the characteristics of their parts. Hence, they are grouped as like terms and each group of like terms is assigned a different singular or multi-objective function identified with that particular group. Any of these groups will possess a spatial view of the urban form which stems to be a representation of an urban system from their common concerns.

D. Spatial Dominance

There is almost never the best system, but there is an optimal system at any given point in space. While in many real-world situations, optimal strategies are unknown or unknowable [15], the city is not one of those. Enabling urban intelligence fueled by urban technological innovations begins as a pragmatic, engineering-based attempt to improve the operation of individual urban infrastructure and services; it can also be seen as perturbing unconsciously the interactions of the many systems within a city. Urban networks consist of infrastructure systems, interconnected service delivery mechanisms and social networks.

In the context of the city, spatial dominance represents the estimation of interconnectedness of cities. Regardless of how minuscule it might be, it is important for a city to achieve a preferred status, in-other-words, be known as the go-to in an area relative to another city with which is shares relation. It's possible for multiple cities to be equally preferred in enumerated areas or metrics.

E. *Self-Orchestration*

While making a city think may be a new research domain, the study of cities as systems dates back to at least the mid-1950s. Cities were first treated formally as systems when General System Theory and Cybernetics came to be applied to the softer social sciences in the 1950s. It is worth mentioning that the structure of a digital urban space is not static, that is, with the continuous improvement of theory and practice related to urban management and operations, urban components and their systems can be dynamically optimized and adjusted so that they can better cover all areas of the city [16].

With self-orchestration, there is an end-to-end function of cities as systems within systems of cities, such that multiple areas of the city function autonomously and at the same time controlled. Example, the automatic detection of a pothole and the prevention of a pothole. It is a trusted, integrated state.

F. *Astute*

This is the final stage and a culmination of insulation, micro-functional, macro-functional, spatial dominance and self-orchestration. Thinking in systems or systems thinking can be said to hold the city in its dichotomy: it helps to show how local processes and interactions give rise to global structures considering a plethora of local views and constraints and how these global structures feedback into local interactions.

VI. CONNECTING THE DOTS

Studies on cities as socio-technical systems are recent and not well developed. Either there have been undue emphases on creating diminutive *artificial societies* – a technology lead approach or a 180 degree turn to emphasize the value of social welfare. The study of cities as socio-technical systems recognizes an eminent social part and an important technological dependency. The COVID-19 crisis made it clear that cities suffer if their citizens do, and that without the well-being of the latter, they are merely empty structures [17]. This approach reduces the evidence of social and technical polarization cited in earlier works such as [18], [19].

The ability to deal with commonsense knowledge about the world is fundamental for any intelligent system that acts in the real world and it has been early recognized as one of the central topics of Artificial Intelligence to represent and reason about commonsense knowledge. Space has always been considered to be an important part of commonsense reasoning given the physical world has a spatial dimension and all objects which are dealt with are located in space relative to other objects. Early approaches involving commonsense knowledge about the physical world were trying to solve text book physics and math problems, e.g., [19, 17]. but it soon turned out that mathematical equations were not sufficient for solving most problems.

VII. CONCLUSION

Strong linkage between the state of cities and information technology is a function of time and obligate symbiosis. In order words, technological innovation, regardless of the geography within which it occurs: be it in a basement in India, Bangladesh, Nairobi, or in well-organized centers in Silicon Valley, mostly occur in cities. Technology evolves when actors nurture and develop ideas directly impacting existing spatial dynamics of their living squatters'. Because money begets money, actors are attracted to disproportionally work towards where such technology will be needed. The law of disproportionality does not deny but delay diffusion into other areas.

By employing systems thinking and systems engineering, we think about how a set of "city events" are governed and function as a function of nested complexities. We acknowledge learning in city spaces require abilities to decrypt, analyze, synthesize, apply, predict [actions] and re-configure an integral knowledge base. Such information, where gathered can be molded into patterns of behavior, develop predictive models of likely outcomes allowing better decisions and informed actions [20]., *learning* in space require Networked Infrastructure, Information Systems and City Citizens as principal agents.

Cities are complex spatial systems with social and technical rules, structures and networks. In the most general terms, there is a network of cities or a network *in* cities. Of more interest is network in cities where the city becomes less obtrusive and reinforce a network dependency of a system among systems, rightly called a *system of systems*. By extension, it is important to realize these relationships because they serve a building blocks to understand how logical and physical networks work in cities. When we say a city is connected, more 'smartly' connected we mean it is capable of reinventing itself through appropriate and optimal communications between local nodes enabled by the network and in addition, it engages in interconnectedness with foreign entities relevant to local sustenance and/or evolution.

In this paper, we have presented the background of the problem and introduced five stages of assessment and measurement. Further research will expand on guidance and evaluation of the proposed stages.

REFERENCES

[1] J. Jacobs, The Death and Life of Great American Cities Part, New York: Random House, 1961.

[2] J. G. Miller, Living Systems, The Basic Concepts, 1978.

[3] D. V. Philippe Blanchard, Mathematical Analysis of Urban Spatial Networks, Springer, 2007.

[4] M. Batty, Cities as Complex Systems: Scaling, Interactions, Networks, Dynamics and Urban Morphologies, UCL Working Paper Series: London, 2008.

[5] J. Forrester, Urban Dynamics, MIT Press, 1969.

[6] J. Muvuna, T. Boutaleb, S. Mickovski, and K. J. Baker, "Systems engineering approach to design and modelling of smart cities," *International Conference for Students on Applied Engineering (ICSAE)*, pp. 437-440, 2016.

[7] R. Giffinger, and H. Gudrun, "Smart cities ranking: An effective instrument for the positioning of the cities," *Journal of the Center of Land Policy and Valuations*, vol. 4, no. 12, pp 13-18 2010.

[8] E. Glaeser, Triumph of the City, How our Greatest Invention Makes Us Richer, Smarter, Greener, Healthier and Happier, New York: Penguin press, 2011.

[9] B. F. Skinner, "Are theories of Learning Necessary?," *The Psychological Review, Volume*, vol. 57, no. 4, pp. 193-216, 1950.

[10] E. Tolman, "Cognitive Maps in Rats and Men," *The Psychological Review*, vol. 55, no. 4, pp. 189-208, 1948.

[11] R. Hollands, "Will the real smart city please stand up?," *Analysis of Urban Change, Theory, Action*, vol. 12, no. 3, pp. 303-320, 2008.

[12] A. Bahadori, "Design and Application of Thermal Insulation," *Thermal Insulation Handbook for the Oil, Gas, and Petrochemical Industries*, 2014.

[13] The Wor;d Bank Group, 2010.

[14] H. Simon, "Rational Choice and the Structure of the environment," 1956. [Online].

[15] H. Simon, "Rational decision making in business organizations," *Advances in behavioral economics*, vol. 1, pp. 18-47, 1987.

[16] L. S. Souza, S. Misra and M. S. Soares, "SmartCitySysML: A SysML Profile for Smart Cities Applications," *Computational Science and Its Applications*, 2020.

[17] IESE, "IESE Cities in Motion Index," IESE, Pamplona, 2020.

[18] A. Smith, A. Stirling, and F. Berkhout, "The governance of sustainable socio-technical transitions," Research Policy, pp. 1491-1510, 2005.

[19] J. Peck, "Struggling with the Creative Class," International Journal of Urban and Regional Research, vol. 29, no. 4, pp. 740-770, 2005.

[20] IBM Institute for Business Value, "A vision of smarter cities, How cities can lead the way into a prosperous and sustainable future," IBM Global Business Services, 2011.

```
function IMPROVE_QUALITY_OF_ LIFE(target)        returns  an action

        cognition:  localPercept,   access local conditions, initially set to null [0, 1]

                    foreignPercept  , excepted opportunities for goal attainment [0, 1]

                     Goal , access short term and long term

        DEFINE:     localState  ['current local State' based on performance measure]

                futureState       ['perceived future State' based on performance measure]

    if {

     localPercept    approaches   1 && foreignPercept   approaches   0, then

      Goal  ← foreignPercept

      VERIFY

      Problem ((futureState – currentState) < (currentState – futureState))

       execute   ← MIGRATIONDIRECTION     (foreignPercept)

         ELSE if

          localPercept  approaches   0 then

          break thought;

      return action

           if

                SOLUTION   is null [0]   after 'x  LOOPS  '

                AGENT  is content  ← SET  localPercept (   approaches   0 )

      }

    END IF

      return state
```

Figure. 3 The core problem fueled by migration

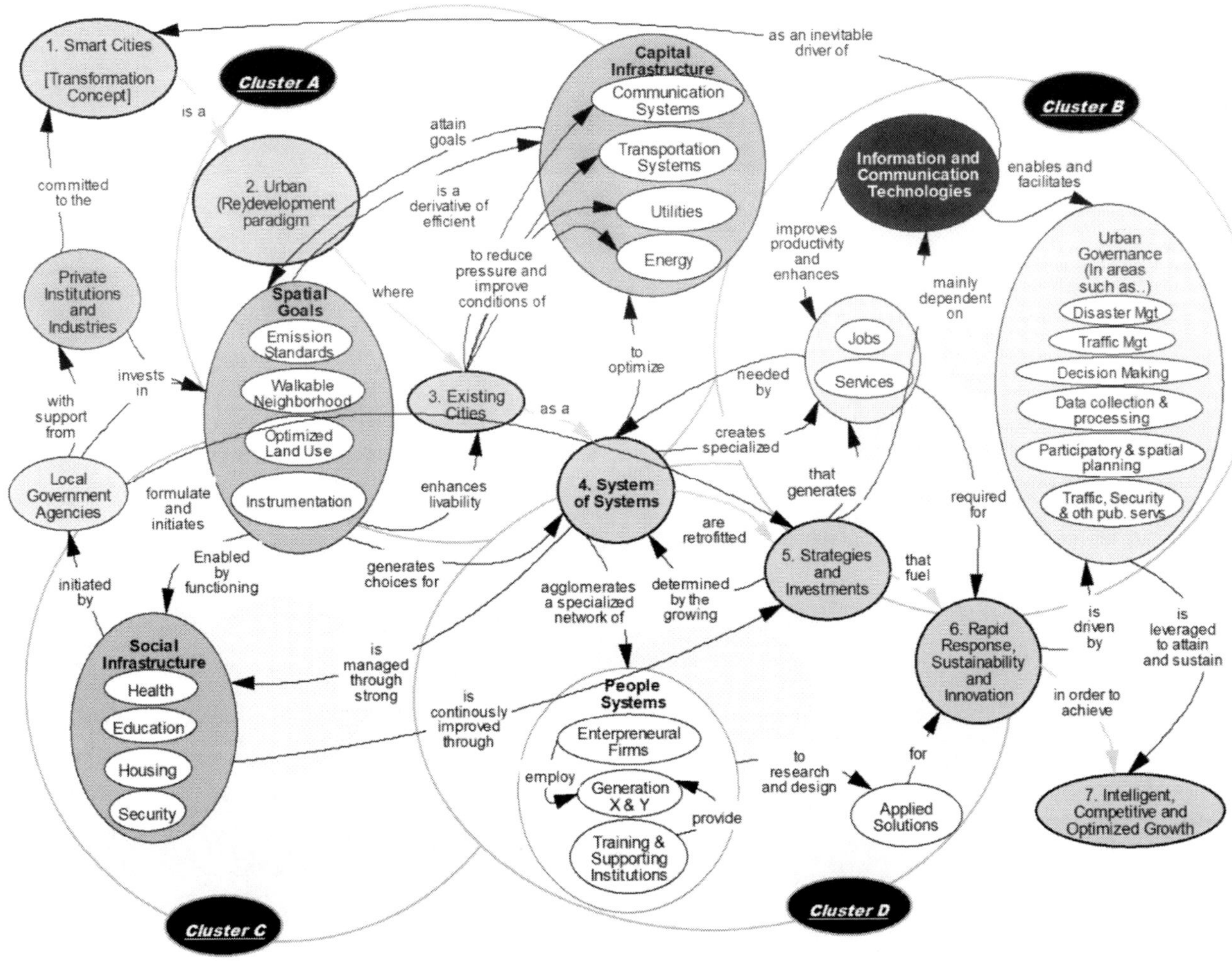

Figure. 4. The Systemigram of a Smart City

International Academy, Research, and Industry Association (IARIA)
412 Derby Way
Wilmington, DE 19810

ISBN 978-1-7138-6958-0

CURRAN ASSOCIATES INC.
proceedings.com

Fifth International Conference on Building and Exploring Web Based Environments (WEB 2017)

Held at InfoSys 2017

Barcelona, Spain
21 - 25 May 2017

IARIA